DORDT INFORMATION SERVICES

3 6520 0080305 W

D1234308

Clinical Applied
Psychophysiology

THE PLENUM SERIES IN BEHAVIORAL PSYCHOPHYSIOLOGY AND MEDICINE

Series Editor:
William J. Ray, *Pennsylvania State University, University Park, Pennsylvania*

BIOLOGICAL BARRIERS IN BEHAVIORAL MEDICINE
Edited by Wolfgang Linden

CLINICAL APPLIED PSYCHOPHYSIOLOGY
Edited by John G. Carlson, A. Ronald Seifert,
and Niels Birbaumer

ELECTRODERMAL ACTIVITY
Wolfram Boucsein

HANDBOOK OF RESEARCH METHODS IN CARDIOVASCULAR
BEHAVIORAL MEDICINE
Edited by Neil Schneiderman, Stephen M. Weiss,
and Peter G. Kaufmann

INTERNATIONAL PERSPECTIVES ON SELF-REGULATION AND
HEALTH
Edited by John G. Carlson and A. Ronald Seifert

PHYSIOLOGY AND BEHAVIOR THERAPY
Conceptual Guidelines for the Clinician
James G. Hollandsworth, Jr.

THE PHYSIOLOGY OF PSYCHOLOGICAL DISORDERS
Schizophrenia, Depression, Anxiety, and Substance Abuse
James G. Hollandsworth, Jr.

THE PSYCHOLOGY AND PHYSIOLOGY OF BREATHING
In Behavioral Medicine, Clinical Psychology, and Psychiatry
Robert Fried with Joseph Grimaldi

SOCIAL SUPPORT AND CARDIOVASCULAR DISEASE
Edited by Sally A. Shumaker and Susan M. Czajkowski

A Continuation Order Plan is available for this series. A continuation order will bring delivery of each new volume immediately upon publication. Volumes are billed only upon actual sipment. For further information please contact the publisher.

Clinical Applied Psychophysiology

*Sponsored by the Association for
Applied Psychophysiology and Biofeedback*

Edited by

John G. Carlson
*University of Hawaii
Honolulu, Hawaii*

A. Ronald Seifert
*Behavioral Institute of Altanta
Atlanta, Georgia*

and

Niels Birbaumer
*University of Tübingen
Tübingen, Germany*

Plenum Press • New York and London

Library of Congress Cataloging-in-Publication Data

Clinical applied psychophysiology / edited by John G. Carlson, A.
Ronald Seifert, and Niels Birbaumer.
      p.   cm. -- (The Plenum series in behavioral psychophysiology
and medicine)
    Collection of papers and key note addresses at the Second
International Conference on Biobehavioral Self-Regulation and Health
held at the University of Munich, Germany, Sep. 15-20, 1991.
    Includes bibliographical references and index.
    ISBN 0-306-44555-7
    1. Medicine, Psychosomatic--Congresses. 2. Psychophysiology-
-Congresses.   I. Carlson, John G.   II. Seifert, A. Ronald.
III. Birbaumer, Niels.   IV. Association for Applied Psychophysiology
and Biofeedback.   V. International Conference on Biobehavioral Self
-Regulation and Health (2nd : 1991 : University of Munich, Germany)
VI. Series.
    [DNLM: 1. Biofeedback (Psychology)--congresses. 2. Behavior
Therapy--congresses.   WL 103 C6414 1994]
RC49.C49 1994
616.08--dc20
DNLM/DLC
for Library of Congress   94-961
                                                               CIP

ISBN 0-306-44555-7

©1994 Plenum Press, New York
A Division of Plenum Publishing Corporation
233 Spring Street, New York, N.Y. 10013

All rights reserved

No part of this book may be reproduced, stored in a retrieval system, or transmitted
in any form or by any means, electronic, mechanical, photocopying, microfilming,
recording, or otherwise, without written permission from the Publisher

Printed in the United States of America

To the memory of Hisashi Hirai
Professor, Department of Psychology, Sophia University, Tokyo, Japan.
His international efforts in self-regulation and health,
and his gentle humanity, will be greatly missed.

Contributors

Sonia Ancoli-Israel, Department of Psychiatry, University of California, San Diego, California; Veterans Affairs Medical Center, San Diego, California

Elisabetta Angelino, Psychology Service, Clinica del Lavoro Foundation, Institute of Care and Research, Medical Center of Rehabilitation, Veruno, Italy

Giorgio Bertolotti, Psychology Service, Clinica del Lavoro Foundation, Institute of Care and Research, Medical Center of Rehabilitation, Veruno, Italy

Ornella Bettinardi, Psychology Service, Clinica del Lavoro Foundation, Institute of Care and Research, Medical Center of Rehabilitation, Veruno, Italy

Niels Birbaumer, Department of Clinical and Physiological Psychology, University of Tübingen, Tübingen, Germany; Department of General Psychology, Universitá degli Studi, Padova, Italy

M. M. Brown, Psychology Department, Victoria University of Wellington, Wellington, New Zealand

John G. Carlson, Department of Psychology, University of Hawaii, Honolulu, Hawaii

Irene Daum, Department of Clinical and Physiological Psychology, University of Tübingen, Tübingen, Germany

Johannes Dichgans, Department of Neurology, University of Tübingen, Tübingen, Germany

Andreas Düchting-Röth, Epilepsy Center Bethel, Bielefeld, Germany

Thomas Elbert, Institute of Experimental Audiology, University of Münster, Münster, Germany

Robert L. Fell, Department of Psychiatry, University of California, San Diego, California; Veterans Affairs Medical Center, San Diego, California

Herta Flor, Department of Clinical and Physiological Psychology, University of Tübingen, Tübingen, Germany

Robert R. Freedman, C. S. Mott Center, Wayne State University, Detroit, Michigan

Robert Fried, Hunter College, City University of New York, New York; Institute for Rational Emotive Therapy, New York, New York

Iris B. Goldstein, Department of Psychiatry, University of California at Los Angeles, Los Angeles, California

Larry Jamner, University of California, San Francisco, California

Lynne A. Kenney, Department of Psychiatry, University of California, San Diego, California; Veterans Affairs Medical Center, San Diego, California

Melville R. Klauber, Department of Family and Preventive Medicine, University of California, San Diego, California

Werner Lutzenberger, Department of Clinical and Physiological Psychology, University of Tübingen, Tübingen, Germany

Giorgio Mazzuero, Division of Cardiology, Clinica del Lavoro Foundation, Institute of Care and Research, Medical Center of Rehabilitation, Veruno, Italy

P. G. F. Nixon, Charing Cross Hospital, London, England

Linda Parker, Department of Psychiatry, University of California, San Diego, California; Veterans Affairs Medical Center, San Diego, California

Martin Reker, Epilepsy Center Bethel, Bielefeld, Germany

Brigitte Rockstroh, Department of Psychology, University of Konstanz, Konstanz, Germany

J. P. Rosenfeld, Department of Psychology, Northwestern University, Evanston, Illinois

Ezio Sanavio, Department of General Psychology, University of Padova, Padova, Italy

A. Ronald Seifert, Behavioral Institute of Atlanta, Atlanta, Georgia

David Shapiro, Department of Psychiatry, University of California at Los Angeles, Los Angeles, California

Edward Taub, Department of Psychology, University of Alabama at Birmingham, Birmingham, Alabama

A. J. W. Taylor, Psychology Department, Victoria University of Wellington, Wellington, New Zealand

Tores Theorell, National Institute of Psychosocial Factors and Health, Stockholm, Sweden

Wolfgang Tunner, Department of Clinical Psychology, Institute of Psychology, University of Munich, Munich, Germany

Jan van Dixhoorn, St. Joannes de Deo Hospital, Haarlem, The Netherlands

Giulio Vidotto, Department of General Psychology, University of Padova, Padova, Italy

Richard Willens, Department of Psychiatry, University of California, San Diego, California; Veterans Affairs Medical Center, San Diego, California

Peter Wolf, Epilepsy Center Bethel, Bielefeld, Germany

Anna Maria Zotti, Psychology Service, Clinica del Lavoro Foundation, Institute of Care and Research, Medical Center of Rehabilitation, Veruno, Italy

Foreword

Although the injunction "Know thyself" was inscribed over the site of the Delphic Oracle, the concept is of much more ancient lineage. Thousands of years ago, the wise men of the East had learned to exert authority over a broad range of bodily experiences and functions using techniques that are still taught today. But it is only in the past few decades that the West has become aware once again of the range of control that the central nervous system can maintain over sensation and body function. Medicine has moved slowly in integrating these concepts into the classic medical model of disease despite a growing body of evidence that links emotional state, thought, and imagery to immunocompetence, tissue healing, and bodily vigor.

It is precisely the role of a volume such as this, reflecting a fascinating conference in Munich, to emphasize and reemphasize these ideas. We are fortunately well beyond the sterile behaviorism of Watson with its complete negation of the significance of mental operations. But many still consider suspect those forces and mechanisms, however powerful, that seem to originate from brain–mind activity. The chapters in this book, with their emphases on the mind–body continuum as a bridge to self-regulation and health, provide a modern "School of Athens" in bringing these concepts to wider acquaintance.

One of the necessary bridges to such an appreciation is a growing understanding of the structure and modes of function of the nervous system. The neural substrates for our ability to self-regulate experience and body function are becoming less mysterious. If it can be shown that the structures and mechanisms are present and describable, even the skeptic must eventually see the possibilities.

One of the more powerful insights into such candidate neural connections has emerged from study of the relations among prefrontal cortex, nucleus reticularis thalami, and thalamocortical projections. Neuroanatomical, neurophysiological, and immunocytochemical studies have confirmed the role of the n. reticularis thalami as a filter or gating system, sitting athwart all sensory communication between thalamus and cortex. En route to cortical receptive areas, sensory thalamic activity activates localized neuron clusters of the n. reticularis thalami. Short, high-frequency bursts of these n. reticularis cells then play back onto the thalamus, causing brief periods of profound thalamic cell inhibition. Each thalamocortical burst thus selectively closes reticularis gates during the period of its activation, thereby delimiting and emphasizing its own content—temporally and spatially.

In contrast, ascending connections from the mesencephalic reticular formation exert a strong inhibitory bias on the cells of the n. reticularis thalami, effectively opening the gates. This is undoubtedly the system that is activated in a period of stress or maximal emergency (e.g., when someone shouts "Fire" in a crowded theater). The sudden voluminous opening of n. reticularis gates tends to flood the cortex with information, powerfully stimulating some individuals and totally paralyzing others (i.e., freezing them in a panic state).

There is a third series of connections to this gating system, which is most relevant to our interest. The prefrontal cortex projects to the intra-laminar nuclei of the thalamus and indirectly to the mesencephalic reticu-lar core. Through these pathways, neurons of the n. reticularis can be driven or inhibited by prefrontal activity. Although the prefrontal cortex remains one of the more functionally enigmatic areas of the entire brain, it is increasingly seen as an executive area for decision, focus, and projec-tion. It is at once the head end of the keel-like fronto–septo–hypothalamo–tegmental axis and a source for connections to the entire cerebral cortex, basal ganglia, and thalamus. As closely as one can make such an analogy, it is simultaneously the site of the decisionary "I" involved in conscious choice and life planning and the ultimate source of modulation over hypothalamus-controlled visceral activity. In the latter case, the demon-strated immunocompetence of the nude mouse may correlate with a thinner, less developed frontal cortex. Similarly, experimental destruction of the murine left frontal cortex also results in diminished immunocompe-tence. In humans, devastating life experiences (e.g., loss of mate, child, or job) have equally destructive effects on the immune system. And guided imagery may enhance immunocompetence for the cancer patient.

In making conscious choices, such imagery helps shape our plans for the evening or for our career. And it is undoubtedly the ultimate agency involved when we "think positively," "determine to get well," or enter a psychophysiological program to diminish chronic pain, control hyperten-sion, and so forth. The mechanisms are just as valid for the Hindu fakir lying calmly on his bed of nails as for our own attempts to attain greater relaxation during stress or to diminish the pains of migraine.

The remarkable ability of the prefrontal cortex, operating through the thalamic intralaminar system and the brainstem reticular core to open or close the multiple gates of the n. reticularis thalami, provides the control mechanism we seek. Our conscious decision to effect change is apparently impressed on the neuronal substrate through these connections, and with repetition (the Hebb paradigm), the links are reinforced and the technique of control is learned.

This volume and the clinical research organization that it represents serve an invaluable function in highlighting the various phenomena and the therapeutic potential inherent in appropriate utilization of this neural system. Their efforts represent medically relevant education at its highest level.

ARNOLD B. SCHEIBEL

Brain Research Institute
UCLA Medical Center

Preface

The collection of papers in this volume represents a broad spectrum from the invited presentations in a series of symposia and keynote addresses at the Second International Conference on Biobehavioral Self-Regulation and Health. The conference was held at the University of Munich, Germany, September 15–20, 1991, in accordance with plans announced at the first of these conferences (in Honolulu, Hawaii, 1987). A third conference in the series is planned (to be held in Japan in 1993). The advisory committee for the Munich conference—Niels Birbaumer (Germany), the late Hisashi Hirai (Japan), M. Barry Sterman (United States), and Holger Ursin (Norway)—was coordinated by the Chairmen of the International Committee of the Association of Applied Psychophysiology and Biofeedback, A. Ronald Seifert (United States) and John G. Carlson (United States). The advisory committee and chairs together developed the program and solicited presentations from six keynote speakers and thirty-one individual symposium presenters, all eminent and internationally known researchers representing eleven countries. The invited presentations at the conference were organized into eight topical areas, including the applied psychophysiology of epilepsy, cardiovascular disorders, sleep disorders, exercise, pain, breathing, stress in the workplace, and man in hazardous environments. In addition, in these and other content areas, thirty-five posters were contributed and presented at the meeting, the authors of which represented eight countries (Carlson & Seifert, 1992).

This collection of papers represents the second volume from these international meetings, the first also published in the *Plenum Series in Behavioral Psychophysiology and Medicine* (Carlson & Seifert, 1991). That collection was focused mainly on pure and applied research in the field of self-regulation and health. In this volume, the focus is more on clinical applications of psychophysiological principles and methods. The fifteen chapters largely comprise outstanding selections from the conference oral presentations, organized into those that discuss disorders of the central nervous system (two chapters), the cardiovascular system (three chapters), the applied psychophysiology of breathing (four chapters), the neuromuscular system (two chapters), and long-term stress (two chapters). These papers should be an asset for the applied psychophysiologist-clinician who keeps abreast of the latest developments and techniques of the field. Additional details on the individual chapters and the Munich meeting are to be found in the Introduction (Chapter 1).

Sincere thanks for efforts that helped to make this second meeting a successful one are due to many individuals—foremost, the presenters themselves. The many formal and informal exchanges at the meeting were always lively and packed with fascinating and new approaches and data. Behind the scenes, the local coordinator, Ulrich Birner, and his always helpful and gracious assistants, Barbara Steinkopf and Ida Kukarski, all of the University of Munich, provided invaluable organization and attention to details. Various forms of financial support for the meeting were provided by the Association of Applied Psychophysiology and Biofeedback, the German Research Society, and the European Space Agency.

We also wish to thank Eliot Werner, Executive Editor, Plenum Press, for his ever-positive encouragement of our editing efforts, and William Ray, the supportive and keen-eyed editor of the *Plenum Series in Behavioral Psychophysiology and Medicine*.

JOHN G. CARLSON
A. RONALD SEIFERT
NIELS BIRBAUMER

Honolulu, Atlanta, and Tübingen

References

Carlson, J. G., & Seifert, R. (Eds.) (1991). *International perspectives on self-regulation and health*. New York: Plenum Press.
Carlson, J. G., & Seifert, A. R. (1992). Abstracts of papers presented at the Second International Conference on Biobehavioral Self-Regulation and Health. *Biofeedback and Self-Regulation, 17*, 221–244.

Contents

PART I. OVERVIEW

PART II. DISORDERS OF
THE CENTRAL NERVOUS SYSTEM

PART III. DISORDERS OF
THE CARDIOVASCULAR SYSTEM

Chapter 6

Psychological Factors Affecting Ambulatory Blood Pressure in
    a High-Stress Occupation 73

David Shapiro, Iris B. Goldstein, and Larry Jamner

Chapter 7

Mechanisms and Treatment of Raynaud's Disease and
    Phenomenon 89

Robert R. Freedman

PART IV. APPLIED PSYCHOPHYSIOLOGY
AND RESPIRATION

Chapter 8

Sleep-Disordered Breathing: Preliminary Natural History and
    Mortality Results 103

*Sonia Ancoli-Israel, Melville R. Klauber, Robert L. Fell, Linda Parker,
Lynne A. Kenney, and Richard Willens*

Chapter 9

Significance of Breathing Awareness and Exercise Training for
  Recovery after Myocardial Infarction 113

Jan van Dixhoorn

Chapter 10

Respiration in Clinical Psychophysiology: How to Assess Critical
  Parameters and Their Change with Treatment 133

Robert Fried

PART V. NEUROMUSCULAR DISORDERS

PART VI. LONG-TERM STRESS

Chapter 14

A. J. W. Taylor and M. M. Brown

Chapter 15

Tores Theorell

PART I

Overview

CHAPTER 1

Clinical Applied Psychophysiology
Introduction

A. Ronald Seifert, Niels Birbaumer, and John G. Carlson

The Conference and a Changing World Order

This edited volume is derived primarily from the Second International Conference on Biobehavioral Self-Regulation and Health held at the University of Munich, Germany on September 15–20, 1991. A preceding edited volume, *International Perspectives on Self-Regulation and Health*, was based on papers submitted to the inaugural conference in this series, held in Honolulu, Hawaii, in 1987. The Third International Conference on Biobehavioral Self-Regulation and Health will be held in Tokyo, Japan, September 21–25, 1993.

The Second International Conference on Biobehavioral Self-Regulation and Health again drew on the expertise of a scientific advisory committee to select the participants for oral presentation. The committee was composed of Drs. Niels Birbaumer of Germany, the late Hisashi Hirai of Japan, M. Barry Sterman of the United States, and Holger Ursin of Norway. As a result of their efforts, the meeting was truly international in both intent and execution—a total of twenty-one countries were repre-

A. RONALD SEIFERT • Behavioral Institute of Atlanta, Atlanta, GA 30342.   *NIELS BIRBAUMER* • Department of Clinical and Physiological Psychology, University of Tübingen, Tübingen, Germany D-72074; Dipartimento di Psicologia Generale, Universitá degli Studi, Padova, Italy.   *JOHN G. CARLSON* • Department of Psychology, University of Hawaii, Honolulu, HI 96822.

Clinical Applied Psychophysiology, edited by John G. Carlson, A. Ronald Seifert, and Niels Birbaumer. Plenum Press, New York, 1994.

sented in the conference through oral presentation, poster presentation, workshops, attendance, or in some or all of these ways.

No one could anticipate that the inaugural international conference in 1987 would be followed by the fall of the Iron Curtain, the collapse of the former Russian empire, and the consequent and continuing redefinition of the geography and governments of a large part of the world. While we are not attempting to attribute any of these events to the unifying efforts of this meeting, there certainly has been profound change. Many conflicting ideologies and restriction of borders were to all but vanish overnight, or so it seemed at the time. Unforeseeably, out of these changes, dramatic as they were, there has arisen yet another set of circumstances that does not contribute to the timely progress of science and health care.

With the replacement of governments that had engaged in arguments of conflicting ideology and cold war rhetoric came a corresponding loss of certainty that science and business would go on as usual. The historical problems of funding for science paled by comparison with the priorities of some new governments, the compelling requirements of which are for stable economies to meet the basic needs of their people. Even more devastating, some countries became immediately embroiled in new armed conflicts.

In some situations, where strong scientific organizations and reliable funding previously existed, there was now a total disruption of those processes. Conditions were so adverse for some scientists that they attempted an exodus to other countries. For those not able to leave, often there was (and there still remains) an impoverishment of funds to maintain even the most prestigious institutes. New restrictions were imposed on the activities of researchers and clinicians and on the flow of scientific information and health care. Thus, while the intellectual freedom for the pursuit of scientific inquiry may have improved in this new world order, adequate funding and opportunities to conduct scientific work have not necessarily followed. In fact, opportunities for international communication between scientist and clinician actually may have been worsened in some dimensions.

One of our original stated goals during the inaugural planning of this series of conferences was to provide a forum in which some of the leading scientists and practitioners in biobehavioral self-regulation and health could meet and share their theories, data, and clinical experiences. In addition to this formal venue, it was deemed equally important that the participants have the opportunity for informal person-to-person communication. To our great satisfaction, the participants in these conferences have rated the content of the meetings to be of the highest caliber. They have also rated the opportunity for informal communication as having contributed significantly to the overall high quality of the experience. While not yet attained, therefore, the goal of these meetings—to enhance international scientific communication—appears to have been approached a step nearer. One measure of the vitality, development, and growth of clinical applied psychophysiology is the increasing number and geographical diversity of the participating scientists and practitioners. The excitement of their individual efforts and accomplishments is further enhanced when viewed from an international perspective.

It also was explicitly intended that the second international conference go beyond the scope of nontraditional treatment of medical disorders. The intent was to include strategies that focused on optimization of health and survival through disease prevention. There was no intent to distract from applications within medicine, but rather to be more inclusive of the broader arena of biobehavioral self-regulation and health. Again, this was to be accomplished by bringing together outstanding researchers representing both pure and applied science in the field of self-regulation and health, through the dissemination of their previous research, as well through promoting new efforts via the interchange of ideas and collaboration.

The challenge in assessing issues of mind/body, body/mind relationships demands a biopsychosocial understanding of the human condition. We can no longer be content to describe the human as an isolated organic system, as a solely psychological being, or as a person without environmental context. The nature of clinical applied psychophysiology requires more than the mere acknowledgment of the whole person. It requires that the dynamic individual be referenced and studied in context, while continuously adapting to an ever-changing environment. Clinical applied psychophysiology often requires unique procedures that depart from more traditional static research designs. To assess human adaptation as if it were a static event is to deny the very nature of this truly dynamic process.

Moreover, the issues of health and wellness demand not only the treatment but also the prevention of the various disease states through the attainment of homeostasis for optimal health. The conceptual and theoretical models of clinical applied psychophysiology contribute uniquely to the description and empirical assessment of contributors to disease states. Also, through the integrated approaches of the biopsychosocial model, the resulting inquiry offers the opportunity for health promotion through prevention. For some of our most compelling health care issues, prevention may be the single most useful solution available to date. Such a strategy, in the long run, undoubtedly will prove to be the most cost-effective and the most viable solution to the world's escalating health care problems and costs. By increasing the number of international participants contributing to and sharing the data base, it is believed that this goal can be more quickly attained.

Turning to the organization of the content areas in the present data base—this volume—the several sections provide only one possible structure for the individually prepared chapters. These topical areas were selected mainly because they are familiar to the reader and help to organize the diverse theory, data, and application in the papers. No existing organization, however, can satisfactorily account for all the diversity of the field. Research in clinical applied psychophysiology reflects the efforts of many to confront challenging demands. These chapters are well written, reflect sound research and treatment strategies, and often represent an ongoing series of studies. It is hoped that in reading them, you will share with us the enjoyment that was ours when we heard the oral presentations and again when we read the manuscripts for editing. More compelling is the hope that the unique theory and observations contained within may help to define the problems that confront you in your own work.

The Chapters

I. Overview

If we are to progress, the assumptions of inquiry must be examined, as well as the methodology. Following this introductory first chapter, Chapter 2 is the first philosophical presentation in the conference series. Wolfgang Tunner examines the concept of behavioral self-regulation from the vantage point of Schopenhauer's ethics and sets a standard for future presentations.

Chapter 3, by Niels Birbaumer and co-workers, examines a specific approach to a traditional medical condition, epilepsy, while making comparisons to alternative efforts. The clinical outcome of their approach is significant in and of itself; however, the greatest contribution to understanding may be in how the brain processes and modulates its own function as reflected through electrophysiology. Chapter 4, by J. P. Rosenfeld, may be the most technologically and procedurally sensitive chapter. The systematic manner in which Rosenfeld presents his theory and empirical findings makes it possible for the reader unfamiliar with the P300 event-related potential to quickly become familiar with it. Familiarity should provide the basis for an appreciation of the uniqueness of Rosenfeld's work.

Chapter 5, by Giorgio Bertolotti and associates, provides one of the few opportunities for cross-cultural comparison of a heavily investigated problem, Type A behavior. The assumptions one might make without the benefit of this comparison would surely be less empirically valid. Chapter 6, by David Shapiro and colleagues, provides a clear challenge to incorporate his methodological approach to improve diagnosis, selection of treatment, and assessment of treatment for essential hypertension. It seems clear that if this incorporation does not take place, the best we have to offer is not being utilized, and this neglect is unacceptable. Chapter 7, by Robert Freedman, employs the scientific process for the understanding of Raynaud's disease in a manner that is truly representative of what can be accomplished. Not only is there an improved understanding of the benefits of the treatment protocol, but also the elucidation of the basis on which it is accomplished enhances our understanding of human physiology.

Chapter 8, by Sonia Ancoli-Israel and colleagues, presents findings on sleep-disordered breathing (SDB). Their research on both the assessment of SDB and the effect on mortality helps to define this relatively new area of study. It not only challenges existing assumptions but also points the way for a better understanding of the prevalence and consequence of the problem. Although most people assume the benefit of relaxation, Jan van Dixhoorn provides in Chapter 9 one of the relatively few studies of the effects of relaxation and breathing training on cardiovascular disorders. His results not only provide data to support the approach but also bring into question the present strategies for the rehabilitation of cardiac patients. In Chapter 10, Robert Fried presents his protocol for the assessment of the role of respiration in a wide range of disorders. Fried's work on hypoxia provides a challenge to all who are interested in the physiology of respiration as well as to the clinician confronted by a host of diagnostic categories. P. G. F. Nixon, in Chapter 11, challenges the reductionistic approaches to the role of hyperventilation. Instead, he provides a systems approach utilizing a modified performance–arousal curve as a model. He advocates the uncoupling of breathing from arousal and coupling it with the body's need for making and sustaining effort. His conceptualization will challenge even those who currently acknowledge a role for breathing.

Herta Flor and Niels Birbaumer attempt in Chapter 12 to apply psychophysiological theory to the study of chronic musculoskeletal pain. They not only first establish that a specific need exists, but then also conduct their study of biofeedback after providing the electrophysiological rationale for treatment and assessment of treatment efficacy. In Chapter 13, by Edward Taub, the reader is presented with both the research leading to the theory of learned nonuse and the results of its application to specific patient populations. This chapter should be required reading for anyone working in chronic pain, continence training, and neurological injury.

A. J. W. Taylor and M. M. Brown present in Chapter 14 data from a series of four-person parties who wintered over in Antarctica each year from 1986 to the present. Conducting research under these conditions as well as the challenges of long-term stress are examined. Such extreme conditions require adequate selection of participants for a number of factors, especially the ability to maintain group relationships lest they all be seriously compromised. In Chapter 15, Tores Theorell presents data obtained in the workplace. The complexity of the factors monitored and the context of the measurement, as well as the short- and long-term effects, are all of importance in understanding the effect on health. Theorell's concern is to establish relationships of monitored factors that persist and serve as predictors for the effects of long-term stress.

Chapter 2. Schopenhauer's Ethics and the Concept of Behavioral Self-Regulation

Wolfgang Tunner's precedent-setting treatise articulates his thoughts on self-regulation as related to the metaphysics of Arthur Schopenhauer. Self-regulation, as defined, means the functioning of behavior and physiology without external assistance. Self-regulation becomes possible only when one can predict and control his internal psychological and physiological activities. Tunner directs us to define what "self" really means—which, in turn, he acknowledges is impossible. The intent to control is goal-directed; therefore, it leads us from the present to the future. The uncertainty of one's ability to accomplish the task leads to a basic insecurity and concern over whether self-control will work or not.

The intentionality of self-control is equated to Schopenhauer's concept of Will. The short "Gedankenexperiment" in which the audience at the conference participated cannot be captured by words. If one directs his or her attention to the activity of inner organs, eliminates the sources of expectation, and takes things as they appear, a feeling of being alive—uniquely alive and different from all others—becomes for that moment the only fact without doubt. Schopenhauer's metaphysics begins at this point of certainty. Tunner skillfully guides the reader to the realization that the constant struggle for existence and pleasure is the Will. Self-control, then, can be viewed as a free decision of will. The ethic of will is not based on the "you should" that is demanded of reason, but rather on the feeling of compassion. Science shows how we function, while metaphysics allows the development of ideas to determine whether our functioning makes sense. Tunner affords the readers of this chapter an opportunity to relate their scientific concepts of self-regulation to Schopenhauer's philosophical framework. Whether the resulting conjunction makes sense or not will be dependent on individual Will.

II. *Disorders of the Central Nervous System*

Chapter 3. Biofeedback of Slow Cortical Potentials in Epilepsy

This chapter by Niels Birbaumer, Brigitte Rockstroh, Thomas Elbert, Peter Wolf, Andreas Düchting-Röth, Martin Reker, Irene Daum, Werner Lutzenberger, and Johannes Dichgans focuses on their research directed at the approximately 20–50% percent of patients with seizures who do not respond to antiseizure medication. The authors describe a procedure that relies on biofeedback and instrumental conditioning of surface-negative slow cortical potentials (SCPs). The SCP is understood to represent the extent to which apical dendrites of the cortical pyramidal cells are depolarized and therefore to indicate cortical excitability. The contingent negative variation (CNV), a slow negative shift in electrical potential, is one of the brain's responses between a warning signal and a second imperative signal representing expectancy or mobilization of the subject's brain.

Birbaumer and colleagues hypothesized that patients with seizures suffer from impaired control over their cortical excitability and decided to investigate SCP regulation as a means of reducing seizures. Their data support the hypothesis that abnormal increases in cortical excitability covary with a risk for seizures to develop. The first study presented consisted of a group of patients suffering from varied types of drug-refractory seizures and was conducted in a double-blind setting. The double-blind protocol was used to assess and rule out the role of placebo effects. It is unlikely that placebo effects accounted for seizure reduction secondary to this learning. The second study investigated learned control over SCPs in a larger group of drug-refractory seizure patients. The results of the study indicate that the majority of drug-refractory patients did achieve control over their SCPs after extended biofeedback training and instrumental conditioning. While learned control over the SCPs can be strengthened utilizing feedback and instrumental conditioning, not every patient was able to achieve SCP control and not every patient who did demonstrate control experienced a reduction in seizures. Only when the self-control was successfully transferred to the everyday environment was it effective for seizure reduction.

Continued systematic investigation provides the promise that a greater understanding of procedures to reduce seizures for these refractory populations will be attained.

*Chapter 4. The P300 Event-Related Brain Potential in Psychiatric and
Neurological Diagnosis*

In his chapter, J. P. Rosenfeld provides a definition of the P300 as an
EEG-derived event-related potential (ERP) recordable from the human
scalp using EEG-type electrodes and physiological recording parameters.
The word "event" in the term ERP refers to the external physical or internal
psychological event that causes the deflection in ongoing EEG, defining
the ERP.
Chapter 4 is based on a method called the "oddball paradigm."
Rosenfeld adapted this paradigm and presents his assumptions why the
P300 appears to represent a psychological event. Thus, it might be utilized
in psychological diagnosis for conditions in which psychological dysfunction is basic to a neurologically or psychiatrically defined state. Rosenfeld's
work defines the P300 as a form of lie detector to signify special guilty or
personal knowledge that a subject will behaviorally deny (in an attempt to
escape detection). The neurological and psychiatric applications of this
paradigm are closely related to the forensic applications that are described. Rosenfeld believes that this paradigm might be used in the
neurological setting to assess memory loss or to detect whether there is
specific recognition even when there is verbal denial of the ability to recall
or remember.
Another potential use of the P300-based dual-task paradigm is being
considered in Rosenfeld's laboratory for use in psychodiagnosis. The
potential detection and discrimination of depressed and nondepressed
subjects has already been investigated. Although fewer than ten subjects
were utilized in the first study, the differential effect of the P300 was
positive for such a discrimination. Whether all of Rosenfeld's assumptions
are empirically validated remains to be determined. Either way, the work is
provocative and offers the reader an opportunity to be at the cutting edge
of the use of the EEG in clinical psychophysiology.

III. Disorders of the Cardiovascular System

*Chapter 5. Type A and Cardiovascular Responsiveness in Italian
Blue Collar Workers*

This chapter by Giorgio Bertolotti, Ezio Sanavio, Elisabetta Angelino,
Ornella Bettinardi, Giorgio Mazzuero, Giulio Vidotto, and Anna Maria
Zotti presents a brief review of the Type A behavior literature plus a
description of the authors' original research on the characteristics of Type
A blue collar workers in Italy. This work is one of the few structured

interview studies in a Latin country. The authors' question is whether the assessment of Type A behavior pattern with the structured interview, largely confined to the United States and Northern European countries and to middle class working men, demonstrates a clear link between the Type A behavior pattern and cardiovascular variables. They also question whether there is adequate proof that physiological hyperresponsiveness is indicative of autonomic nervous system activation and, in turn, is a risk factor for coronary heart disease. Equally critical for all such research is whether studies conducted in the laboratory hold up when tested in real-life situations.

Given the lack of structured interview research in Italy, it is interesting to learn that in a group of blue collar workers in that country, 67% may be classified as Type A. By comparison, in the United States, one study found 45% Type As among blue collar workers. Such cross-cultural comparison provides an increased understanding of the possible variables affecting the condition under study.

The present research employed three different tasks to address the issue that different behavioral demands might produce different cardio-vascular responses. The analysis took account not only of the task period but also of the recovery period following the challenges, the latter perhaps being of greater use clinically. The findings of Bertolloti's group are not only relevant to the field of clinical applied psychophysiology in Italy but also valuable for anyone interested in cardiovascular response.

Chapter 6. Psychological Factors Affecting Ambulatory Blood Pressure in a High-Stress Occupation

The chapter by David Shapiro, Iris B. Goldstein, and Larry Jamner confronts the known problems of blood pressure (BP) monitoring, and its relationship to the establishment of the diagnosis of hypertension, as well as the onset and assessment of the efficacy of treatment. With 24-hr ambulatory BP monitoring, the variability of an individual's BP can be assessed, a good means of predicting target-organ damage. It is this variability that is of special interest to the clinical applied psychophysiologist. Comparison of subjects across more or less fixed variables, such as age, sex, body weight, level of exercise, and use of caffeine, provides one level of understanding. By comparing subjects across settings, such as home vs. work and daytime vs. nighttime, one can also assess the role of the setting. When subjects are asked to rate themselves for a given event and a specific BP measurement, individual differences in perception of the stressfulness of an event or place become clearer.

Shapiro and associates cite a related growing body of evidence that job stress might be a primary factor in the etiology of hypertension and cardiovascular disease. They present their research findings on the assessment of job stress as a contributor to hypertension and cardiovascular disease for paramedics. First, they assessed both high and low stress as related to cynical hostility and defensiveness. Next, they assessed the role of ambivalence and conflicting attitudes to determine whether individuals who are motivated by social approval would inhibit the expression of such "sociably unacceptable" behavior. Also assessed and compared were workdays and days off.

Among other findings, the results of Shapiro's group indicate that inhibition of anger and hostility is toxic in hypertension. Both diagnosis and treatment may be improved by adopting ambulatory BP monitoring procedures to account for individual differences and reaction to environmental events. Whether such findings will be incorporated into the medical management of hypertension and cardiovascular disease remains to be seen. Meanwhile, it is clear that anyone wishing to do quality clinical applied psychophysiology in the area of essential hypertension cannot ignore these procedures and findings.

Chapter 7. Mechanisms and Treatment of Raynaud's Disease and Phenomenon

In this chapter, Robert R. Freedman first reviews the etiology and distinguishing features for classification of Raynaud's disease and phenomenon. Research in Freedman's laboratory points to a "local fault" that renders small peripheral blood vessels hypersensitive to local cooling. No differences were found between patients with primary Raynaud's disease and control subjects in their response to a variety of sympathetic stimuli, such as reflex cooling, indirect heating, and intra-arterial infusion of tyramine. Freedman demonstrated that a sympathetic nerve block of one hand did not significantly alter the frequency of vasospastic attacks when compared to the nonanesthetized contralateral hand. Using a radioisotope clearance procedure, Freedman further demonstrated that temperature-feedback-trained vasodilation occurred in finger capillary beds. Also, sympathetically mediated finger-skin conductance was demonstrated to increase, rather than decrease, during temperature training. By measurement of circulating catecholamine levels, it was also demonstrated that the assumption of decreased sympathetic activation during temperature-feedback training is not warranted. It is noted that surgical procedures to abolish sympathetic influence to control Raynaud's disease have not been successful. These findings argue against the role of sympathetic innervation as the explanation for Raynaud's disease.

Using brachial artery infusion of α_1- and α_2-adrenergic agonist, Freedman demonstrates that patients with primary Raynaud's disease have increased peripheral vascular α_1- and α_2-adrenergic receptor sensitivity and/or density. Thus, the "local fault" appears to be sensitization of peripheral vascular α_2-adrenergic receptors, which can probably also be induced by emotional stress and corresponding normal catecholamine elevations. In previous research, Freedman had shown that temperature feedback was physiologically different from autogenic training or frontalis EMG feedback. Using the brachial artery infusion model, Freedman demonstrated that propranolol significantly attenuated vasodilation, but had no effect on autogenic training. Presented is a comparison of temperature training, temperature training under mild cold stress, and other methods.

Freedman's research demonstrates that previously held assumptions about Raynaud's disease are inaccurate. The manner in which this was demonstrated by this careful researcher is exemplary and sets a standard for clinical applied psychophysiology. For the clinician treating these patient populations, a giant step forward has been taken.

IV. Applied Psychophysiology and Respiration

Chapter 8. Sleep-Disordered Breathing: Preliminary Natural History and Mortality Results

Sonia Ancoli-Israel, Melville R. Klauber, Robert L. Fell, Linda Parker, Lynne A. Kenney, and Richard Willens provide in this chapter a brief review of the literature on sleep-disordered breathing, prompting the question as to how predictive inpatient recordings of apnea status are for predicting outpatient apnea. The role of breathing must be determined relative to context to accurately appreciate the implications. The authors report preliminary results on male patients in a Veterans Administration Medical Center ward, yielding two major observations: (1) that inpatient sleep recordings may not be predictive of outpatient apnea status and (2) that moderate sleep-disordered breathing predicts mortality. Their results have implications both for assessment and for the necessity to initiate treatment of sleep-disordered patients.

Chapter 9. Significance of Breathing Awareness and Exercise Training for Recovery after Myocardial Infarction

In this chapter, Jan van Dixhoorn points out that the treatment of choice for cardiac rehabilitation has been exercise. The author summarizes a variety of research suggesting that relaxation can impact positively on risk factors for cardiovascular disease as well as related psychological factors. In van Dixhoorn's research, the relative effects of a comprehensive program of exercise, breathing awareness training, and relaxation are compared with those of exercise alone in a sample of patients recovering from myocardial ischemia due to exercise. The comprehensive program enhances heart rate variability and reduces the occurrence of cardiovascular events, as well as produces psychological improvement. One important implication of van Dixhoorn's findings is that sufficient attention to both sides of the psycho/physiological equation yields measurable benefits in clinical applications.

Chapter 10. Respiration in Clinical Psychophysiology: How to Assess Critical Parameters and Their Change with Treatment

Robert Fried outlines in this chapter the respiration physiology that underlies his work and provides a review of his psychophysiological respiration profile—affording a comprehensive view of cardiovascular, pulmonary, temperature, and neuromuscular reactions during rest and various activities imposed in the clinic. Fried points out that most persons with psychiatric, psychosomatic, and stress disorders have hyperventilation-related complaints, and it is not coincidental that hyperventilation symptoms are indistinguishable from these disorders. One problem, of course, is what is stress? Fried selects Selye's definition, that stress is the "nonspecific response of the body to any demand made upon it." This definition does not explain the phenomenon but does provide a general description of what follows chronic exposure to stressors. Fried further elects to follow the Pavlovian Society's notion that all nonspecific reactions begin with an orienting response (OR), whereby activity—especially breathing—is inhibited and is followed by an excitatory increased metabolic demand for oxygen. Based on his extensive literature review, it is Fried's opinion that the body cannot sustain intermittent OR and sympathetic arousal for any considerable time period and still meet the increased metabolic demand for oxygen. The nonspecific stress response then can be defined as a specific consequence of increased tissue air hunger.

To better understand how metabolic arousal and homeostatic hypoxia with chronic lacticacidemia account for this observation, Fried argues, it is essential that one be more knowledgeable about respiration/ventilation and the O_2 and CO_2 transport systems. He argues that the acid and alkaline relationship that shifts in this process is the critical variable in respiration psychophysiology and is dependent on CO_2 and not O_2. Fried integrates the role of the parasympathetic activity and the respiratory sinus arrhythmia, which is typically absent before training but may become pronounced and involved in changing a breathing style. He presents other markers that may be significant, one of which is EEG change. Fried argues that the assessment of the EEG must incorporate the status of appropriate ventilation.

Based on ten years of clinical and research efforts, Fried has developed breathing-assessment techniques and protocols as well as therapeutic strategies. He presents assessment and treatment protocols to help the reader understand how they might duplicate his process. In addition to his protocols, he presents typical findings that help one to assess whether one is obtaining results that are similar to those he would obtain in his clinical research setting.

Chapter 11. Breathing: Physiological Reasons for Loss of Self-Control

In his chapter, P. G. F. Nixon first makes the point that respiratory dysregulation does not appear on its own—rather, dysregulation appears as one element of the multiple systems disturbances that occur in people who are stretched beyond the boundaries of their physiological tolerance by effort and distress. Nixon focuses on arousal as the chief enemy of order and stability. However, arousal is only one end of the spectrum, and it has both positive and negative effects. The inference is, of course, that the lower end of the physiological spectrum can have a similar positive or negative benefit. Nixon observes that when one goes beyond the physiological tolerance of the individual, there is likely to be homeostatic degradation, catabolic disorders, and acceleration of entropy.

Nixon believes that the performance–arousal curve appears to be the most useful model for solving the riddles of failure of respiratory self-control. For those individuals who fail to accommodate to distress, the loss of order, stability, and control of the internal milieu results in a continuing spiral downward of failures to adequately compensate for the expenditures of the resources of the body. Failure to resolve the stress and recovery phase leads to a hypersensitivity to any stimulation with increased reactivity.

Nixon believes that two phases correspond with and are probably caused by biphasic neuronal responses to hypocapnia. The early phase generates anxiety and stimulates breathing to any given level of carbon dioxide in the blood. The catabolic shifts that take place in high arousal states add to the burdens of effort in distress, which consequently encourages further hyperventilation. It is probable that hyperventilation-related cardiac disorders are generated in the first phase and the fatigue syndrome in the second. Sleep provides the opportunity for anabolism, a powerful promoter of order and stability in the internal systems. Unfortunately, inadequate ventilation during sleep often reduces the anabolic effect. This leads to further changes affecting the brain and the sleep cycle itself, and again another vicious cycle leads to further disregulation.

Nixon points out that in assessment, one must keep in mind that the loss of control of breathing behavior is likely to present so that further and greater sustained effort is exerted—trying harder only makes the condition worse. To assess patients, Nixon employs the physiological measures of the clinical capnograph, which continually records the partial pressure of the carbon dioxide in the exhaled air drawn through a fine plastic tube held by a light headband in one nostril.

The reductionistic approaches of conventional medicine to hyperventilation have yielded little of value for everyday diagnosis and management. By using Nixon's suggested systems approach, with a modified performance arousal curve, one can look at hyperventilation as a marker of loss of order and stability of the internal systems through failure of homeostatic and cognitive control. His procedure not only provides a methodology for assessing performance but also offers a means of assessing treatment effects.

V. Neuromuscular Disorders

Chapter 12. Psychophysiological Methods in the Assessment and Treatment of Chronic Musculoskeletal Pain

Herta Flor and Niels Birbaumer point out in their chapter that the psychophysiological assessment of chronic musculoskeletal pain, specifically chronic lower back pain, has become very popular over the last decade. Bilateral asymmetries, abnormal resting tension levels, abnormal movement patterns, and an abnormal reactivity to stressors have all been investigated. However, there have been few attempts to apply psychophysiological theories to the study of chronic musculoskeletal pain. The authors have begun to address the aforementioned issues as well as to establish a program of research based on hypotheses regarding psychophysiological specificities that may contribute to the development or maintenance of chronic pain or to both.

Two theoretical concepts are identified as having value in the study of the psychophysiology of musculoskeletal pain. The first is that respondent conditioning of tension and pain serves as a basic mechanism for the development of chronic musculoskeletal pain syndromes. Based on this model, it is assumed that pain leads to reflex muscle spasms and sympathetic activation that can become conditioned to innocuous stimuli present in the pain-eliciting situation. It is believed that over time, the increases in muscle tension are frequent and of sufficient magnitude and duration that these physiological processes lead to persistent pain and suffering. Often, this newly acquired pain is unrelated to the original source of pain, although the patient may attribute it to its original pain-eliciting event. Flor and Birbaumer examine this model to demonstrate that muscle tensions can be classically conditioned, that the obtained muscle tension levels induce pain, and that chronic pain patients overreact physiologically to stimuli associated with the original pain episode.

The second theoretical concept examined is that of response stereotypy (or symptom specificity). It has been suggested that pain patients are prone to show maximum physiological reactivity in the muscular system and that this overutilization might induce musculoskeletal pain syndromes. This concept was extended by Sternbach, who noted that prolonged return to baseline levels following the response to a stressor might be more indicative of physiological dysregulation than the amplitude of the response itself. The focus then becomes to demonstrate whether there is an increased amplitude and/or duration of the response as a means to understand the pathophysiology of chronic musculoskeletal pain.

Flor and Birbaumer provide a related series of findings based on their systematic research. Both chronic back pain and temporomandibular pain were treated with EMG biofeedback and cognitive behavior therapy as well as traditional medical treatment. In these studies, biofeedback treatments proved to be the most effective. Thus, it remains the case that psychophysiological assessments that are based on a sound theoretical rationale are a useful tool in patient selection for psychophysiological treatment and are themselves valuable predictors of probable treatment outcome. While the data are being collected, the clinician remains in the real-world situation, having to frequently treat pain patients without an adequate data base. It is felt that this particular chapter will be of benefit in the process of developing that base.

Chapter 13. Overcoming Learned Nonuse: A New Approach to Treatment in Physical Medicine

In his chapter, Edward Taub examines the assumptions underlying any injury to the nervous system or other part of the body that results in an initial loss of motor ability. A long-term result of these types of injuries leads to the assumption of two possible outcomes: First is that the injury permanently destroys an anatomical substrate or structure upon which the movement was based, and therefore motor function will not return. The second is that the injured substrate will recover or heal either entirely or in part, and motor function will then return to the maximum extent permitted by whatever that underlying restitution of the anatomical substrate might be.

The purpose of Taub's chapter is to advance the possibility of a new mechanism, which he has termed "learned nonuse." Taub attacks the assumption that failure to regain motor function can be caused only by a failure at some anatomical or transmitter level. His notion is that learning can and is of sufficient influence to explain the deficits. This theory was developed during Taub's own research on somatosensory deafferentation in monkeys. The theory comes from the failure of his findings to explain the outcomes that followed deafferentation in monkeys. Taub applies his animals research to human conditions and begins to make parallel observations at this level. Specifically, Taub begins with deafferentation of one limb and notes its specific effects on that limb and the sensual failure to recover. In subsequent research on the bilateral deafferentation of the upper extremities in monkey, Taub demonstrated that recovery was actually better than if he had deafferented one limb.

Taub's initial work demonstrated that contrary to the accepted view, there are a variety of techniques that can lead monkeys to exhibit purposive movement of the affected extremity following somatosensory deafferentation. Thus, he demonstrated that the chained stretch reflexes are not necessary for the learning and performance of most types of movements in monkeys. With these findings, he then proceeded to elucidate the mechanism responsible for this phenomenon. Through a series of well-conceived and systematic experiments, Taub was able to demonstrate that a forced-use paradigm would lead to increased recovery of the single-limb-deafferented monkey.

These techniques have been applied to humans. One series of studies demonstrated that in fact the motor control of the affected limbs could be readily demonstrated in the laboratory. That is, a human patient could evidence with electrophysiological feedback control over muscles in an affected arm. However, it was also found that even though this could be readily accomplished in the laboratory, it did not generalize to the real world; the limb was not used and continued to be a dysfunctional extremity. In humans, Taub demonstrates a learned recovery similar to that of monkeys. This is done by initiating a forced-use paradigm—restraining the unaffected limb with a soft sling and thereby forcing the use of the affected limb. With this technique, it has been demonstrated that increased recovery can be attained and that it will in fact generalize to the real world. Taub goes on to extend the implications of his theory to other conditions as well, including pain of a nature such that use of the particular extremity or engagement in a particular movement results in pain or a punishment for that attempted function.

Taub has therefore elegantly clarified an assumption long held to be true in the relationship regarding the anatomical substrates and the essential requirements for motor function. He has also advanced the understanding of treatment for those conditions, going beyond the assumption that absence of function is sufficient evidence to indicate that there is a defect or some absence of anatomical substrate. This particular series of research studies and this particular theory of learned nonuse go a very long way in suggesting means for enhancing the quality of life for numerous conditions affected by this phenomenon.

VI. Long-Term Stress

The work environment is one context wherein the interaction of stress and health is becoming more clearly documented and understood. People who perform in hazardous environments provide an opportunity to study the extreme demands placed on human function.

Chapter 14. Quartets in Antarctic Isolation

This chapter by A J. W. Taylor and M. M. Brown presents work on the preparation and debriefing of a series of four-person parties that wintered over in the Antarctic each year from 1986 until the present. The purpose of the work was to detect changes in the health, personality, and social interaction of these individuals and to relate the findings to those of previously studied larger isolated groups.

A variety of interesting effects were observed, many of them related to group dynamics and leadership. The data acknowledged are not accumulated and compared with a matched control group. But this is the beginning of systematic assessment of these groups, which are originally assembled for other purposes. This is another opportunity for behavioral scientists to participate and share their expertise as they have with the various space agencies and undersea programs.

Chapter 15. Notes on the Use of Biological Markers in the Study of Long-Term Stress

Finally, Tores Theorell points out in this chapter the possibility of monitoring in work settings minute changes in blood and urinary concentration of hormones, immunoglobulins, and lipoproteins, as well as blood pressure and electrical activity of the brain and heart. The shortage of parameters to monitor is not the problem; quite the contrary, it is the question of which parameters to select. Whatever parameters are chosen, the short-term changes typically associated with a stress reaction are not the only variables of interest. The relationship of the long-term effects of stress reactions to health may be more important. What is sought are relationships that persist despite all the difficulties of day-to-day function as well as the various mechanisms of adaptation along the way.

Theorell presents findings that afford the opportunity not only to determine the effects of stress but also to then use that information in a systematic manner to determine whether prevention can then follow. The reader will be drawn to the obvious—that the circumstance and the individual in interaction remain critical to the understanding of the effects of stress for both immediate and long-term consequences. The continuous monitoring of blood pressure and heart rate may be especially valuable tools in the determination of the effects of long-term stress.

Conclusion

The individual chapters of this text are excellent representations of the quality and type of work undertaken in the area of clinical applied psychophysiology. This rapidly growing field of theory, research, and application advances only through the efforts of individual researchers, individuals who could benefit from even greater opportunity for collegial exchange and collaboration. In that sense, this series of international conferences has not lost momentum due to the suddenly transformed politics of the world, but rather has gained impetus for remaining focused on the original goals of the meetings. The changing world has increased the urgency for such international endeavors. Comparisons across differing cultures offer a unique means of assessing various biopsychosocial influences on health and well-being. It is possible to learn from our mutual experiences and to correct for those efforts that prove not to contribute to health. There exists the possibility of another order for humankind to follow—one of collaboration through promotion of the well-being of all!

CHAPTER 2

Schopenhauer's Ethics and the Concept of Behavioral Self-Regulation

Wolfgang Tunner

I would like to talk to you about philosophy, but by "philosophy" I mean the metaphysics of philosophy. Metaphysics is the core of philosophy. The content of metaphysics cannot be comprehended by the human mind. The great philosophers speak of the incomprehensible. It is the unspeakable for which language lacks the word of proof.

On their road to the limits of understanding, philosophers have made many discoveries, for example, the axioms of logic and mathematics or the laws of planetary movement. However, these discoveries are not the primary goal of philosophy.

I would like to present you with some thoughts on self-regulation, and I will try to relate these thoughts to the metaphysics of Arthur Schopenhauer (1788–1860).

Self-regulation means the functioning of behavior and physiology without external assistance. A homeostatic system, in which the variable to be regulated is the structure of the system itself, is a technical example of self-regulation. In psychology, self-regulation has in principle the same connotation: It is the ability to think and behave independently. One of the problems with self-regulation is that in order to function normally, self-control is necessary. Self-regulation is possible only if we can predict and control our internal psychological and physiological activities.

Self-regulation is in a sense like labor: I have to create the conditions

WOLFGANG TUNNER • Department of Clinical Psychology, Institute of Psychology, University of Munich, D-80802 München, Germany.

Clinical Applied Psychophysiology, edited by John G. Carlson, A. Ronald Seifert, and Niels Birbaumer. Plenum Press, New York, 1994.

for work before I can actually work. If hindrances and inhibitions occur, the problems of self-regulation become clear. Self-regulation seems to be more an idea than a reality. The ability to regulate one's self is limited. Furthermore, if self-control works, it often impedes and obstructs the way we want to live. This conflict leads us to the question of what "self" really means. Even though everybody directly experiences the self and everybody knows that he or she possesses a self, it is impossible to say what it is. It probably consists of a feeling for the knowledge of our own abilities and weaknesses and the sum of our present and past experience.

The control we have over ourselves implies that we have to separate the self. Self-regulation of a highly pleasurable emotion in order to complete certain work is a good example. The impulse to work and the pleasure impulse are unified in one person. One's self is the place where the fight between impulses takes place. The commanding and dictating part of the self usually identifies itself with the ego. The obeying part is the emotion. You see, ego and self are not the same. The self consists of all my abilities and inabilities as they are; the ego has to do with certain intention that directs itself—as our example shows—against parts of the self.

The intention to control has a further characteristic. It directs the attention away from the present to the future. Control is always directed toward a certain goal. Because my intention, "I want, I wish," does not mean that I can really do it, basic insecurity and concern arise as to whether the control will work or not.

To summarize, we may say that self-control separates and splits the self, directs attention away from the present, and causes concern about unpredictability. The more I want to control myself, the more my self is split and the more I am concerned about the future.

Let me now jump to Schopenhauer. His philosophy is highly interesting in the effort to understand self-control. Schopenhauer based his thoughts on the philosophy of Immanuel Kant, the holy writings of the Hindu, and the philosophy of ideas of Plato. Without knowledge of these sources, it is difficult to understand Schopenhauer. Despite this difficulty, I will try to illustrate the most important concept of his philosophy: This concept is WILL. Will is the basis of the axiomatic structure of his philosophy.

I would like to ask you to do a short "Gedankenexperiment" in order to follow the methodology of the philosopher. The starting point is the naïve and focusing concentration on object-oriented perception. Schopenhauer calls it "contemplation." He totally leaves himself to the impressions as they are present in the immediate experience. He eliminates the sources of his expectations and takes things as they appear. If he directs his attention to the activity of his inner organs, then it becomes clear to him that there is nothing that is of greater conscious certainty than the feeling that arises in this process of concentration. Feeling is directed to nothing else than the fact that he is alive. It is the basic awareness that cannot be traced back any further. Life, as his own life and that which can be found everywhere in nature, is the only unquestionable fact, the only fact without a doubt. Nothing is as certain as the physical awareness of life.

Since science has shown that our perception does not reflect reality, and that our sensual experience never leads to certainty, philosophers have tried to find a pure consciousness that cannot be doubted. Descartes found this certainty in thinking—the *cogito me cogitare, ergo sum*. That is an inner experience for which we need no senses that normally assure us of reality. Kant, too, saw the last certainty in the thinking ego. For Schopenhauer, on the other hand, certainty is not a cognitive activity, but the body-bounded feeling for the fact that one is alive.

Schopenhauer's metaphysics begins at the point of this certainty. Something that is undoubtable must also have undoubtable reasons for its existence. Just as science searches out the experiences of our sense organs and our perceptions, metaphysics looks behind this knowledge for a last certainty. In contrast to science, the philosopher believes that we lack reason and mental abilities to find the last causes of appearances. Beyond the limits of reason, there are laws other than those of reason. For reason we need space, time, and causality. Without these factors, there is no reasoning and understanding. It therefore seems plausible to assume the nonunderstandable without space, time, and causality.

For us, things seem real that can be proven by measurement. But what we experience is real too. The subjective world is real, even without measurement and number, even if measurement and number contradict the subjective world. No measurement and no theory can predict what the fantasy of the subjective world creates. In fantasy, we can totally exchange the order of spatial and temporal relationships. The nonreversibility of time is not valid in fantasy. Fantasy is that part of reality that allows one to think the unreal. Fantasy enables us to have an idea of the metaphysical causes of appearance. It makes metaphysics possible.

For Schopenhauer, the last causes of everything are all the same; all suffering and pleasure, even if they appear in totally different individuals and are separated by time and space, are all the same. Everybody lives in everybody else, so that all passion of the world has the same basic origin and returns to this origin. What we perceive and understand from this basic origin is the realization of WILL. The realization of will is perceived as the constant struggle for existence and pleasure. In this respect, each individual is a victim of his or her egotistical drives. It is a strange contradiction that will, which manifests itself as the fight of life, is viewed as perfect unity in its basis.

Man always acts only on his will, and at the same time acts out of necessity—thus the affix of the philosopher. This, however, is based on the fact that he or she is what he or she wants to be. Subjectively, everyone feels that one does only what one wants. This means only that his or her action is the pure expression of his or her own being. The same would therefore be felt by anyone, even the most primitive being in nature if it had had the power of feeling. If this opinion is correct, then self-control, viewed as a free decision of will, is impossible. Nevertheless, Schopenhauer proposed an ethic in which man is free of the urges of his or her egotistical drives. However, he or she does not base his or her ethics on the "you should" that is demanded by reason, but on the feeling of compassion.

At this point, I would like to build another bridge to psychology. Earlier, it was noted that the controlling impulse, "I want to," divides the self, distracts attention away from the present, and elicits insecurity with regard to the success of the action. These are no optimal conditions for the motivation of self-control. Nevertheless, self-control is possible. The first reason is that we are capable of learning and that we are imaginative. Self-control is not present from the very beginning, but is learned over time and under the influence of imagination. Imagination anticipates reward and punishment contingent on behavior, no matter how distant it may be. Second, the disruption of the unity of the self is not only a consequence of self-control. Emotions and cognitions are naturally created as opposites. Because there is hunger, eating is pleasurable. Work makes feasts enjoyable, and love makes hatred so terrible. Third, self-control does not divide reason and feelings. Normally, these two cannot be separated. Usually, there are opposing motives that stem from emotional and rational reasons and may be judged as positive or negative, depending on the current attitude. Fear, for example, has a positive factor of curiosity, and love has the negative factor of exhaustion. Thus, it is possible to say that there are also pleasurable motives for self-control and that these motives are probably the reason that self-control sometimes prevails.

If self-control is directed at altruistic actions, ethics is not content with this latter statement of the psychologist. The ethicist demands an action that is not founded on one's own pleasure. Schopenhauer views compassion as the motive for altruistic actions. If I take an action only because of another, then the other's joy or suffering must be my own motive. "The other turns into the last purpose of my will," writes the philosopher. When my will becomes that of someone else, then I want his or her joy and do not want his or her suffering. This implies that I have some kind of identification with him or her. The difference between us and the other is to some extent suspended. Schopenhauer calls this process mysterious because it is something reason cannot account for. I believe that psychologists have to concur with this. From the metaphysical point of view, this mystery can be an indication that beyond the egotistical struggle of motives there is unity.

Through empathy, one's self extends into the self of the other. Doing so appears to be possible if the ego gives up issuing commands. If one has the conviction that everything is one in the beginning and in the last aim of our being, it may be possible to have self-control without too bitter a fight of motives. The opponents no longer seem so alienated in their knowledge of unity. And this is the condition for an easier reconciliation of motives. Whatever thoughts and emotions may come into being, they are still always part of myself.

Metaphysics may be useful in that it influences the everyday conflict of motives. It is not sufficient to function. It is always important to know what one functions for. Science has shown how we function, but metaphysics develops ideas on whether or not it all makes sense—and it is clear that these ideas influence the way things work.

Reference

Schopenhauer, A. (1819). *Die Welt als Wille und Vorstellung* (4th ed.). Hübscher (Ed.), Stuttgart: Brockhaus (1988).

PART **II**

Disorders of
the Central Nervous System

Included in this section are Chapter 3, by Niels Birbaumer and colleagues, Brigitte Rockstroh, Thomas Elbert, Peter Wolf, Andreas Düchting-Röth, Martin Reker, Irene Daum, Werner Lutzenberger, and Johannes Dichgans, and Chapter 4, by J. P. Rosenfeld. The first is on the biofeedback of slow cortical potentials (SCPs) in the treatment of epilepsy; the second provides a look at the very recent work on the use of the P300 event-related brain potential (ERP) in various types of psychiatric and neurological diagnoses.

The presentation by Birbaumer and colleagues in their chapter provides an overview of several animal and human studies suggesting a link between abnormal SCPs and epilepsy. These studies support the hypothesis that abnormal increases in cortical excitability are correlated with epileptic seizures. Relatedly, other studies in Birbaumer's laboratory show that with biofeedback, healthy subjects can achieve control of SCPs in a few sessions of training, but that epileptics have difficulty with this response. In recent research reported in the chapter, Birbaumer and associates extend the amount of biofeedback training and obtain positive results in terms of seizure frequency in some epileptic patients. This research, as with all of that by Birbaumer's team, provides a prototype for the use of applied psychophysiology assessment and training in dealing with a serious clinical disorder.

Rosenfeld's chapter is a fascinating discussion of the use of the "oddball paradigm" (the presentation of a relatively infrequent stimulus) to elicit the P300 potential in efforts to diagnose such problems as potential suicide, depression, schizophrenia, and others. Rosenfeld proposes a variation on the method, termed the "dual-task paradigm" (providing a second task that draws off cognitive–attentional resources and reduces P300 amplitude), to provide better individual assessment of psychiatric and neurological disorders. Several manipulations yield an effective means for differentiating subjects undergoing (ischemic) pain stimulation.

An innovative extension of the technique for psychodiagnosis along thematic dimensions is described and simulated using films with differing attentional value. Rosenfeld's applied psychophysiology is consistently at the leading edge of conceptual and technological innovation, and the studies described here are no exception. The reader will invariable be led to additional hypotheses for the application of the P300 techniques outlined by Rosenfeld.

CHAPTER 3

Biofeedback of Slow Cortical Potentials in Epilepsy

Niels Birbaumer, Brigitte Rockstroh,
Thomas Elbert, Peter Wolf,
Andreas Düchting-Röth, Martin Reker,
Irene Daum, Werner Lutzenberger,
and Johannes Dichgans

Introduction: Behavioral and Psychophysiological Treatment of Epilepsy

It remains a pertinent problem that dependent on the type of epilepsy, 20–50% of patients are not sufficiently controlled with antiepileptic medication. Alternative approaches such as behavioral treatment have therefore been explored. The behavioral research was stimulated by a famous single case study published by Efron (1975) documenting the classical conditioning of seizure depression. Reduction in seizure frequency has been re-

NIELS BIRBAUMER • Department of Clinical and Physiological Psychology, University of Tübingen, D-72074 Tübingen, Germany; Department of General Psychology, Universitá degli Studi, I-35122 Padova, Italy. BRIGITTE ROCKSTROH • Department of Psychology, University of Konstanz, D-78434 Konstanz, Germany. THOMAS ELBERT • Institute of Experimental Audiology, University of Münster, D-48149 Münster, Germany. PETER WOLF, ANDREAS DÜCHTING-RÖTH, and MARTIN REKER • Epilepsy Center Bethel, D-33617 Bielefeld, Germany. IRENE DAUM and WERNER LUTZENBERGER • Department of Clinical and Physiological Psychology, University of Tübingen, D-7274 Tübingen, Germany. JOHANNES DICHGANS • Department of Neurology, University of Tübingen, D-72074 Tübingen, Germany.

Clinical Applied Psychophysiology, edited by John G. Carlson, A. Ronald Seifert, and Niels Birbaumer. Plenum Press, New York, 1994.

ported following the application of desensitization and extinction procedures (Forster, 1969, 1972, 1977; Rockstroh & Elbert, 1990), self-control procedures implying self-perception, self-control, and relaxation (Dahl, Brorson, 1985; Dahl, Melin, & Leissner, 1988; Bühring & Weltek, 1990), biofeedback of respiratory parameters (Fried, Rubin, Carlton, & Fox, 1984), and instrumental modification of EEG spectra (Lubar, 1984; Sterman, 1984; Rockstroh, Elbert, Birbaumer, Wolf, Düchting-Roth, Reker, Daum, Lutzenberger, & Dichgans, 1993). For recent overviews, see Birbaumer, Elbert, Canavan, and Rockstroh (1990) and Elbert, Rockstroh, Canavan, Birbaumer, Lutzenberger, von Bülow, and Linden (1991).

Our approach described in this chapter relies on biofeedback and instrumental conditioning of *surface-negative slow cortical potentials (SCPs)*. The underlying neurophysiology of SCPs is fairly well understood. SCPs represent the extent to which apical dendrites of the cortical pyramidal cells are depolarized and therefore indicate cortical excitability (Elbert & Rockstroh, 1987; Elbert, 1991). The SCPs originate in the cerebral cortex, when unspecific excitatory thalamic or intracortical input depolarizes the apical dendrites (for reviews, see Birbaumer *et al.*, 1990; Rockstroh, Elbert, Canavan, Lutzenberger, & Birbaumer, 1989). Cortical excitability is regulated according to the constantly varying environmental and metabolic demands, and feedback mechanisms within the brain control the range of this excitability.

Overexcitability of cortical tissue, as during seizures, can be initiated by a transient failure in down-regulating mechanisms and allow an explosive chain reaction of excitation among neuronal networks (Braitenberg, 1978; Elbert & Rockstroh, 1987). Extreme negative shifts that result from overexcitability of cortical neuronal networks indicate a high risk for seizures to develop. For example, pronounced negative DC shifts develop under hyperventilation—a procedure known to increase excitability in neuronal tissue due to metabolic changes (von Bülow, Elbert, Rockstroh, Lutzenberger, Canavan, & Birbaumer, 1989; Rockstroh, 1990). Anticonvulsants significantly *reduce* surface negativity in healthy subjects (Rockstroh, Elbert, Lutzenberger, Altenmuller, Diener, & Birbaumer, 1987; Rockstroh, Elbert, Lutzenberger, & Altenmuller, 1991).

Animal experiments as well as observations from human subjects suggest a link between abnormal negative SCPs and epileptic activity. In the cat, the negative shift with onset of seizure activity in the EEG (induced by epileptic agents such as pentylentetrazol or penicillin) coincides with paroxysmal depolarization shifts in cortical neurons (Caspers & Speckmann, 1969; Caspers, Speckmann, & Lehmenkuehler, 1984). A widespread negativity appears during generalized seizure activity and is followed by a positive repolarization with termination of the seizure. Patients who undergo an epileptic attack during hyperventilation tend to exhibit extreme potential shifts exceeding 200 μV (von Bülow et al., 1989; Chatrian, Somasundaram, & Tassinari, 1968). Slow negative potential shifts can be considered a sign of cortical excitability, and that excitability that increases beyond control reduces thresholds for an epileptic attack. Epileptic patients are vulnerable to cortical excitement that is beyond their control, and they suffer from an impaired or at least transiently failing regulation of their cortical excitability. Such a deficit could manifest itself in an impaired capacity for self-regulation of SCPs.

For the biofeedback of SCPs (the self-regulation paradigm used by Elbert, 1991; Elbert, Birbaumer, Lutzenberger, & Rockstroh, 1979; Elbert, Rockstroh Lutzenberger, & Birbaumer, 1980), subjects receive on-line feedback of their surface-recorded SCPs and are reinforced for increasing or reducing their SCPs above or below a prestimulus baseline level depending on discriminative stimuli. Studies from different laboratories have replicated our original finding that healthy human subjects can achieve "control" through their SCPs in this paradigm—that is, they produce significant differences between required negativity increase and negativity suppression—within 100–200 training trials (or two training sessions) without mediation from other physiological systems (for a recent review, see Rockstroh et al., 1989). A preliminary study with epileptic patients revealed a reduced ability for self-control compared to healthy subjects— that is, only 1 of the total 18 patients demonstrated SCP differentiation within two feedback sessions (Birbaumer, Elbert, Rockstroh, Daum, Wolf, & Canavan, 1992; Elbert et al., 1991). These results support our hypothesis that epileptic patients suffer from impaired control over their cortical excitability (SCPs). It is also of interest whether and to what extent SCP regulation could be improved if feedback and instrumental conditioning are extended to many training sessions. Since control over cortical excitability is represented in the regulation and control over surface-recorded SCPs and since acquisition of SCP control seems to be related to a stabilization of an impaired excitability regulation in epileptic patients, then patients should profit from extended training.

Study 1

A total of 14 patients suffering from drug-refractory epilepsy (complex-focal, grand mal, and absence type of seizures) participated in 28 1-hr training sessions. In a double-blind setting, 7 patients received feedback of their vertex-recorded SCPs and were reinforced for systematically increasing or suppressing surface negativity relative to the pretrial baseline level, while another 7 patients received feedback of the activity in the alpha frequency range (9–15 Hz) and were reinforced for increasing or reducing the activity in the alpha band depending on the discriminative stimuli. The same visual feedback was given to both groups, and it was carefully assessed that patients could not discriminate between SCP and alpha feedback conditions. The control group served to control for the specificity of excitability control by means of SCPs. Of the 7 patients, 4 demonstrated SCP control at the end of the training period (Elbert, Birbaumer, & Rockstroh, 1990; Elbert et al., 1991). Only the group receiving SCP feedback demonstrated a significant reduction in seizure frequency. We concluded that nonspecific "placebo" effects of the biofeedback procedure were unlikely to affect seizure frequency.

Study 2

The second study was planned to expand the investigation of the acquisition of control over SCPs to a larger group of drug-refractory patients. Because of the evidence that alpha feedback did not affect seizure frequency in the preceding study, and out of ethical considerations, we decided not to use a (placebo) control group. In addition to the acquisition of SCP control and its relationship to a change in seizure frequency, possible determinants (such as age, medication, type of epilepsy, and pretraining seizure frequency) of acquisition and learning progress were evaluated. The methodology is described in detail elsewhere (Rockstroh et al., 1993); only an overview of the basic procedure is given here.

A total of 25 patients (13 females, 12 males) participated in a standardized training program (age range 15–49 yrs). Patients suffered from complex-focal seizures ($N = 20$), secondary generalized grand mal ($N = 1$), and petit mal epilepsy or absences ($N = 4$). The patients' seizure history ranged from 3 to 15 years. A minimum of 1 seizure per week was required for patients to be included in the sample. The average seizure frequency varied from 1/week to more than 60/week (series of absences) around a mean of 11.5 (calculated from individual medians during baseline). Patients with progressive neurological conditions, pseudo- or nonepileptic seizures, or psychiatric complications were not included in the sample, nor were patients suffering primarily from attacks during sleep.

Of the 25 patients, 15 were trained at Tübingen University and 10 at the Epilepsy Center in Bethel, Bielefeld. (Training procedures, data acquisition, and data analyses were the same at both sites.)

Medication remained constant throughout the baseline, training, and follow-up periods. Anticonvulsant blood levels were checked at regular intervals. Medication regimes were highly variable, ranging from mono-therapy to regimens with various types of antiepileptics.

Biofeedback Procedure

Within each training session, continuous visual feedback from the vertex (Cz) SCP was provided to the subject during intervals of 8 sec each by means of the outline of a rocket ship appearing on a TV screen in front of the subject (see Fig. 1). Its movements were a linear function of the integrated SCP referred to the mean of a 4-sec pretrial baseline. Depending on visual discriminative stimuli (the letters "A" or "B" presented on the TV screen simultaneously with the feedback stimulus), the subject was asked to modulate the SCP response in either a negative or a positive direction. Forward movements of the rocket ship signaled the required SCP shift, while backward movements indicated inadequate performance. The letter "A" signaled that an increase in negativity above the mean of the pretrial baseline would move the rocket ship forward, while the letter "B" asked for negativity suppression. On-line artifact-control procedures prevented movements of the signal from being affected by eye movements, muscular

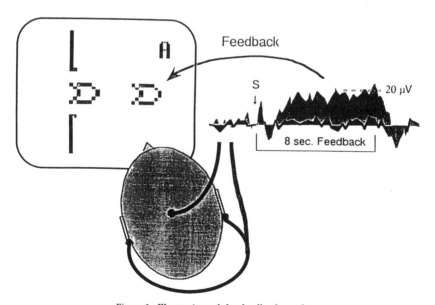

Figure 1. Illustration of the feedback mode.

artifacts, or tiny electrode displacements. The effects of conditioning or "transfer of learning" were tested in transfer trials in which only the signal stimuli (e.g., "A" or "B") were presented and no feedback was provided. Each patient completed 28 sessions. Within each session, an initial block of 20 transfer trials was followed by two blocks of 30 feedback trials each, while the session terminated with another 30 transfer trials. Within each trial block, "A" and "B" trials alternated pseudorandomly.

Training sessions were held for 2 weeks (two 1-hr sessions per day with a 2-day break separating each training week). After an intermission of 8 weeks, patients underwent another eight sessions of training (the "booster" sessions). Sessions 10–28 included playing a radio program chosen by the subject in order to simulate conditions of real life. Patients were instructed to practice the acquired SCP during the intermission by realizing their strategies for SCP control on "A" and "B" trials 5 times per day for about 5 min each. The year after the "booster" sessions, patients continued this home practice, which was verified by daily ratings and regular contacts with the attending staff member. Throughout the entire time period (from baseline until the end of follow-up), patients kept diaries specifying seizure frequency and completed a behavior-analysis question-naire on symptoms, antecedents, and consequences for every seizure.

EEGs were recorded from Cz with a time constant modified to 30 sec for SCP recording. Vertical eye movements were monitored throughout the training.

Computers (DEC PDP 11/73) were utilized to acquire and store the physiological data, to detect artifacts, and to compute the feedback values on-line. These values were passed via a serial line to a Commodore Amiga computer, which served to generate the visual feedback.

For every patient, median seizure frequency was calculated for the baseline period (8 weeks) and for the 1-year follow-up period (beginning with the end of the 28 training sessions). In order to evaluate factors that might have caused a change in seizure frequency, the group was divided into subjects who became completely seizure-free, into those with reduc-tions, and into those with little or no change in symptomatology. Analyses of variance with this between-subject factor were computed for (1) the SCP differentiation achieved under feedback; (2) the amount of transfer, com-puted as the fraction transfer differentiation divided by feedback differen-tiation; and (3) the patient variables; age, diagnosis, and seizure frequency during baseline.

The possible impact of age, medication, and diagnosis on learning criteria (t-values and regression coefficients for the four different trial blocks) as well as on the change in seizure frequency was examined by simple and multiple regressions.

Learning of Slow-Cortical-Potential Control

Figure 2 illustrates a typical example of SCPs during transfer trials. Little systematic differentiation in SCP, and often none, was achieved during the first few sessions, but a significant increase in SCP differentiation was demonstrated toward the end of the training period. Figure 3 shows the mean differentiation (averaged across all 25 patients) between "A" and "B" trials, i.e., between required negativity increase and negativity suppression. Under feedback conditions, differentiation was close to zero (-1.9 μV) during the first session; it increased to $+13.2$ μV on the 28th session.

SCP differentiation across the 28 sessions was significant under all

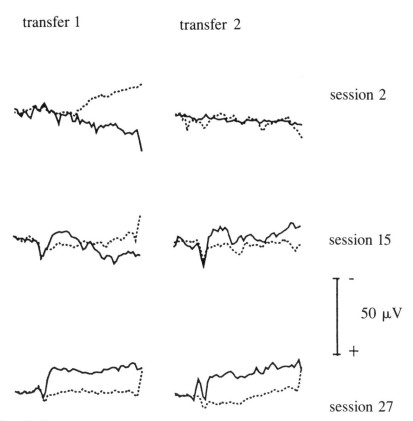

Figure 2. Example of averaged slow waves during transfer trials from an arbitrarily selected patient. (——) Required negativity; (····) required positivity. From Rockstroh *et al.* (1993).

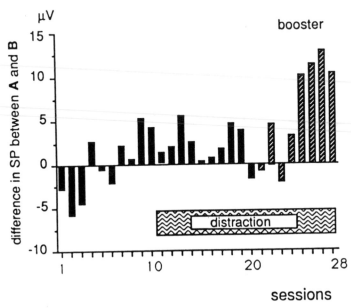

Figure 3. Mean differentiation in SCPs (in μV, ordinate) as achieved by the patient group (*N* = 25) during each of the 28 training sessions (abscissa) under feedback conditions (mean of first and second feedback block in each session). Each bar represents the group mean of one session. Note the significant simple and cubic trend indicating the progress of SCP differentiation across sessions and mainly during sessions 21–28. From Rockstroh *et al.* (1993).

conditions (for the first feedback block: $z = 5.2$, $p < 0.01$; the second feedback block: $z = 6.8$, $p < 0.01$; the first and the second transfer blocks: $z = 2.3$ and 2.2, respectively, $p < 0.05$). Of the 25 patients, 17 achieved significant SCP differentiation under at least one condition (feedback or transfer); 9 of the 17 demonstrated significant transfer.

Figure 3 illustrates the increase in SCP differentiation under feedback conditions across sessions, which turned out to be the most pronounced during the second training period, from sessions 21 to 28. At 4 months after the end of the training period, generalization of SCP control and correctness of home practice were evaluated in a session in which patients are asked to produce "A" and "B" states as they did at home, while the EEG was monitored. This testing was realized in an office in which the patient had never been, in order to avoid possible effects of conditioning to experimental context. However, this examination could not be obtained for every patient; therefore, the results for the group are not reported. Of the 9 patients that were examined for generalization of SCP control 4 months after completion of the training, 5 patients could still produce a systematic change in their EEG potential when asked to produce the "A" or the "B" response.

Treatment Effects

The change in seizure frequency and its relationship to SCP control was analyzed for 18 subjects, because 7 subjects stopped monitoring. Compared to baseline levels, seizure incidence was significantly lower during the follow-up period [F (1,17) = 21.7, $p < 0.01$]. Of the 18 patients, 6 have become completely seizure-free, 7 showed reductions of seizure incidences compared to baseline, and the remaining 5 did not exhibit changes in seizure frequency. The frequency distribution of the change in seizure frequency demonstrates these three groups (see Fig. 4).

While the success in SCP differentiation was in about the same range in all three outcome groups, the rate of *transfer* (defined as transfer differentiation divided by feedback differentiation) was different [F (2,15)

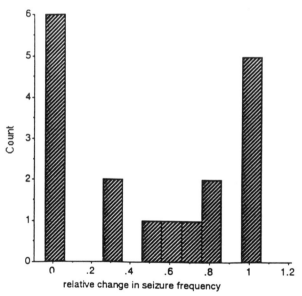

Figure 4. Frequency distribution of the relative changes in seizure frequency, computed as the fraction of median seizure incidence during the follow-up divided by the median during a 3-month baseline. A value of 0 on the abscissa means that a patient has become seizure-free during the follow-up period; a value of 1 means that seizure incidence has remained unchanged. From Rockstroh *et al.* (1993).

$= 4.5, p < 0.05$]. Compared to patients who did not experience a change in seizure frequency or to those demonstrating seizure reduction, the transfer rate was 5–20 times higher in patients who became seizure-free.

The type of epilepsy or the amount of medication did not influence treatment outcome. Patients becoming seizure-free were younger than members of the other two groups [22 ± 3 years vs. 36 ± 3 years and 35 ± 5 years, respectively; F (2,15) $= 5.0, p < 0.02$].

A stepwise multiple regression was performed to explain the variance in this measure; dependent variables were the criteria for SCP control, age, diagnosis, amount of medication, and baseline seizure frequency. The resulting significant multiple correlation of $R = 0.82$ [F (3,14) $= 9.6$, $p = 0.01$] indicates that 65% of the variance in seizure reduction can be explained by the SCP differentiation during the second feedback block ($t = 4.0, p < 0.01$), SCP differentiation during the second transfer block ($t = 2.7$, $p < 0.05$), and age ($t = 3.2, p < 0.05$). The ability to "transfer" SCP control into real life seems to be the relevant variable for the reduction in seizure frequency. The transfer is better achieved by younger patients.

Factors That Determine the Outcome of the Behavioral Slow-Cortical-Potential Treatment

The majority of drug-refractory patients can achieve control over their SCPs after extended training involving biofeedback and instrumental conditioning. In particular, control over SCPs under *transfer conditions* covaries with a reduction in seizure frequency. These results support our theory that surface-negative SCPs indicate cortical excitability, that the regulation of this excitability is impaired in epileptic patients, and that the control over one's own cortical excitability can be strengthened utilizing feedback and instrumental conditioning.

Not every patient is able to achieve SCP control, and not every patient who demonstrates reliable SCP control experiences a reduction in seizure frequency. Only when the self-control is successfully transferred and applied in the everyday environment is it effective. *Age* seems to be an important mediating variable: Younger patients seem to learn and generalize SCP control better than the older ones; none of the patients over 35 was successful. A detrimental effect of age on the ability to achieve self-control over brain activity has also been suggested by the observations of Sterman (personal communication). The age effect may be confounded with intellectual deterioration: Sterman reports age–IQ correlations with treatment success, and Daum, Rockstroh, Birbaumer, Elbert, Canavan, and Lutzenberger (1993) found correlations of verbal IQ with learning success in the present patient sample.

Apart from various impairing side effects of antiepileptic medication on psychological functioning (as described by Penry & Rahel, 1986), we demonstrated dampening effects of two antiepileptic drugs, carbamazepine and the benzodiazepine (Clonazepam), on EEG and SCP regulation in healthy humans (Rockstroh *et al.*, 1987, 1991). In study 2, two patients who became completely seizure-free following SCP training were not under current antiepileptic medication. On the other hand, some patients who did not show such substantial changes in seizure frequency were under heavy and long-term medication.

The present sample was too small and too homogeneous with respect to type of epilepsy (most patients suffering from complex-focal seizures) to allow any conclusion about the mediating role of the type of epilepsy for treatment success.

Motivation of the patient seems to be a crucial variable, but was not quantified in our studies. The most important variable is *training time.* For this study, 28 training sessions within 2 months were chosen. For successful SMR (sensory motor-rhythm) training, 18 sessions (Sterman, Lantz, Bruckler, & Kovalesky, 1981) and training periods of 4 months (Lubar, 1984) have been reported. The time needed to learn a specific task varies a great deal from subject to subject, but unlike motor-skill learning, the simple rule—the more extensive the training, the higher the skill—seems not to apply for operant learning of EEG parameters. The present data suggests that learning occurs in steps rather than smoothly across time.

The evidence that epileptic patients can achieve control over their SCPs and the evidence that this control can affect seizure frequency, at least in some patients, encourages us to further explore feedback and instrumental conditioning of cortical excitability as an alternative and additional instrument in the treatment of epileptic patients.

Summary

This study aimed at investigating the extent to which the regulation of excitability in cortical networks, as indicated by surface-negative slow cortical potentials (SCPs), is impaired in epileptic patients, and the extent to which training of SCP self-regulation by means of biofeedback and instrumental learning procedures might affect seizure frequency. A total of 25 patients suffering from drug-refractory epilepsies (complex-focal, grand mal, and absence type of seizures) participated in 28 1-hr sessions of feedback and instrumental conditioning of their SCPs. The subjects' EEG were obtained from the vertex. Depending on discriminative stimuli, DC shifts toward increased or suppressed negativity relative to the pretrial baseline were demonstrated by on-line visual feedback during intervals of 8 sec. each. While performance on the SCP self-regulation task was initially below normal (as compared to healthy subjects), significant increases in SCP control were achieved by the patients across the 28 training sessions. In 18 patients, at least 1-year follow-up data are available. Changes in seizure frequency were related to transfer of SCP control, with 6 of the 16 patients becoming seizure-free. Age affected the ability to acquire SCP control and its impact on seizure frequency.

ACKNOWLEDGMENTS.   This research was supported by the Deutsche Forschungsgemeinschaft and the Foundation Michael. The data presented in this chapter were first described in Rockstroh *et al.* (1993).

References

Birbaumer, N., Elbert, T., Canavan, A., & Rockstroh, B. (1990). Slow potentials of the cerebral cortex and behavior. *Physiological Reviews, 70*, 1–41.

Birbaumer, N., Elbert, T., Rockstroh, B., Daum, I., Wolf, P., & Canavan, A. (1992). Clinical-psychological treatment of epileptic seizures: A controlled study. In A. Ehlers, I. Florin, W. Fliegenbaum, & J. Margraf (Eds.), *Perspectives and promises of clinical psychology*, New York: Plenum Press.

Braitenberg, V. (1978). Cell assemblies in the cerebral cortex. In R. Heim & G. Palm (Eds.), *Theoretical approach to complex systems* (pp. 171–188). Berlin/Heidelberg: Springer.

Bühring, M., & Weltek, H. (1990). Entwicklung eines systematischen Anfallsunterbrechungstrainings, dargestellt anhand einer exemplarischen Fallstudie. In P. Wolf (Ed.), *Epilepsie 89* (pp 216–220). Reinbeck: Einhom.

Caspers, H., & Speckmann, E. J. (1969). DC-potential shifts in paroxysmal states. In H. H. Jasper, A. A. Ward, & A. Pope (Eds.), *Basic mechanisms of the epilepsies*. Boston: Little Brown.

Caspers, H., Speckmann, E. J., & Lehmenkuehler, A. (1984). Electrogenesis of slow potentials of the brain. In T. Elbert, B. Rockstroh, W. Lutzenberger, & N. Birbaumer (Eds.), *Self-regulation of the brain and behavior* (pp. 25–41). Berlin/Heidelberg: Springer.

Chatrian, G. E., Somasundaram, M., & Tassinari, C. A. (1968). DC-changes recorded transcranially during "typical" 3/sec spike and wave discharges in men. *Epilepsia, 9*, 185–209.

Dahl, J., Brorson, L. L. (1985). Effects of a broad-spectrum behavior modification treatment program on children with refractory epileptic seizures. *Epilepsia, 26*, 303–309.

Dahl, J., Melin, L., & Leissner, P. (1988). Effects of a behavioral intervention on epileptic seizure behavior and paroxysmal activity: A systematic replication of three cases of children with intractable epilepsy. *Epilepsia, 29*, 172–193.

Daum, I., Rockstroh, B., Birbaumer, N., Elbert, T., Canavan, A., & Lutzenberger, W. (1993). Behavioural treatment of slow cortical potentials in intractable epilepsy: Neuropsychological predictors of outcome. *Journal of Neurology, Neurosurgery, and Psychiatry, 56*, 94–97.

Efron, R. (1975). Conditioned inhibition of uncinate fits. *Brain, 80*, 251–260.

Elbert, T. (1991). Slow cortical potentials reflect the regulation of cortical excitability. In W. C. McCallum (Ed.), *Slow potentials in the human brain*. New York: Plenum Press.

Elbert, T., & Rockstroh, B. (1987). Threshold regulation—a key to the understanding of the combined dynamics of EEG and event-related potentials. *Journal of Psychophysiology, 1*, 317–333.

Elbert, T., Birbaumer, N., Lutzenberger, W., & Rockstroh, B. (1979). Biofeedback of slow cortical potentials: Self-regulation of central autonomic patterns. In N. Birbaumer & H. D. Kimmel (Eds.), *Biofeedback and self-regulation* (pp. 321–342). Hillsdale, NJ: Lawrence Erlbaum Associates.

Elbert, T., Rockstroh, B., Lutzenberger, W., & Birbaumer, N. (1980). Biofeedback of slow cortical potentials. *Journal of Electroencephalography & Clinical Neurophysiology, 48*, 293–301.

Elbert, T., Rockstroh, B., Lutzenberger, W., & Birbaumer, N. (Eds.) (1984). *Self-regulation of the brain and behavior*. Berlin/Heidelberg: Springer.

Elbert, T., Birbaumer, N., & Rockstroh, B. (1990). Regulation of slow cortical potentials (SCP) in epileptic patients. In C. H. M. Brunia, A. W. K. Gaillard, & A. Kok (Eds.), *Psychophysiological brain research* (pp. 231–235). Tilburg: University Press.

Elbert, T., Rockstroh, B., Canavan, A., Birbaumer, N., Lutzenberger, W., von Bülow, I., & Linden, A. (1991). Self-regulation of slow cortical potentials and its role in epileptogenesis. In J. G. Carlson & R. Seifert (Eds.), *International perspectives on self-regulation and health*. New York: Plenum Press.

Forster, F. M. (1969). Conditioned reflexes and sensory-evoked epilepsy: The nature of the therapeutic process. *Conditional Reflex, 4*, 103–114.

Forster, F. M. (1972). The classification and conditioning treatment of the reflex epilepsies. *International Journal of Neurology, 9*, 73–86.

Forster, F. M. (1977). *Reflex epilepsy, behavioral therapy, and conditional reflexes*. Springfield, IL: Charles C. Thomas.

Fried, R., Rubin, S. R., Carlton, R. M., & Fox, M. C. (1984). Behavioral control of intractable idiopathic seizures: I. Self-regulation of end-tidal carbon dioxide. *Psychosomatic Medicine, 46*, 315–332.

Lubar, J. (1984). Application of operant conditioning of the EEG for the management of epileptic seizures. In T. Elbert, B. Rockstroh, W. Lutzenberger, & N. Birbaumer (Eds.), *Self-regulation of the brain and behavior* (pp. 107–125). Berlin/Heidelberg: Springer.

Penry, K., & Rahel, R. E. (1986). *Epilepsy: Diagnosis, management, quality of life*. New York: Raven Press.

Rockstroh, B. (1990). Hyperventilation-induced DC-potentials in human subjects. *Epilepsy Research, 7*, 146–154.

Rockstroh, B., & Elbert, T. (1990). On the regulation of excitability in cerebral cortex—A bridge between EEG and attention? In H. G. Geissler, M. Muller, & W. Prinz (Eds.), *Psychophysical explorations of mental structures* (pp. 323–332). Gottingen: Hogrefe.

Rockstroh, B., Elbert, T., Lutzenberger, W., & Birbaumer, N. (1984b). Operant control of slow brain potentials: A tool in the investigation of the potential's meaning and its relation to attentive dysfunction. In T. Elbert, B. Rockstroh, W. Lutzenberger, & N. Birbaumer (Eds.), *Self-regulation of the brain and behavior* (pp. 227–239). Berlin/Heidelberg: Springer.

Rockstroh, B., Elbert, T., Lutzenberger, W., Altenmuller, E., Diener, H. C., & Birbaumer, N. (1987). Effects of the anticonvulsant carbamazepine on event-related brain potentials in humans. In R. Nodar, C. Barber, & T. Blum (Eds.), *Evoked potentials III* (pp. 361–369). London: Butterworths.

Rockstroh, B., Elbert, T., Canavan, A., Lutzenberger, W., & Birbaumer, N. (1989). *Slow cortical potentials and behavior*. 2nd ed. Munich: Urban & Schwarzenberg.

Rockstroh, B., Elbert, T., Lutzenberger, W., & Altenmuller, E. (1991). Effects of the anticonvulsant benzodiazepine Clonazepam on event-related potentials in human subjects. *Journal of Electroencephalography and Clinical Neurophysiology, 78,* 142–149.

Rockstroh, B., Elbert, T., Birbaumer, N., Wolf, P., Düchting-Roth, A., Reker, M., Daum, I., Lutzenberger, W., & Dichgans, J. (1993). Cortical self-regulation in patients with epilepsies. *Epilepsy Research, 14,* 63–72.

Sterman, M. B. (1984). The role of sensorimotor rhythmic EEG activity in the etiology and treatment of generalized motor seizures. In T. Elbert, B. Rockstroh, W. Lutzenberger, & N. Birbaumer (Eds.), *Self-regulation of the brain and behavior* (pp. 95–106). Berlin/Heidelberg: Springer.

Sterman, M. B., Lantz, D., Bruckler, R. M., & Kovalesky, R. A. (1981). Effects of sensorimotor EEG normalization feedback training on seizure rate in poorly controlled epileptics. *Proceedings of the Biofeedback Society of America, 12th Annual Meeting,* Louisville.

von Bülow, I., Elbert, T., Rockstroh, B., Lutzenberger, W., Canavan, A., & Birbaumer, N. (1989). Effects of hyperventilation on EEG frequency and slow cortical potentials in relation to an anticonvulsant and epilepsy. *Psychophysiology, 3,* 147–154.

Chapter 4

The P300 Event-Related Brain Potential in Psychiatric and Neurological Diagnosis

J. P. Rosenfeld

The electroencephalogram (EEG) is the record of voltage recorded from the human scalp (as a function of time) that is thought to be attributable to underlying cortical (brain) activity. P300 (P3) is an EEG-derived event-related potential (ERP) recordable from the human scalp using EEG-type electrodes and physiological recording parameters (for a detailed description, see Fabiani, Gratton, Karis, & Donchin, 1987). The word "event" in "event-related potential" refers to the external physical or internal psychological event that causes the deflection (in the ongoing EEG) that defines the ERP. A quarter of a century ago, the term "evoked potential" was used to describe EEG deflections caused by external stimuli (e.g., light flashes, tones). The deflections were known to be related to cortical sensory neuronal activity occurring synchronously on the arrival in the cortex of the neuronal activity evoked by the discrete sensory–physical event. It is now known that other events, i.e., events not of a sensory nature, are also associable with distinct EEG deflections, and thus the more general term ERP was developed and understood to include such special cases or subcategories as sensory evoked potentials. Hillyard (1985) has provided a concise review of the approximately half dozen well-studied psychologically related ERPs, including the P3 wave.

J. P. ROSENFELD • Department of Psychology, Northwestern University, Evanston, IL 60208.

Clinical Applied Psychophysiology, edited by John G. Carlson, A. Ronald Seifert, and Niels Birbaumer. Plenum Press, New York, 1994.

There are various ways that P3 can be elicited (for a comprehensive review, see Fabiani *et al.*, 1987). This chapter is based on the use of one of these methods, called the "oddball paradigm" (Duncan-Johnson and Donchin, 1977). In this basic situation, a subject wired for EEG recording sits in a comfortable chair while a series of (typically) two types of stimuli is presented in a random order, e.g., a series of high and low acoustical tones (bright vs. dim light flashes, strong vs. weak hand taps, or other pairs of stimuli would also work). One of the tones is typically designated as a *task-relevant oddball*—say, for present purposes, the low tone. To make the low tone an "oddball," its probability is reduced to less than 0.5 (although the series of tones is still presented in a random order). Typically (and in our situation), the oddball has $p = 0.2$, whereas the nonoddball (frequent) high tone has a complementary $p = 0.8$. To further make the low tone "task-relevant," the subject is given a task to perform whenever the low tone is presented; typically (and in our situation), the subject is instructed to keep a count of the oddballs.[1] The ERPs in response to the oddballs (also called "targets" in the present situation, since a counting response is required when they occur) are averaged into one accumulating average ERP, and the frequents (nonoddballs or nontargets) into another. The typical result of using this situation is seen in Fig. 1, which shows superimposed, averaged target- and nontarget-evoked entire ERP waveforms beginning 100 msec prior to the tone stimulus and ending 1100 msec later. Figure 1 shows that a large positive deflection occurs in response to the target oddballs, but not in response to the nontarget frequent tones. This deflection, which peaks at about 400–450 msec in Figure 1 and which is largest parietally (Pz electrode) and smallest frontally (Fz), is called the P3 or P300 response.[2] The response clearly represents a psychological event, rather than a physical one; this assertion can be supported in various ways: First, one could replicate Figure 1 regarding P3 with the opposite designation of target and nontarget; i.e., it is irrelevant whether or not the oddball is a physically high or low tone. It matters only that it be rare ($p < 0.5$) and task-relevant. Second, one could occasionally substitute *no tone at all* for the oddball, and a P3-like deflection would appear where it

---

[1]There are, of course, many variations on this basic set of arrangements that we use for our purposes (see Fabiani, Gratton, Karis, & Donchin, 1987).

[2]P300 was the original name of the wave because when first reported (Sutton, 1965), it had a latency more like 300 msec as opposed to the 400 msec we often see. The precise latency varies with the physical nature of the stimulus used, other experimental parameters (e.g., ITI, intensity), and, most important, stimulus evaluation time unique to a given experimental situation (Duncan-Johnson, 1981). Thus, P300s have been reported at peak latencies of 250–1000 msec. What defines them is the polarity, latency *range*, and especially scalp distribution, usually with Pz>Cz>>Fz, as in Fig. 1 (see Fabiani *et al.*, 1987).

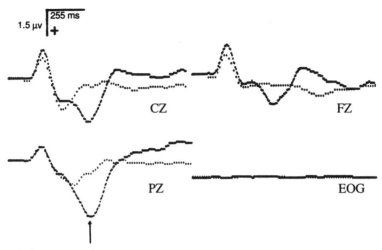

Figure 1. Superimposed group-grand-averaged ERPs in response to oddball targets (———) and frequent nontargets (·········) from three scalp sites (FZ, CZ, PZ) and the artifact-detector channel (EOG). The downward-going (positive) wave in the target/oddball ERPs (↑ in the PZ waveforms) is P3. The traces are 1200 msec long and begin 100 msec prior to the tone presentation. P3 thus has a *poststimulus* latency of about 400 msec and is largest at PZ, smallest at FZ. From Rosenfeld *et al.* (1992).

would have appeared had the oddball tone been presented. The absent tone obviously has no physical properties, but when it "occurs" at the time that the actual tone was expected to occur, it has the obvious psychological property of representing something expected but absent.

That P3 represents a psychological event immediately suggests that it can be utilized in psychological diagnosis for conditions wherein psychological dysfunction is basic to various states that are definable neurologically or psychiatrically or both. Clearly, this kind of application requires some specification of what the psychological event is that P3 signifies. There is as yet no final, universally accepted answer to this question. On the contrary, the fundamental meaning of P3 has been vigorously debated since its discovery (e.g., see Donchin and Coles, 1988). Despite the controversy, there is agreement that P3 can be successfully used in *specified situations* to index various psychological processes that may inhere in these variously given situations. For example, because P3 is an *objective*[3] response to rare meaningful stimuli, it can be used as a kind

---

[3]An objective event is publicly confirmable, like a yardstick measurement. It does not depend on unique subjective experience.

of lie detector to signify special guilty or personal knowledge that a subject will deny behaviorally (vocally) in his attempt to escape detection [see Rosenfeld, Angell, Johnson, & Qian (1991) and papers cited therein]. The neurological and psychiatric applications of this same paradigm are closely related to the forensic one. For example, a subject may be trying to conceal his recent thoughts about suicide. One presents him with the following series of verbal stimuli: *aspirins, antihistamines, antibiotics, Tylenol, sleeping pills,* and the like. If he has been thinking of overdosing with sleeping pills, he should respond with a P3 to that stimulus. In the neurological setting, one can help assess the nature of a memory loss by seeing if there is recognition defined by a large P3 to a stimulus that is behaviorally (vocally) unrecognized (see also Brandt, 1988).

P3 (amplitude and especially latency) has also been used in the straightforward oddball paradigm (as described above with tone stimuli) to attempt diagnosis in aging, schizophrenic, and depressive disorders, and in other conditions (e.g., Diner, Holcomb, & Dykman, 1985; Grillon, Courchesne, Ameli, Geyer, & Braff, 1990; Polich, Ladish, & Bloom, 1990; Syndulko, Hansch, Cohen, Pearce, Goldberg, Morton, Tourtellotte, & Potvin, 1982). The conceptual foundation of this approach, very simply, is that whatever the basic meaning of P3 (in the oddball paradigm), it surely represents cognitive processing, and since there are clear cognitive deficits in such conditions as aging, Alzheimer's disease, late-stage AIDS, schizophrenia, and depression, there should be some difference between the P3 responses of normals and persons with these various pathologies. The literature on this subject is vast; suffice it here to say that while there have surely been significant group effects reported, the P3 of the simple oddball paradigm has not produced a clear enough differentiation of well and ill persons on an *individual* basis, to be used diagnostically. It is certainly not implied here that the group effects are without great value, for group effects do allow rigorous testing of theories of pathogenesis. However, *individual hit rates* for *diagnostic* purposes are another matter.

Some years ago, investigators at the University of Illinois in Champaign–Urbana utilized a more elaborate variation of the oddball paradigm, called the *dual-task* paradigm, to help index the cognitive demands created by task situations of interest to human engineers (see Donchin, Kramer, & Wickens, 1986). If, for example, it was desired to see whether a given simulated flight task was more demanding than another task, the subject would be called on to perform the oddball (P3-evoking) task at the same time as he performed the simulated flight tasks to be tested. It was expected and confirmed that since P3 amplitude indexes cognitive–attentional resource availability for oddball detection, burdening a subject with a simultaneous second task would drain some of these resources, thereby producing a P3 amplitude *decrement*, the size of which would be in proportion to the difficulty of the secondary task.

We reasoned that this basic approach could be readily adapted for diagnostic applications in all conditions in which oddball-available attention would be compromised. The first application we attempted was in pain diagnosis and measurement. We reasoned that the experience of pain *during the oddball task* would constitute a cognitive (and perhaps also emotional) demand that would bring about a reduction in P3 amplitude in comparison to its ordinary baseline level in the single (no-pain) oddball task).

In our first study (Rosenfeld & Kim, 1991), we developed a finger-press pain inducer for the laboratory. It consisted of a dull blade that pressed down on the nail of the middle finger of a subject's hand, which rested palm down on a restraining board. After a baseline (no-pain) condition in which the subject's single-task (oddball detection only) oddball-evoked P3 was obtained, the subject was asked to adjust the blade-press to a pain tolerance level defined as the maximum painful pressure he was willing to withstand for two 15-min test periods. In the first period ("pain only"), the subjects merely endured the pain as the oddball task was re-presented. In the second period ("pain-tracking"), subjects were required to track their pain by mentally rating it continuously on a 1–10 point scale. The experimenter would solicit an oral rating about every minute. Two groups of subjects were actually run: a *real-pain* group, run just as described above, and a *pain-feigning* group. In the latter group, no actual pain was experienced; the subjects were told to imagine they were in pain in the *pain-only* condition and rate their *feigned* pain in the *pain-tracking* condition. The results, for a first study, were encouraging: Significant differences in oddball-evoked P3 amplitudes between real pain and pain-feigning groups were obtained during *pain tracking* (see Fig. 2). On the other hand, the results were far short of ideal for a number of reasons: First, there were no significant differences between real- and feigned-pain groups during the *pain-only* condition, and this finding was unexpected. Second, the nature of the laboratory method of pain induction—the finger press—made it impossible for us to determine whether the dual-task approach could successfully index the *degree* of real pain subjects experienced, since only one level of pain, the tolerance threshold, could be used. Finally, and perhaps most disappointing and important, although significant group effects, as noted above, were obtained, the individual diagnostic (real vs. feigned) classification accuracy (based on P3 amplitude only) was poor: less than 70% correct.

We therefore did a second study (Rosenfeld, Johnson, & Koo, 1993) designed to overcome these limitations. In the second study, we used a

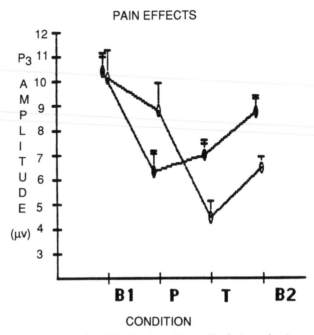

Figure 2. Computer-calculated, oddball-evoked P3 amplitude in real-pain group (○) and feigned-pain group (●) in first baseline (B1), last baseline (B2), pain-only (P), and pain-tracking (T) conditions. From Rosenfeld and Kim (1991).

different method of pain induction, the more familiar ischemic pain-producing arm cuff. This cuff is ordinarily used clinically for brief periods to obtain blood pressure. However, when left on for more than 5 min, it produces a well-documented discomfort that, though harmless, rises to agonizing levels by 15 min after application. Although subjects could wiggle in the finger press, even unintentionally, thereby reducing the pain, and although the finger-press pain did show some habituation, the ischemic pain produced by the blood-pressure tourniquet (inflated to about twice the systolic pressure) is inescapable, consistently mounting, and, probably for these reasons, much less variable in its noxious effect than the finger press. The reason we did not use it initially—we obviously were aware of it—was that it has the inherent confound of pain duration and intensity. For the second study, we accepted this confound and got the benefit of its lower variability, plus, of course, the possibility of testing differing *levels* of pain, since the ischemic pain is well documented to rise monotonically as a function of time.

Again, real-pain and pain-feigning subject groups were run in *baseline* conditions, *low* pain conditions (about 6 min of ischemia pain), and *high* pain conditions (about 13 min of ischemia pain). We also utilized the tracking/no-tracking variable, but this time on a between-subject basis. In all, there were four groups of subjects: (1) real-pain/nontracking (RP/N), (2) real-pain/tracking (RP/T), (3) feigned-pain/nontracking (FP/N), and (4) feigned-pain/tracking (FP/T). Consistent with the finding of our original study, we found in the real-pain groups a significant difference in P3 amplitude between tracking and nontracking groups in the low-pain condition. Also in the RP/N group, we found a near-significant difference ($p < 0.06$) in P3 amplitude between low- and high-pain conditions; this latter finding suggests that it will be possible to use this new method to index *amount* of pain, not just its simple presence. A novel finding was a parallel increase (in the RP/N group) in P3 *latency* from low- to high-pain conditions. We found robust differences between RP and FP nontracking subjects in high pain using both P3 latency and amplitude. On this basis, we developed an index for *individual* diagnosis in which a subject was classified as being in real pain if his P3 amplitude decreased *and* his P3 latency increased from baseline to high-pain conditions; he was classified as not being in pain otherwise. This time, using this new index, our diagnostic accuracy reached 91%.

By no means do we think our method for pain measurement is as finely tuned as it can be, and, of course, there is a major difference between clinical and experimental pain diagnosis. We remain optimistic that further study will yield an objective pain index that will add to the diagnostician's toolbox.

There is one further potential use of the P3-based dual-task paradigm (i.e., *not* the single-oddball paradigm) to be considered here: in psycho-diagnosis. This application is at a primitive stage of development in our laboratory. It has the following conceptual foundation: It is assumed that differing populations of psychiatric subcategories will be differentially responsive to audiovisual materials—films—of a given subject matter. To vastly oversimplify, a paranoid individual would be expected to become much more engaged in a film about a person against whom many others were plotting than in a film about happy family life. A nonparanoid person seriously depressed over the recent loss of his family might be expected to show exactly the opposite pattern of interests. On this basis, it would be predicted that the paranoid individual watching the plot film while simultaneously performing the oddball task would show a greater degree of P3 amplitude reduction than that obtained when watching the family film. The reason is that he would invest more attention in the plot film (and away from the oddball-detection task) than in the family film. The depressed individual would show the opposite pattern of P3-amplitude decrements, hence the differential diagnosis.

A first question to be posed, however, en route to such a (*hypothetically*) good diagnostic instrument is: Can P3-amplitude decrements be used to index differing attention investments in differentially engaging films in normals? Answering this first question, by the way, is about as far as we have gone at the moment. We (Rosenfeld, Bhat, Miltenberger, & Johnson, 1992) ran five groups of subjects, 11–18 subjects per group. In three of the groups, oddball probability was 0.22; it was 0.33 in the other two groups. In each study, the subjects had a baseline/single-oddball-task run, followed by 15-min viewings of two films, a boring film and an exciting film, with order counterbalanced. The films were viewed/heard simultaneously with execution of the oddball task, and they were expected to cause a drop in oddball P3 amplitude, since they drained attentional resources, hopefully in proportion to their interestingness. The films were rated as boring or exciting by a panel of undergraduates, and for each film-pair used in each study, the ratings of the two films differed at $p < 0.05$–0.0001 levels of significance. The sound tracks of the segments of boring and exciting films used in the study were chosen to be equivalent in sound level so that any effects would not be trivially attributable to sound differences, but to genuine differences in film engagingness. The structure of the entire study is shown in Table 1.

The reason for repeating the same basic study using various boring–exciting film-pairings was our interest in replicability of the basic effect, even when using different movies in each hypothesis test. The findings were most encouraging. There was always a main effect of boring vs. interesting films on oddball P3 amplitude. The effect was clearer at the lower than at the higher oddball probability (for reasons discussed in Rosenfeld *et al.*, 1992). All movies reduced P3 amplitude relative to base-

Table 1. *Structure of the Film-Pair Study*

Group	Boring film[a]	Exciting film[a]	Oddball probability	N
1	AND	RAIDERS	0.22	11
2	WHALE	GOLD	0.22	16
3	WHALE	GOLD	0.33	18
4	AND	GOLD	0.22	11
5	AND	GOLD	0.33	13

[a](AND) "My Dinner with Andre"; (RAIDERS) "Raiders of the Lost Ark"; (WHALE) "Whales of August"; (GOLD) "Goldfinger."

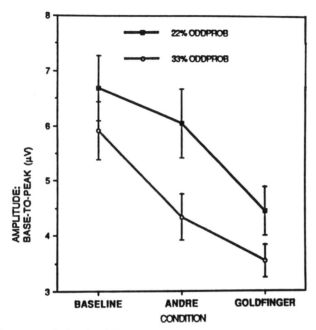

Figure 3. Computer-calculated, oddball-evoked P3 amplitudes in a baseline and two film-watching conditions. (ANDRE) "My Dinner with Andre," rated boring; (GOLDFINGER) the movie of the same name, rated exciting; (ODDPROB) the two oddball probabilities used. From Rosenfeld *et al.* (1992).

line. Figure 3 illustrates all these findings, although it shows results for only the last pair of groups run. An additional, unanticipated positive result was that the *non*oddball (nontarget, frequently occurring) tone-evoked P3 amplitudes also robustly discriminated boring and interesting films. This adds yet another index for use with real psychopathology populations.

We (Leiphart and Rosenfeld, 1991) did one preliminary study of whether or not films differentially affect oddball P3 ERPs in normal vs. depressed subjects. The group results were positive, although there were fewer than ten depressed subjects in this preliminary report. We look forward to extending this work in the future.

References

Brandt, J. (1988). Malingered amnesia. In R. Rogers (Ed.), *Clinical assessment of malingering and deception* (pp. 65–84). New York: Guilford Press.

Diner, B. C., Holcomb, P. J., & Dykman, R. A. (1985). P300 in major depressive disorder. *Psychiatry Research, 15,* 175–184.

Donchin, E., & Coles, M. G. H. (1988). Is the P300 component a manifestation of context updating? *Behavioral and Brain Sciences, 11,* 357–374.

Donchin, E., Kramer, A., & Wickens, C. (1986). Applications of brain event-related potentials to problems in engineering psychology. In M. Coles, S. Porges, & E. Donchin (Eds.), *Psychophysiology: Systems, processes and applications.* New York: Guilford Press.

Duncan-Johnson, C. (1981). P300 latency: A new metric of information processing. *Psychophysiology, 18,* 207–215.

Duncan-Johnson, C. C., & Donchin, E. (1977). On quantifying surprise: The variation of event-related potentials with subjective probability. *Psychophysiology, 14,* 456–467.

Fabiani, M., Gratton, G., Karis, D., & Donchin, E. (1987). The definition, identification, and reliability of measurement of the P300 component of the event-related potential. In P. K. Ackles, J. R. Jennings, & M. G. H. Coles (Eds.), *Advances in psychophysiology,* Vol. 2. Greenwich, Conn.: JAI Press.

Grillon, C., Courchesne, E., Ameli, R., Geyer, M. A., & Braff, D. L. (1990). Increased distractibility in schizophrenic patients: Electrophysiological and behavioral evidence. *Archives of General Psychiatry, 47,* 171–179.

Hillyard, S. A. (1985). Electrophysiology of human selective attention. *Trends in Neurosciences,* September 1985, 400–405.

Leiphart, J. W., & Rosenfeld, J. P. (1991). Study of depression using P300 in the dual task paradigm. *Psychophysiology, 28,* S37 (abstract).

Polich, J., Ladish, C., & Bloom, F. E. (1990). P300 assessment of early Alzheimer's disease. *Electroencephalography and Clinical Neurophysiology, 77,* 179–189.

Rosenfeld, J. P., & Kim, M. (1991). Ongoing pain as a mental workload indexed by P300 depression: Discrimination of real and feigned pain conditions. *Psychophysiology, 28,* 336–343.

Rosenfeld, J. P., Angell, A., Johnson, M., & Qian, J. (1991). An ERP-based control-question lie detector analog: Algorithms for discriminating effects within individual waveforms. *Psychophysiology, 28,* 320–336.

Rosenfeld, J. P., Bhat, K., Miltenberger, A., & Johnson, M. (1992). Event-related potentials in the dual task paradigm. *International Journal of Psychophysiology, 12,* 221–232.

Rosenfeld, J. P., Johnson, M. M., Koo, J. (1993). Ongoing ischemic pain as a workload indexed by P3 amplitude and latency in real–versus feigned-pain conditions. *Psychophysiology, 30,* 253–260.

Sutton, S., Braren, M., Zubin, J., John, E. R. (1965). Evoked potential correlates of stimulus uncertainty. *Science, 150,* 1187–1188.

Syndulko, K., Hansch, E. C., Cohen, S. N., Pearce, J. W., Goldberg, Z., Morton, B., Tourtellotte, W. W., & Potvin, A. K. (1982). Long-latency event-related potentials in normal aging and dementia. In J. Courjon, F. Mauguiere, & M. Revol (Eds.), *Clinical applications of evoked potentials in neurology* (pp. 279–285). New York: Raven Press.

PART III

Disorders of
the Cardiovascular System

Included in this section are Chapter 5, by Giorgio Bertolotti and his co-workers, Ezio Sanavio, Elisabetta Angelino, Ornella Bettinardi, Giorgio Mazzuero, Giulio Vidotto, and Anna Maria Zotti; Chapter 6, by David Shapiro, Iris B. Goldstein, and Larry Jamner; and Chapter 7, by Robert R. Freedman. The first chapter includes a brief review of the Type A behavior pattern literature plus a description of the authors' original research on the characteristics of Type A blue collar workers in Italy. The second, on ambulatory assessment of blood pressure, provides a brief review of the related literature including studies in the authors' own laboratory. The third provides a review of the research on biofeedback and other treatments of Raynaud's disease—digital vasospasms induced by cold or emotional stressors—and a related discussion of mechanisms for the disorder.

In their chapter, Bertolotti and colleagues make the point that assessment of Type A behavior pattern with the structured interview has been largely confined to the United States and Northern European countries and to middle class, working men. Moreover, although a wealth of studies and related meta-analyses support the view that Type As are more reactive than Type Bs on many cardiovascular variables, methodological considerations render the link between Type A behavior pattern and cardiovascular hyperreactivity less than conclusive. In the authors' own research with a large sample of Italian blue collar workers reported in this chapter, subjects were classified with the structured interview into Type A and other behavior patterns. Assessment during baseline and cognitive or noise stressor tasks yielded no differences in cardiovascular reactivity on any of the variables. These negative results provide a clear challenge to the generality of previously reported hyperreactivity in Type A individuals—perhaps related to cultural differences, subpopulation differences (i.e., blue collar workers), or a fundamental weakness in the relationship between Type A behavior pattern and cardiovascular responsiveness, among other possibilities.

In a very clear presentation of some complex material, Shapiro and co-workers provide in their chapter a useful summary of a number of studies of the use of ambulatory blood pressure assessment methods in both research and clinical settings. The advantages of ambulatory assessment in terms of reliability and enhanced predictive power for cardiovascular morbidity and mortality are cited. From their own research with para-medics, the authors outline several personality and situational variables that were significantly related to blood pressure in natural settings, includ-ing cynical hostility, defensiveness, and job site. Conflicting and ambiva-lent expression of hostility appears to be a dominant issue in predicting elevated blood pressure. The researchers also detail several clinical impli-cations of their work, including the usefulness of ambulatory assessment for diagnoses and documentation of treatment effects, as well as the role of anger and hostile outlook in hypertension. This is a chapter that re-searchers in the area of essential hypertension will want to attend closely to for a sample of methods and directions that will impact in a major way of future research.

Shifting to the peripheral vasculature in his chapter, Freedman con-trasts two early theoretical conceptions of Raynaud's disease—Raynaud's notion that it is due to heightened sympathetic activity and Lewis's view that it is a "local fault" that causes small peripheral blood vessels to become hypersensitive to cooling. The latter view implies that the disorder will occur without involvement of the sympathetic nervous system. Freedman cites a number of studies, including several ingenious experiments in his laboratory, to support a position on the pathophysiology of Raynaud's disease that is closer to Lewis's position. These studies include demonstra-tions that temperature biofeedback is superior to therapies aimed at general sympathetic reduction, that temperature biofeedback induces vasodilation despite blockade of the sympathetic system in the fingers, and that there are no changes in circulating catecholamine levels in patients who are successful in learning temperature increases with biofeedback. These and other results support Freedman's contention that Raynaud's is caused by hypersensitive peripheral vascular α_2-adrenergic vascular re-ceptors during cooling or emotional stress, rather than by sympathetic activity *per se*. Freedman's research is a model for clinical applied psycho-physiology and has implications not just for behavioral treatments of Raynaud's but also for medical interventions.

CHAPTER 5

Type A and Cardiovascular Responsiveness in Italian Blue Collar Workers

Giorgio Bertolotti, Ezio Sanavio,
Elisabetta Angelino, Ornella Bettinardi,
Giorgio Mazzuero, Giulio Vidotto,
and Anna Maria Zotti

Introduction

Since great importance is attached in behavioral medicine and in health psychology to problems of prevention, it is only right that one of the most explored areas should be the assessment of psychosocial coronary risk factors. The best known of these factors is probably the Type A behavior pattern (TABP), a construct defined as the outcome of a person–situation interaction that emerges in certain individuals in appropriately stressful or challenging situations (Friedman & Rosenman, 1959). Since the TABP has come into use, there have been a host of studies clarifying the construct, its modes of assessment, and its association with the development of coronary heart disease (CHD). These studies have generated two meta-

GIORGIO BERTOLOTTI, ELISABETTA ANGELINO, ORNELLA BETTINARDI, and ANNA MARIA ZOTTI • Psychology Service, Clinica del Lavoro Foundation, Institute of Care and Research, Medical Center of Rehabilitation, 28010 Veruno, Italy.   EZIO SANAVIO and GIULIO VIDOTTO • Department of General Psychology, University of Padova, 35100 Padova, Italy.   GIORGIO MAZZUERO • Division of Cardiology, Clinica del Lavoro Foundation, Institute of Care and Research, Medical Center of Rehabilitation, 28010 Veruno, Italy.

Clinical Applied Psychophysiology, edited by John G. Carlson, A. Ronald Seifert, and Niels Birbaumer. Plenum Press, New York, 1994.

analyses (Booth-Kewley & Friedman, 1987; Matthews, 1988), which lead to the conclusion that the linkage between Type A and CHD is not particularly strong and may be considered meaningful only for certain populations and with certain modes of assessment. Both find that the strength of the linkage between TABP and CHD varies with the tools of assessment— significant if the assessment is conducted with the structured interview (SI), but less so with self-report inventories (Houston, 1988). It also appears that the value of the SI as predictor is proven in cross-sectional researches and in population-based prospective studies, but is drastically reduced in studies conducted on high-risk populations.

The SI is a semistructured interview in which the subject is confronted with questions designed to elicit Type A behavior characteristics (Rosenman, Friedman, Straus, Wurm, Kositchek, Hahn, & Werthessen, 1964; Rosenman, 1978). Videotape recordings of the interview are then rated by judges as belonging to the following categories: A1, extreme Type A behavior; A2, mild Type A or incompletely developed Type A behavior; X, Types A and B characteristics coexisting; and B, absence of Type A characteristics. The classification rests chiefly on behavioral features: on speech and motor stylistics, on the manner rather than the matter of the responses.

Both the characteristics that define the TABP and the characteristics tested in the SI are heavily colored by the middle-class American life style. About 10 years ago, a panel of biomedical and behavioral scientists in the United States assessed the body of research into coronary-prone behavior and CHD on behalf of the National Heart, Lung and Blood Institute (Review Panel, 1981). This authoritative review panel reckoned that the TABP is an independent coronary risk factor only in employed middle-aged United States citizens, and the panel was doubtful whether this construct and the related assessment techniques would be relevant to other populations. In the past decade, research into the TABP and the SI has burgeoned outside the United States, signally in Europe. But here again, the vast bulk of the data comes from Anglo-Saxon countries, very little from the Latin area. This applied to Italy, too, for only 1 of the 21 prospective studies on which the meta-analysis of Matthews (1988) is based comes from Italy (De Leo, Caracciolo, Berto, Mauro, Magni, & Miraglia, 1986); furthermore, in the larger meta-analysis of Booth-Kewley and Friedman (1987), which includes cross-sectional studies and psychological variables other than Type A, only 1 of 86 comes from Italy (Maggini, Guazzelli, Castrogiovanni, Mauri, De Lisio, Chierchia, & Cassano, 1976/1977).

Although there is no adequate proof that physiological hyperresponsiveness indicative of autonomic nervous system activation may be a risk factor for CHD, numerous researches have examined the psychophysiological responsiveness induced in the laboratory by behavioral or psychological methods or both (for reviews, see Krantz & Manuck, 1984; Manuck, Kasprowicz, Monroe, Larkin, & Kaplan, 1989). For example, numerous studies have found that Type A subjects present larger episodic increases in arterial pressure, heart rate, catecholamines, and cortisol when confronted with appropriately challenging or stressful tasks. Krantz and Manuck (1984) considered 37 studies on the association between TABP and psychophysiological reactivity: 11 found no differences in reactivity between Type A and Type B, while the others (about 71%) found greater reactivity among Type A subjects, at least on the cardiovascular and endocrine measures. A more recent review (Houston, 1988) concludes that the differences in reactivity between Types A and B emerge on tasks "moderately high in difficulty," whereas on tasks of greater difficulty and incentive, the Type Bs appear to be as aroused as the Type As. In such a context, it seems that the SI not only predicts reactivity more strongly than the Jenkins Activity Survey (JAS), the principal self-report inventory for the assessment of TABP, but also predicts it in a wider range of situations and laboratory tasks. The meta-analysis procedures (Harbin, 1989) also show that the SI is a much more effective instrument in this context than is the JAS.

The main upshot of the Harbin meta-analysis of 71 studies of adult subjects in situations of psychological challenge (excluding, that is, cold-pressor testing, body tilt, physical exercise, and other physical challenges) is that "there is strong evidence for the conclusion that Type As are more reactive than Type Bs for HR, sBP, and dBP" (p. 112), but rather weak evidence in the case of norepinephrine and insufficient for cortisol and epinephrine responses. It has been calculated, however, that this meta-analysis, insofar as it concerns SI and cardiovascular responsiveness, covers 33 studies for a total of only 509 subjects, and hence a mean of fewer than 16 subjects per study, a dangerously small number (Ganster, Schaubroeck, Sime, & Mayes, 1991). Further, many of these studies were of postinfarction patients and other clinical populations; the researches on healthy subjects were mainly of college students, and the criteria of health were not always clearly stated. Another point to bear in mind is that these differences in responsiveness, even when statistically significant, are small—so small that many researchers do not consider them to have a credible role of mediation in the pathogenesis of CHD.

There are, then, more clinically oriented researchers who emphasize the complexity of the dynamic interactions that the cardiovascular responses may present, pointing out that cardiovascular responsiveness may manifest in various ways and with various patterns. By this reasoning, only a small proportion of Type A subjects present an exaggerated autonomic response to laboratory challenges; the frequency of these "hot reactors" is thought to be greater among Type A subjects and is rated at about twice the frequency that occurs among Type Bs (Dembrowski & Mac-Dougall, 1983, p. 110). If this relative frequency in fact obtains, the customary statistical analyses, which compare separate parameters of groups of subjects, might be unsuitable, and a case-by-case categorization might be preferable.

In short, notwithstanding the wealth of research material available, it would be premature to conclude that there really is association between Type A and cardiovascular hyperreactivity.

The study presented in this chapter seeks to determine whether the TABP as assessed by the current SI is predictive of cardiovascular reactivity in a group of Italian blue collar workers of proven cardiological normality. Since tasks with different behavioral demands may produce different patterns of cardiovascular responses, we used three tasks, one passive (noise) and two active, one involving human confrontation (mental arithmetic) and the other not (interaction concentration test). We expected, first, greater cardiovascular reactivity changes in the Type A subjects for the two active stressors only and, second, some evidence of stimulation among subjects categorized as Type A1—that is, those more inclined to exhibit anger/hostility, at least during the mental arithmetic task (which involves human confrontation in contrast to the interaction concentration task, which does not).

Method

Subjects

The subjects included in this study formed part of a larger sample on which a previous study had been conducted to determine the relevance of the workload to the ischemic heart disease risk variables in a steel plant. All the data were collected in the interval from June 1986 to December 1988. The subjects, 73 healthy male volunteers aged between 35 and 59 years (mean 44.18, SD 4), were all living in the area around Bergamo (north Italy). Their level of education ranged from 5 to 8 years. All were blue collar workers at the Dalmine SpA plant in Bergamo, which produces steel tubes. All had undergone a medical examination beforehand. Cardiac health was assessed on a history, clinical examination, electrocardiogram, echocardiogram, and forced exertion on a bicycle ergometer test. All participants had been informed that the study was an occupational health survey concerned with disease prevention.

Procedure

Every subject underwent: (1) a structured interview (Chesney, Eagleston, & Rosenman, 1981) in the Psychology Service and (2) a psychophysiological profile recording in the Stress Laboratory. Both were conducted on the same day between 09:00 and 12:00 hours. All the structured interviews, which were videotaped, were administered by a psychologist (O.B.) who had been in the training course held by Dr. Ray Rosenman at the Veruno Medical Center in 1985. The SIs were rated independently by two judges, one of whom (G.B.) had attended Rosenman's training course and another (E.A.) who had taken the training course held by G.B. and O.B. at the Veruno Medical Center. Every subject was categorized as Type A1, A2, X, or B.

Every subject's profile was analyzed, based on the curves for the indices of heart rate and systolic and diastolic blood pressure, one measure each 60 sec, and the subject was classed as a high (H) or low (L) responder. The first criterion of H responder was based on the mean rise in one of the cardiovascular parameters during one or more tasks. For example, any or any combination of a rise of 20 mm Hg in systolic pressure, of 15 mm Hg in diastolic pressure, or of 10 beats/min in heart rate classified the subject as an H responder, and no such rise in any of these parameters marked an L responder [for the choice of criteria, we drew on Schmidt (1983) and Zotti, Bettinardi, Soffiantino, Tavazzi, & Steptoe (1991)]. The second criterion was failure of any one of these cardiovascular values to return to the baseline during the recovery period, this too classifying a subject as an H responder.

Equipment and Measures

The psychophysiological assessment was conducted in the Stress Laboratory, in a soundproof, air-conditioned room (T = 22–24°C, humidity 40–60%). The parameters measured were heart rate (HR), systolic blood pressure (sBP), and diastolic blood pressure (dBP). The cardiovascular indices were recorded from a Mingocard 3 electrocardiograph (Siemens Elema) in the standard 12-lead arrangement and an automatic sphygmomanometer (Siemens model Diasyst TA) for the noninvasive measurement of blood pressure at set intervals (60 sec). The subject was placed in a semirecumbent position on the bed and connected to the equipment for recording the various physiological parameters. An interval of 10 min was allowed to elapse for adaptation before the test started. Recording of the psychophysiological profile started with a baseline lasting 5 min, followed by administration of the three tasks, each lasting 10 min. Each task was followed by a 5-min rest interval, the last 2 min (4th and 5th) of which ranked as the baseline for the next task. The tasks were set in the following order: (1) interactive concentration test (ICT), (2) mental arithmetic test (MAT), and (3) workside noises (WN). The first two tests have been used repeatedly in the research laboratory on heart disease patients (Pagani, Mazzuero, Ferrari, Liberati, Cerutti, Vaitl, Tavazzi, & Malliani, 1991; Tavazzi, Mazzuero, Giordano, Zotti, & Bertolotti, 1984; Tavazzi, Zotti, & Rondanelli, 1986; Tavazzi, Zotti, & Mazzuero, 1987; Zotti et al., 1991).

The ICT is a computer-controlled task that does not entail human confrontation. This attention test is based on a computer program that controls the sequential presentation of 60 different slides, each containing a 6×6 matrix of two-digit numbers. Among these numbers, the presence or absence of two numbers (43 and 63) provides four possibilities (neither number is present in the slide, both are present, or only 43 or 63 is present). The participant is requested to press one of four microswitches located on a handrest according to which possibility the slide presents. The advancement of the slides is accelerated or decelerated by the computer to induce the subjects to make approximately 50% errors in categorizing the slides. If no selection is made before the presentation time is over, the computer program considers this omission an error. By decreasing (or increasing) the presentation time, the task is made more difficult (or easier). Whenever there is a mistake, a negative acoustic reinforcement is also given (Kuhmann, Lachnit, & Vaitl, 1985).

The MAT was performed aloud with three levels of difficulty: serial subtraction of the number 17 beginning from 1013 for subjects with an IQ higher than 110, of 7 beginning from 251 for subjects with an IQ of 90–110, or of 3 beginning from 101 for subjects with an IQ lower than 90 (Wechsler, 1955). By this means, the task is adjusted as far as possible to the subject's ability. The subject gives the answer orally, and a psychometric technician calls out "right" or "wrong" in a harsh, driving tone, pressing the subject to give the right answer smartly with the continuous presence of human confrontation and challenge.

WN was produced by tape recordings taken in the workplace, where smelting, refining, scorching, and flame cutting are carried on. The noises were low frequency with pure tone at 125 Hz and medium-high frequency with the possible presence of a pure tone at 4000 Hz. The intensities were between 90 and 110 decibels.

Results

The rating on the SI assessment divided the group into the four Type A behavior patterns (Table 1). Rater concordance (A vs. B) was 85%. In four cases, a third judge was called in. In all, Type A accounted for 67.1% of the subjects and the non-A for 32.9%. Table 1 shows that age did not affect the category to which the subjects belonged. Category X subjects were grouped with the non-A, i.e., Type B.

The number of subjects analyzed was reduced to 70 because in three cases, numerous data for the cardiovascular parameters measured during the psychophysiological profile were missing. All statistical analyses were carried out using BMDP (Dixon, Brown, Engelman, Frane, Hill, Jennrich, & Toporek, 1983).

The relation between TABP and physiological responsiveness was investigated by analysis of variance, both parametric (one-way ANOVA) and nonparametric (Kruskal-Wallis test), with categories A1, A2, X+B as independent variables and the following as dependent variables: (1) the mean values recorded during the baseline (2 min), stress task (10 min), and recovery (3 min) for the cardiovascular parameters, HR, sBP, dBP, and RPP (rate × sBP product calculated) and (2) the variations in these parameters during the three tasks, i.e., subtracting the mean value for the 2 min before the start of the task from the mean value for the 10-min task.

Table 2 lists the baseline, task, and recovery period levels for HR, sBP, dBP, and RPP. The results clearly indicate that there were no differences in the cardiovascular parameters across the three groups in any of the periods considered.

Table 3 supplies an easier, more immediate view of the variations recorded in the three groups. Inspection of these data reveals that the mean cardiovascular response to laboratory challenges was substantial for

Table 1. Characteristics of the Study Population

TABP	N	%	Age	± SD
A1	15	20.5	43.8	3.5
A2	34	46.6	44.8	3.8
X	15	20.5	43.8	5.0
B	9	12.4	43.4	4.1
	Total		Mean	
	73	100	44	4.1

Table 2. Type A Behavior Pattern and Cardiovascular Responses during Mental Stress Testing: Means (M), Standard Deviations (SD), and Probability (p)[a]

		Heart rate (beats/min)						Blood pressure (mm Hg) systolic					
		BSL	ICT	REC	MAT	REC	WN	BSL	ICT	REC	MAT	REC	WN
A1	M	64.6	71	63.8	76.3	64.7	64.9	134.6	145.6	134.7	149.8	134.1	136.8
	SD	10	10.2	11	12.4	10.8	11.5	13.2	15.6	12.6	16.6	12.6	12.8
A2	M	69	74.9	66.6	78.9	66.6	66.6	133.1	144.7	129.5	148.8	130.8	133.9
	SD	9.7	10.3	9.3	10.1	9.5	9.7	13.4	13.9	12.1	13.6	13.4	14.7
X+B	M	64.8	71.09	63.2	75	63	63.2	131.2	140.2	129.0	144.9	128.4	131.6
	SD	9.8	11.8	10.3	11.3	10	9.6	12.1	12.1	9.7	12.4	10.2	11.4
	F	1.6	1.14	0.89	0.87	0.85	0.76	0.32	0.92	1.29	0.73	0.97	0.66
	p	n.s.	n.s.	n.s.	n.s.	n.s.	n.s.	n.s.	n.s.	n.s.	n.s.	n.s.	n.s.
K-W		3.36	2.08	2.15	1.55	2.48	1.46	0.53	2.47	2.14	1.73	1.64	1.32
	p	n.s.	n.s.	n.s.	n.s.	n.s.	n.s.	n.s.	n.s.	n.s.	n.s.	n.s.	n.s.

Table 2. (Continued)

	Blood pressure (mm Hg) diastolic						Rate-pressure product (mm Hg/min)					
	BSL	ICT	REC	MAT	REC	WN	BSL	ICT	REC	MAT	REC	WN
A1 M	88.6	94.8	88.9	99.1	89.4	90.6	8780	10402	8681	11547	8759	8953
SD	10.8	11.4	11.9	12.2	11.7	11.2	2079	2306	2205	2916	2146	2208
A2 M	89.1	95.5	88.9	100.8	89.6	92.1	9175	10862	8619	11763	8686	8916
SD	10.3	11.7	10.9	11.3	11	11.7	1481	1932	1351	1944	1379	1521
X+B M	84.9	90	84	95.6	85.3	86.2	8446	9985	8181	10917	8132	8343
SD	7.9	9.71	8.4	11.8	10	10	1722	1908	1556	2040	1653	1494
F	1.3	1.71	1.6	1.31	1.17	1.9	1.24	1.27	0.6	9.8	0.93	0.92
p	n.s.	n.s.	n.s.	n.s.	n.s.	n.s.	n.s.	n.s.	n.s.	n.s.	n.s.	n.s.
K-W	1.76	2.6	2.39	1.92	2.09	2.43	2.05	1.94	1.08	1.65	4.33	1.18
p	n.s.	n.s.	n.s.	n.s.	n.s.	n.s.	n.s.	n.s.	n.s.	n.s.	n.s.	n.s.

[a]Other abbreviations: (BSL) baseline; (ICT) interactive concentration test; (REC) recovery period; (MAT) mental arithmetic test; (WN) workside noises; (K-W) Kruskal-Wallis test; (n.s.) not significant.

Table 3. Type A Behavior Pattern and Changes of Cardiovascular Responses during Mental Stress Testing: Mean (M) Changes from Baseline, Standard Deviation (SD) and Range, and Probability (p)[a]

| | | Heart rate (beats/min) | | | Blood pressure (mm Hg) | | | | | | Rate-pressure product (mm Hg/min) | | |
| | | | | | Systolic | | | Diastolic | | | | | |
		ICT	MAT	WN	ICT	MAT	WN	ICT	MAT	WN	ICT	MAT	WN
A1	M	6.3	12.4	0.2	11.0	15.1	2.7	6.1	10.2	1.2	1622	2865	194
	SD	4.9	8.0	4.4	7.9	9.1	4.8	3.2	5.1	3.0	1096	1799	785
	Max	14.0	30.0	14.0	28.0	30.0	14.0	12.0	19.0	6.0	3946	6566	2298
	Min	0.0	2.0	-5.0	-4.0	-1.0	-7.0	2.0	1.0	-2.0	-171	233	-1072
A2	M	6.0	12.3	0.0	11.6	19.3	3.1	6.4	11.9	2.5	1706	3169	209
	SD	3.4	4.4	2.3	7.3	7.6	4.5	4.2	3.6	3.7	897	1039	459
	Max	19.0	24.0	6.0	27.0	38.0	13.0	14.0	19.0	13.0	4385	5082	983
	Min	-1.0	5.0	-5.0	1.0	4.0	-5.0	-1.0	6.0	-3.0	452	1252	-846
X-B	M	6.2	11.8	0.1	9.0	15.8	3.3	5.1	11.5	1.0	1539	2736	210
	SD	4.8	3.9	2.5	5.7	5.4	4.5	4.0	4.6	3.9	940	889	631
	Max	20.0	19.0	8.0	22.0	34.0	14.0	14.0	21.0	6.0	3610	4981	1972
	Min	-1.0	5.0	-5.0	0.0	9.0	-3.0	-4.0	7.0	-11.0	252	1146	-1370
	F	0.05	0.07	0.03	0.92	2.33	0.08	0.73	0.86	1.44	0.2	0.91	0.0
	p	n.s.	n.s.	n.s.	n.s.	n.s.	n.s.	n.s.	n.s.	n.s.	n.s.	n.s.	n.s.

[a]See the Table 2 footnote.

the mental arithmetic and interaction concentration tests, but not for workside noise. There were, however, no Type A1 vs. A2 vs. non-A differences in cardiovascular responses.

We then checked whether the high-responder vs. low-responder distinction in qualitative terms—i.e., on visual inspection of the profile curves for each subject—would identify a larger number of high responders among the Type As. Table 4 shows the lack of significant differences ($\chi^2 = 0.13$, $df = 2$).

Discussion

This is one of the few structured interview studies in a Latin country. The principal data on the TABP in an Italian healthy population were provided by Caracciolo and colleagues, who found a significantly higher rate of TABP as measured by JAS in a sample of 1465 Italian workers (assumed to be representative of the whole Italian working population) than in United States normative groups (Caracciolo, DeLeo, Baserga Marchetti, Bellaterra, & Molinari, 1987). Another Italian study done by Zotti and co-workers (Zotti, Ambroso, Ambrosio, Vidotto, Dal Palù, & Tabhis Gruppo Collaborativo, 1989) studied 373 hypertensive patients from the International Primary Prospective Prevention Study in Hypertension (IPPPSH) (IPPPSH, 1984) still on double-blind treatment with or without beta-blocker, by means of JAS form C. Among the hypertensives, 74% showed a Type A pattern and 25% were in the extreme predictive interval for CHD according to the Western Collaborative Group Study (WCGS).

Given the lack of SI research in Italy, it may be of some interest to know that in a group of 73 blue collar workers, 49 (67%) may be classified as Type A. All were healthy subjects who had undergone searching

Table 4. Distribution of the Subjects by Cardiovascular Response and by Behavior Pattern[a]

Response	Behavior pattern			
	A1	A2	X+B	Total
Low	9	19	13	41
High	6	15	11	32
Totals	15	34	24	73

[a]$\chi^2 = 0.13$; $df = 2$; $p = 0.93$.

cardiological examination before being included in the experiment. A recent term of reference is a United States study of 568 fulltime workers, 63% in blue collar occupations (Ganster et al., 1991): 45% were classified as Type A and 55% as Type B, and the majority (65%) of those classed as A were rated A1.

In our study, we recorded sBP, dBP, and HR both at rest and in three challenging situations in the course of a laboratory test. Analysis of those parameters shows that subjects rated Type A1, A2, and non-A (X or B) did not differ from one another either during the rest periods or during the challenges. The analysis took account not only of the task period but also of the recovery period following the challenge, since recovery deficits may serve as a diagnostic index independent of responsiveness and of great use clinically (Dienstbier, 1989; Ganster et al., 1991). But no Type A vs. non-A differences emerged here either.

The main aim of this research was to pinpoint the linkage between TABP and cardiovascular reactivity. As expected, the active stressors (MAT and ICT) elicited moderately high cardiovascular responses (in some subjects decidedly high and out of proportion to the physical load of the test), but contrary to expectations, no Type A vs. Type B difference in cardiovascular responsiveness emerged. What is more, not even subjects categorized as Type A1, i.e., those presenting attributes of hostility and competitiveness, were more stressed by a task involving human confrontation like mental arithmetic then were the others.

We then considered the possibility that stereotyped or idiosyncratic response patterns might have blurred real differences in responsiveness across the groups. There was also the possibility that the number of "hot reactors" present was unequal among the groups but too small to be reflected in the means of the responses and in statistical differences. We therefore conducted a qualitative analysis, closely examining each subject's set of cardiovascular responses in order to categorize him as a high or low responder in global terms. This more clinical and detailed categorization yielded a similar frequency of high responders among the Type A1, A2, and non-A groups. We are thus obliged to conclude that our study affords no support whatsoever for the assumption that Type As (or at least Type A1s) are more responsive than others during the laboratory challenges with which they were confronted.

The primary explanation for the failure to find a linkage between TABP and cardiovascular reactivity may lie in the attributes of the study population, which was Italian, while the TABP construct and the SI were developed in another cultural context. In the second place, the subjects studied represented a nonurban population. They all come from the valleys of Bergamo province, where they live and, more important, have their unique cultural roots and social values, including solidarity rather than competitiveness and drive. In the third place, the study population is strongly marked in terms of language, the Bergamo dialect being among the most assertive and most accented in our country. They were therefore probably better able than most to cope with the confrontation of SI tactics. In the fourth place, the subjects work in a relatively homogeneous milieu—blue collar workers in the same steel plant and all engaged in fairly similar jobs connected with steel production. In contrast, it should be borne in mind that studies of TABP have often focused on businessmen, professional people, and white collar workers, rather than on blue collar workers, among whom the TABP and CHD association is highly doubtful. Further, studies of the TABP and cardiovascular reactivity linkage among healthy subjects are heavily weighted in favor of college students.

Another point worth emphasizing is that the study subjects (all volunteers) had been admitted following a cardiological examination, which certainly purged the research of possible artifacts due to the presence of subjects with borderline hypertension or other pathological conditions. In light of these considerations, the failure to find differences in reactivity is open to three possible interpretations. First, it is conceivable that the SI is not appropriate for the assessment of TABP in a sociocultural and linguistic milieu like that of our study. The lack of SI research in Italy, and more generally in the Latin area, makes it impossible to have an opinion on this.

Second, the failure to find differences in reactivity might be due to the multidimensional character of the TABP construct. TABP is not a unitary construct, but is made up of several components under a global index. Some of these components are known to be more associated with CHD than others, especially those connected with hostility, time urgency (Chesney et al., 1981), or with some traits in the hostility domain (Barefoot, Dodge, Peterson, Dahlstrom, & Williams, 1989; Dembroski, MacDougall, Costa, & Grandits, 1989; Scherwiz, Perkins, Chesney, & Hughes, 1991). When one goes into the specifics of these components, one finds that some are more related to cardiovascular reactivity than others (Ganster et al., 1991; Houston, 1988). This being so, the current mode of categorization of the SI may be unsuitable, and some attention may need to be paid to its components.

The third possibility is that our failure may depend, in some measure, on the weakness of the association between TABP and cardiovascular responsiveness. It is recognized that even when significant, the association is extremely weak in the general population. Houston (1988, p. 224) is inclined to rate it close to 0.20. Similarly, Ganster and colleagues (Ganster et al., 1991, p. 158) recently reported very low correlations (even when significant) between Type A (globally defined by means of the SI) and indices of reactivity in 411 United States workers (male and female, white and blue collar workers), namely, for HR, 0.02, n.s.; for sBP, 0.12, $p < 0.01$; for dBP, 0.08, $p < 0.05$. Quite possibly this association varies in strength with linguistic/cultural attributes and socioeconomic and working conditions and ceases to be detectable in somewhat different contexts from the one in which it was originally found.

Our study suggests some future lines of research. A further analysis of the SI videotape may be productive, especially looking at indicators of anger/hostility, such as, for example, the Potential for Hostility rating derived from the SI (Dembroski, MacDougall, Shields, Pettito, & Lushene, 1978). This might be a test of the hypothesis that specific components of the SI are the ones genuinely predictive of coronary reactivity. A second line is a longitudinal prolongation of the study to find out whether the variables obtained from the SI or from psychophysiological recordings or from combinations of the two have some prognostic bearing on the health of the subjects. Whatever the relation between TABP and psychophysiological responsiveness may be, the combined use of behavioral and psychophysiological measures would definitely heighten the validity of a prospective study.

To sum up, as it stands now, our study simply adds one further example to the minority of studies that have failed to find differences in cardiovascular responsiveness between Type A and Type B. In our study population of Italian steel workers subjected to appropriate tests of cardiovascular responsiveness, there was no sign whatsoever of hyperresponsiveness in Type A1s or in those lumped together as Type A. In the present state of knowledge, this finding suggests that there are limits to the transferability of the construct TABP and its most valid tool of assessment (SI) to cultures such as ours, or that the linkage between Type A and cardiovascular reactivity may be weaker than was thought, or perhaps both.

ACKNOWLEDGMENT.   This research was supported by European Economic Community Grant 7247/24/005.

References

Barefoot, J. C., Dodge, K. A., Peterson, B. L., Dahlstrom, G., & Williams, R. B. (1989). The Cook-Medley hostility scale: Item content and ability to predict survival. *Psychosomatic Medicine, 51,* 46–57.

Booth-Kewley, S., & Friedman, H. S. (1987). Psychological predictors of heart disease: A quantitative review. *Psychological Bulletin, 101,* 343–362.

Caracciolo, S., DeLeo, D., Baserga Marchetti, M. A., Bellaterra, M., & Molinari, S. (1987). Cross-cultural distribution of the Type A coronary prone behavior pattern: Is Italy more Type A than U.S.A.? In S. Lenzi & G. C. Descovich (Eds.), *Atherosclerosis and cardiovascular disease*, Vol. 3. Bologna: Editrice Compositori.

Chesney, M. A., Eagleston, P., & Rosenman, R. H. (1981). Type A behavior: Assessment and intervention. In C. K. Prokop & L. A. Bradley (Eds.), *Medical psychology: Contribution to behavioral medicine*. New York: Academic Press.

De Leo, D., Caracciolo, S., Berto, F., Mauro, P., Magni, G., & Miraglia, G. (1986). Type A behavior pattern and mortality after recurrent myocardial infarction: Preliminary results from a follow up study of 5 years. *Psychotherapy and Psychosomatics*, 46, 132–137.

Dembroski, T. M., & MacDougall, J. M. (1983). Behavioral and psychophysiological perspectives on coronary-prone behavior. In T. M. Dembroski, T. H. Schmidt, & G. Bluemchen (Eds.), *Biobehavioral bases of coronary heart disease* (pp. 106–127). Basel: Karger.

Dembroski, T. M., MacDougall, J. M., Shields, J. L., Pettito, J., & Lushene, R. (1978). Components of the Type A coronary-prone behavior pattern and cardiovascular responses to psychomotor challenge. *Journal of Behavioral Medicine*, 1, 159–176.

Dembroski, T. M., MacDougall, J. M., Costa, P. T., & Grandits, G. A. (1989). Components of hostility as predictor of sudden death and myocardial infarction in the multiple risk factor intervention trial. *Psychosomatic Medicine*, 51, 514–522.

Dienstbier, R. A. (1989). Arousal and physiological toughness: Implications for mental and physical health. *Psychological Review*, 96, 84–100.

Dixon, W. J., Brown, M. B., Engelman, L., Frane, J. W., Hill, M. A., Jennrich, R. I., & Toporek, J. D. (1983). *BMDP statistical software*. Berkeley: University of California Press.

Friedman, M., & Rosenman, R. H. (1959). Association of specific overt behavior pattern with blood and cardiovascular findings. *Journal of the American Medical Association*, 169, 1286–1296.

Ganster, D. C., Schaubroeck, J., Sime, W. E., & Mayes, B. T. (1991). The monological validity of the Type A personality among employed adults. *Journal of Applied Psychology*, 76, 143–168.

Harbin, T. J. (1989). The relationship between the Type A behavior pattern and physiological responsivity: A quantitative review. *Psychophysiology*, 26, 110–119.

Houston, B. K. (1988). Cardiovascular and neuroendocrine reactivity, global Type A, and components of Type A behavior. In B. K. Houston & C. R. Snyder (Eds.), *Type A behavior pattern: Research, theory & intervention*. New York: Wiley.

The International Prospective Primary Prevention Study in Hypertension (IPPPSH). (1984). Objectives and methods. The IPPPSH Collaborative Group. *Europ. J. Clin. Pharmac.*, 27, 379.

Krantz, D. S., & Manuck, S. B. (1984). Acute psychophysiological reactivity and risk of cardiovascular disease: A review and methodologic critique. *Psychological Bulletin*, 96, 435–464.

Kuhmann, W., Lachnit, H., & Vaitl, D. (1985). The quantification of experimental load: Methodological and empirical issues. In A. Steptoe, H. Ruddel, & H. Neus (Eds.), *Clinical and methodological issues in cardiovascular psychophysiology*. New York: Springer-Verlag.

Maggini, C., Guazzelli, M., Castrogiovanni, P., Mauri, M., De Lisio, G. F., Chierchia, S., & Cassano, G. B. (1976/1977). Psychological and physiopathological study on coronary patients. *Psychotherapy and Psychosomatics*, 27, 210–216.

Manuck, S. B., Kasprowicz, A. L., Monroe, S. B., Larkin, K. T., & Kaplan, J. R. (1989). Psychophysiologic reactivity as a dimension of individual differences. In N. Schneiderman, S. M. Weiss, & P. Kaufmann (Eds.), *Handbook of research methods in cardiovascular behavioral medicine* (pp. 365–382). New York: Plenum Press.

Matthews, K. A. (1988). Coronary heart disease and Type A behaviors: Update on and alternative to the Booth-Kewley and Friedman (1987) quantitative review. *Psychological Bulletin, 104,* 373–380.

Pagani, M., Mazzuero, G., Ferrari, A., Liberati, D., Cerutti, S., Vaitl, D., Tavazzi, L., & Malliani, A. (1991). Sympathovagal interaction during mental stress: A study using spectral analysis of heart rate variability in healthy control subjects and patients with a prior myocardial infarction. *Circulation,* Supplement II, *83,* No. 4.

Review Panel (1981). Coronary-prone behavior and coronary heart disease: A critical review. *Circulation, 63,* 1199–1215.

Rosenman, R. H. (1978). The interview method of assessment of the coronary-prone behavior pattern. In T. M. Dembroski, S. M. Weiss, J. L. Shields, S. G. Haynes, & M. Feinleib (Eds.), *Coronary-prone behavior.* New York: Springer-Verlag.

Rosenman, R. H., Friedman, M., Straus, R., Wurm, M., Kositchek, R., Hahn, W., & Werthessen, N. T. (1964). A predictive study of coronary heart disease: The Western Collaborative Group Study. *Journal of the American Medical Association, 189,* 113–120.

Scherwiz, L., Perkins, L., Chesney, M., & Hughes, G. (1991). Cook-Medley hostility scale and subset: Relationships to demographic and psychosocial characteristic in young adults in the CARDIA study. *Psychosomatic Medicine, 53,* 36–49.

Schmidt, T. H. (1983). Cardiovascular reactions and cardiovascular risk. In T. M. Dembroski, T. H. Schmidt, & G. Blumchen (Eds.), *Biobehavioral bases of coronary heart disease.* Basel: Karger.

Tavazzi, L., Mazzuero, G., Giordano, A., Zotti, A. M., & Bertolotti, G. (1984). Hemodynamic characterization in different mental stress tests. In H. M. Wegman (Ed.), *Breakdown in human adaptation to stress* (pp. 923–930). Boston: Martinus Nijhoff.

Tavazzi, L., Zotti, A. M., & Rondanelli, R. (1986). The role of psychologic stress in the genesis of lethal arrhythmias in patients with coronary artery disease. *European Heart Journal, 7* (Supplement A), 99–106.

Tavazzi, L., Zotti, A. M., & Mazzuero, G. (1987). Acute pulmonary edema provoked by psychologic stress. *Cardiology, 74,* 229–235.

Wechsler, D. (1955). *WB-I Scala di intelligenza Wescheler Bellevue Form I (manual).* Firenze: Organizzazioni Speciali.

Zotti, A. M., Ambroso, G., Ambrosio, B. G., Vidotto, G., Dal Palù, C., & Tabhis Gruppo Collaborativo (1989). Comportamento di Tipo A e caratteristiche psicologiche dell'iperteso in trattamento antiipertensivo. *Giornale Italiano di Cardiologia, XIX,* No. 2.

Zotti, A. M., Bettinardi, O., Soffiantino, F., Tavazzi, L., & Steptoe, A. (1991). Psychophysiological stress testing in postinfarction patients. *Circulation,* Supplement II, *83,* No. 4.

CHAPTER **6**

Psychological Factors Affecting Ambulatory Blood Pressure in a High-Stress Occupation

David Shapiro, Iris B. Goldstein, and Larry Jamner

Ambulatory Blood Pressure Monitoring as a Research Tool

Since the first recording of indirect and direct ambulatory blood pressure (BP) in human subjects (Bevan, Honour, & Stott, 1969; Hinman, Engel, & Bickford, 1962), the advantages of recording BP in natural settings have become firmly established. Compared to BP values obtained in a doctor's office or clinic, 24-hr ambulatory BP measurements are less likely to give inflated estimates of an individual's BP (Burstyn, O'Donovan, & Charlton, 1981; Floras, Jones, Hassan, Osikowska, Sever, & Sleight, 1981; Mancia, 1990); they also offer a more precise means of evaluating the efficacy of antihypertensive medications (Des Combes, Porchet, Waeber, & Brunner, 1984; Rion, Waeber, Graf, Jaussi, Porchet, & Brunner, 1985) and provide a better predictor of the development of cardiovascular morbidity and mortality (Cheung & Weber, 1988; Harshfield, Pickering, Kleinert, Blank, & Laragh, 1982; Pessina, Palatini, Di Marco, Mormino, Fazio, Libardoni, Mos, Casiglia, & Dal, 1986). These advantages derive from the fact that the 50–100 readings typically obtained in a single 24-hr ambulatory recording

DAVID SHAPIRO and IRIS B. GOLDSTEIN • Department of Psychiatry, University of California at Los Angeles, Los Angeles, CA 90024.   LARRY JAMNER • University of California, Irvine, CA 92717.

Clinical Applied Psychophysiology, edited by John G. Carlson, A. Ronald Seifert, and Niels Birbaumer. Plenum Press, New York, 1994.

yield a considerably more stable mean level of BP compared to the two or three readings obtained in an office examination. The multiple readings also offer a good means of estimating BP variability in the individual, another significant correlate of target-organ damage (Parati, Pomidossi, Albini, Malaspina, & Mancia, 1987). Most important, as compared to laboratory methods, ambulatory BP measurements are obtained in response to a variety of psychosocial situations in circumstances inherently more realistic and appropriate for the individual. This normality of circumstance increases the likelihood of determining how the person's genetic or behavioral dispositions may interact with different kinds of challenges in affecting BP fluctuations that occur during the day. Unlike the laboratory, however, there is no control over what happens during any one period of recording or whether the day will be typical and provide multiple instances of representative stressful events. This uncertainty greatly complicates the processing and analysis of the data, although the unique quantitative and statistical problems are beginning to be addressed (Clark, Denby, & Pregibon, 1989).

To date, ambulatory BP studies have focused on the following issues: presence of a diurnal BP rhythm, effects of activities, and differences between clinic or casual BP and 24-hr ambulatory BP. There is little evidence for a consistent diurnal rhythm other than the well-known reduction in BP during sleep (Clark, Denby, Pregibon, Harshfield, Pickering, Blank, & Laragh, 1987; Pickering, Harshfield, Kleinert, Blank, & Laragh, 1982; Wallace, Thornton, Kennedy, Pickering, Harshfield, Frohlich, Messerli, Gifford, & Bolen, 1984). With regard to activities, higher levels of ambulatory BP have been obtained at work than at home or during sleep (Harshfield et al., 1982; James, Pickering, Yee, Harshfield, Riva, & Laragh, 1988). Particular activities like walking and driving have been associated with higher levels of pressure than activities like reading and relaxing (Van Egeren & Madarasmi, 1988). On the issue of clinic vs. 24-hr BP, clinic or office BP is generally higher on the average when compared to ambulatory BP in hypertensive patients (Pickering & Gerin, 1988). In healthy subjects, however, there is no consistent difference between the two kinds of BP assessments (Fiedler, Favata, Goldstein, & Gochfeld, 1988).

Studies of the variability of ambulatory BP are complicated by wide individual differences in number and type of activities engaged in during the day. Moreover, individuals may respond differently because of their particular perceptions of the stressfulness of the activity or situation (Langewitz, Ruddel, & von Eiff, 1987). To understand the influence of such perceptions, subjects are typically asked to rate their experiences and moods in diaries filled out at each BP measurement or at other times of the day. Systolic blood pressure (SBP) of hypertensive patients was found to vary according to self-reports of emotional state as well as characteristics of situations (James, Yee, Harshfield, Blank, & Pickering, 1986). In a study of adolescents, average ambulatory BP was positively associated with experience of negative emotions (Southard, Coates, Kolodner, Parker, Padgett, & Kennedy, 1986). However, the concordance between BP and mood or activity may be positive for some persons and negative for others, thus accounting for the weak relationships often reported (Sokolow, Werdegar, Perloff, Cowan, & Brenenstuhl, 1970).

The relative contribution to daytime average levels of ambulatory sBP and diastolic blood pressure (DBP) of situational changes in one's mood and of self-ratings of the stressfulness of situations during the day was evaluated in a recent study in our laboratory (Shapiro, Goldstein, & Jamner, 1990). We wished to investigate the extent to which information on a person's moods and perceptions of stress during the day would account for variations in average ambulatory BP levels over and beyond what could be accounted for by more or less fixed characteristics of the individual, e.g., sex, age, body weight, habitual level of exercise, and use of caffeine. Ambulatory BP was recorded at 10-min intervals during two 6-hr daytime periods in 21 healthy male college students. Subjects made hourly ratings of their moods during the day. Fixed characteristics of subjects accounted for up to 50% of the variance in mean levels and variability of BP (Table 1). Average mood ratings and average change in mood from hour to hour added significantly to the variance explained in 25% of the analyses, accounting for an additional 13% of the variance of daytime mean BP levels and variability.

In this study, subjects were monitored over two days, and average BP levels tended to be consistent from day to day. However, individual differences in overall variability of BP during the day were not consistent over the two days, and the pattern of relationships between mood ratings and ambulatory BP also differed on the two days. There was no simple relationship between the positive or negative quality of the particular moods rated and the ambulatory BP or heart rate values. Of the various moods studied, average daily self-ratings of degrees of stress tended to be negatively associated with mean levels of SBP, while variability in anger ratings during the day was positively associated with variability in DBP.

Although these results indicated that an individual's reactions to events during the day have an impact on ambulatory BP, it was evident that our research framework needed to include an assessment of the circumstances that obtained during the day as well as of an individual's behavioral dispositions and characteristic ways of coping with stress. This strategy was followed in our subsequent research on job stress, in which we studied a single occupation in which the stressful events are relatively pervasive and uniform from one person to the next.

Table 1. Predictor Variables Selected by Stepwise Regression and Proportion of Variance Explained (R^2)[a]

Blood pressure measure	Day 1						Day 2					
	Traits with mood means			Traits with mood changes			Traits with mood means			Traits with mood changes		
	Predictor	Std. Coef.	R^2	Predictor	Std. coef.	R^2	Predictor	Std. coef.	R^2	Predictor	Std. coef.	R^2
Systolic mean	Caffeine	0.614	0.222	Caffeine	0.546	0.222	Weight	0.686	0.364	Weight	0.708	0.364
	Weight	0.454	0.407	Weight	0.368	0.407	Caffeine	0.454	0.501	Caffeine	0.422	0.501
							Stress	-0.343	0.601			
							Alert	0.333	0.704			
Systolic SD	Weight	0.422	0.349	Weight	0.596	0.349						
	Exercise	-0.405	0.485	Anger-C	0.524	0.623						
Diastolic mean	Caffeine	0.604	0.364	Caffeine	0.604	0.364	Caffeine	0.621	0.253	Caffeine	0.629	0.253
							Weight	0.382	0.397	Weight	0.400	0.397
							Stress	-0.361	0.527			
Diastolic SD							Age	-0.509	0.259	Age	-0.456	0.259
										Anger-C	0.501	0.366
										Sad-C	-0.512	0.578

[a]The table is based on a study of 21 healthy college men in whom ambulatory BP was recorded for 6 hr on two separate days (Shapiro et al., 1990). Dependent variables were the mean and standard deviation (SD) of SBP and DBP. Significant trait variables included age, weight, amount of caffeine used, and regular hours of exercise. Significant mood variables included mean daily hourly self-ratings of sadness (Sad), stress, and alertness (Alert) and mean hourly change (C) in self-ratings of Sad and Anger.

Job Stress and Blood Pressure

Job stress is considered to be a primary cause of hypertension and cardiovascular disease (Schnall, Pieper, Karasek, Schlussel, Devereux, Ganau, Alderman, Warren, & Pickering, 1990). Although a direct cause-and-effect relationship has not been demonstrated, job stress is an important factor in investigations of the physical and mental health of workers (Margolis, Kroes, & Quinn, 1974; Shapiro & Goldstein, 1982). When hours at work are compared with hours at home during a typical workday, elevated BP at work reflects physical and emotional demands of the job. This was found when BP was self-monitored once an hour during the day in normotensive and hypertensive young men (Theorell, Knox, Svensson, & Waller, 1985) and when ambulatory recordings were monitored on a 24-hr basis in hypertensive subjects of both sexes (Harshfield *et al.*, 1982). However, higher BP at work is not characteristic of all individuals (Harshfield, Pickering, Blank, & Laragh, 1986). In addition, hypertensive left ventricular hypertrophy bears a strong relationship to ambulatory BP during recurring stress at work as well as to BP obtained at home during a workday (Baba, Ozawa, Nakamoto, Ueshima, & Omae, 1990; Devereux & Pickering, 1988). When BP and heart rate were self-monitored once an hour in healthy white collar workers on both a workday and a nonworkday, BP, heart rate, and epinephrine levels were significantly elevated during the day at work (Frankenhaeuser, Lundberg, Fredrikson, Melin, Tuomisto, & Myrsten, 1989).

Work conditions are particularly stressful if they are characterized by being both psychologically demanding and having low decision latitude (Karasek, Russell, & Theorell, 1982). BP at work is definitely higher in "high-strain" occupations (Theorell *et al.*, 1985). For example, compared to clerical workers, police officers were characterized by higher casual dBP, norepinephrine level, and recent life change scores (Ely & Mostardi, 1986).

In a study of casual BP at seven work sites, Schlussel, Schnall, Zimbler, Warren, and Pickering (1990) found that elevations in BP were related to work site, lack of a high school education, being male, being unmarried, and having a clerical occupation. The job stress of complicated machine operation was a significant predictor of dBP increases (Kawakami, Haratani, Kaneko, & Araki, 1989). Various characteristics of one's job, such as lack of meaningful work tasks, little possibility of seeing results and taking initiative (Harenstam & Theorell, 1988), little opportunity for promotion and participating in work decisions, and uncertain job future (Matthews, Cottington, Talbott, Kuller, & Siegel, 1987), all contribute to the elevation of BP. Ambiguity about job future, dissatisfaction with co-workers, and dissatisfaction with promotions were associated with prevalence of hypertension, but only among men who suppress anger (Cotting-ton, Matthews, Talbott, & Kuller, 1986).

Research on Paramedics

We selected paramedics as an occupational group to study because their job meets the dual criteria of high stress and low decision latitude (Karasek *et al.*, 1982). Having to deal with life and death medical emergen-cies under potentially hazardous situations is psychologically demanding, as is repeated exposure to human tragedy, pressure to perform in uncer-tain situations, low pay, excessive paperwork, and lack of administrative support. These factors all contribute to a high incidence of burnout and job turnover (Dutton, Smolensky, Leach, Lorimor, & Hsi, 1978). Since para-medics keep careful time-based logs of their emergency calls, we were able to get precise information on the circumstances in which the ambulatory recordings were made, allowing us to ascertain the degree to which specific work situations contribute to changes in BP during the day and how these changes may be related to characteristic behavioral dispositions of the subjects. The remainder of this chapter will review selected findings in our previous research on paramedics and include new data on relation-ships between behavioral dispositions and BP level and reactivity obtained from the same subjects on a nonworkday.

The aim of our first study of paramedics was to evaluate the effects of different work contexts on ambulatory BP with reactivity being assessed by differences in BP levels between high- and low-stress circumstances. We then attempted to relate these effects to individual differences in cynical hostility as measured by the Cook-Medley Hostility Scale [Ho Scale (Cook & Medley, 1954)]. Scores on the Ho Scale have been shown to predict increased BP reactivity in situations that elicit high interpersonal conflict or suspiciousness and mistrust (Hardy & Smith, 1988; Suarez & Williams, 1989; Weidner, Friend, Ficarrotto, & Mendell, 1989). Cynical hostility has also been identified as a significant risk factor for coronary heart disease morbidity and all-cause mortality independent of other risk factors (Barefoot, Williams, & Dahlstrom, 1983; Barefoot, Dodge, Peter-son, Dahlstrom, & Williams, 1989; Williams, 1987), as well as for the severity of coronary and peripheral artery disease (Joesoef, Wetterhal, DeStefano, Stroup, & Fronek, 1989; Williams, Haney, Lee, Kong, Blumen-thal, & Whalen, 1980). Negative findings regarding these relationships have also been reported (Hearn, Urray, & Leupker, 1989; Leon, Finn, Murray, & Bailey, 1988; McCranie, Watkins, Brandsma, & Sisson, 1986).

We examined defensiveness as a second individual behavioral disposition. As measured by the Marlowe-Crowne Social Desirability Scale [MC (Crowne & Marlowe, 1960)], defensiveness represents a coping style characterized by an orientation away from threatening information and a denial or minimization of distress and negative emotions. High scores on the MC, either alone or in combination with low scores of trait anxiety or anger, have been found to be associated with increased BP and heart rate reactivity to laboratory stressors in both clinical (Warrenburg, Levine, Schwartz, Fontana, Kerns, Delaney, & Mattson, 1989) and nonclinical populations (A. C. King, Taylor, Albright, & Haskell, 1990; Weinberger, Schwartz, & Davidson, 1979). Moreover, these effects were found to be independent of gender and other cardiac risk factors, e.g., weight and smoking history (A. C. King *et al.*, 1990).

The subjects were 33 male paramedics who were studied on a 24-hr workshift. After completing the Ho and MC scales, they were fitted with the ACCUTRACKER II (Suntech Medical Instruments, Inc.) ambulatory BP monitor. The monitor was programmed to operate every 20 min on a random time schedule. On each operation of the machine, single readings of sBP and dBP were obtained. The ACCUTRACKER II is about the weight and size of a Walkman radio, and it is easily attached to one's belt. Subjects were given a diary and a countdown watch and instructed on their use. For each cuff inflation, subjects were instructed to indicate the time and their location. They were also told that the watch alarm would ring every 2 hr, at which time they were to rate their mood states and somatic symptoms since their last diary entry using 15 6-point scales. Subjects were also asked to rate the same items at the completion of each ambulance run. The work diary is shown in Fig. 1.

In addition to diaries, subjects submitted copies of their ambulance run logs, containing detailed information about their activities from the time they were dispatched to the time their responsibilities were transferred to hospital personnel. The logs indicate time of departure from the station, time of arrival at the scene, time of departure for the hospital, time of departure to the station, and time of arrival at the station. Diary entries were used to verify events in the record and determine whether subjects were awake or asleep while at the station. During the 24-hr work period, paramedics responded to approximately six calls on the average. A single call took between 10 min (false alarm) and 3 hr. The types of calls were as follows: bodily complaints, auto accident injuries, other accidents and injuries, seizures, sudden death, acute illness, domestic fights, psychological complaints, and false alarms.

To evaluate the effects of cynical hostility and defensiveness, approximate median scores on the Ho and MC scales were used to divide subjects into high and low hostility and high and low defensive groups. A signifi-

UCLA Blood Pressure/Stress Study

TIME BEGAN	SMOKING	CAFFEINE	ALCOHOL	ACTIVITY 1-Sleep 2-Eat 3-Sitting 4-Standing 5-Walking 6-Exercise 7-Other	LOCATION 1-Station 2-Ambulance 3-Onscene 4-Hospital 5-Other (ex: store)
	√ yes	√ yes	√ yes		

Complete after each RUN or when CLOCK ALARM sounds
Time:_____
How much of the following did you experience
since the last cuff-inflation

	NOT AT ALL					EXTREMELY MUCH
STRESS	1	2	3	4	5	6
HAPPY	1	2	3	4	5	6
FRUSTRATED	1	2	3	4	5	6
ALERT	1	2	3	4	5	6
TENSE NECK & SHOULDERS	1	2	3	4	5	6
ANGRY/HOSTILE	1	2	3	4	5	6
UNHAPPY	1	2	3	4	5	6
COLD HANDS	1	2	3	4	5	6
SAD/BLUE	1	2	3	4	5	6
RACING HEART	1	2	3	4	5	6
PLEASANT	1	2	3	4	5	6
FATIGUED	1	2	3	4	5	6
WORRIED/ANXIOUS	1	2	3	4	5	6

Figure 1. Paramedic work diary. During the workday, paramedics filled out the top portion of the diary on every BP measurement and the bottom portion after each ambulance run or after each 2-hr period in which an ambulance run did not occur. During a day off, the diary entries were made appropriate to activities and locations occurring on a nonworkday.

cant relationship was found for DBP between hostility and work context (Fig. 2). In the hospital setting, subjects who were high in cynical hostility showed dBP levels about 4 mm Hg higher than subjects who were low in hostility. Subjects scoring high in both defensiveness and cynical hostility showed significantly greater hospital DBP levels (about 10 mm Hg on the average) than other subgroups of subjects (Fig. 3). These findings extend previous research reporting increased BP reactivity in highly hostile subjects to situations involving interpersonal conflict (Hardy & Smith, 1988; Suarez & Williams, 1989).

Moreover, the relationship between cynical hostility and cardiovascular reactivity was improved by taking defensiveness into account. The saliency of the hospital setting was confirmed in postexperimental interviews with subjects. The paramedics reported feeling challenged by hospital emergency room physicians and nurses concerning their care of patients and decisions made in the field as opposed to feeling "more in control" in the ambulance, where they were alone with patients.

To understand the psychology of individuals who are both highly hostile and highly defensive, we examined items of the Ho and MC scales. Responses to the two scales provide an index of a form of ambivalence and conflicting attitudes, as exemplified in Table 2. In light of society's disapproval of and sanctions against hostile behaviors, individuals who are

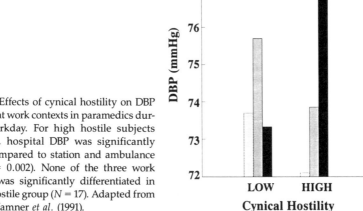

Figure 2. Effects of cynical hostility on DBP in different work contexts in paramedics during a workday. For high hostile subjects ($N = 16$), hospital DBP was significantly higher compared to station and ambulance DBP ($p = 0.002$). None of the three work contexts was significantly differentiated in the low hostile group ($N = 17$). Adapted from Fig. 2 in Jamner *et al.* (1991).

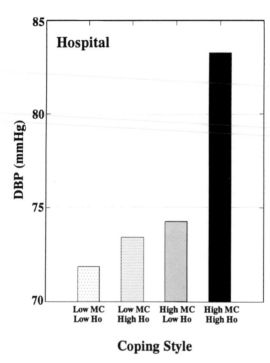

Figure 3. Differences among four subgroups of paramedics, classified according to high and low scores on cynical hostility (Ho) and defensiveness (MC) scales. Subjects scoring high on both scales had higher DBP levels as compared to all other subgroups (p's < 0.05). Based on data discussed in Jamner *et al.* (1991). Numbers of subjects: Low MC/Low Ho, 6; Low MC/High Ho, 10; High MC/Low Ho, 11; High MC/High Ho, 6.

motivated toward gaining social approval would be expected to inhibit the expression of such "unacceptable" behavior (Kiecolt-Glaser & Greenberg, 1981). If coupled with a world-view that others are out for themselves and not to be trusted, this tendency might have the effect of making the individual more conflicted or ambivalent about expressing hostility. Thus, conflicting and ambivalent attitudes about the expression of hostility, rather than hostility *per se*, may be a critical psychological mechanism of increased BP reactivity. This conclusion is in broad agreement with recent findings on the psychological and physiological effects of conflict over emotional expression and of the matching of one's preferred anger coping style with the type of anger expression (Engebretson, Matthews, & Scheier, 1989; L. A. King & Emmons, 1990).

We also examined relationships between the 24-hr ambulatory data and individual differences in hostility and defensiveness. Mean levels of SBP when subjects were awake were higher in high hostile than in low hostile subjects (Fig. 4a). High defensive subjects showed higher awake DBP than low defensive subjects (Fig. 5a). Furthermore, variability of DBP during the day while subjects were awake was higher in high than in low

Table 2. An Index of a Form of Ambivalence and Conflicting Attitudes[a]

Cook-Medley Hostility Scale	Marlow-Crowne Social Desirability Scale
T Most people inwardly dislike putting themselves out to help other people.	T I never resent being asked to return a favor
T No one cares much what happens to you.	T I never hesitate to go out of my way to help someone in trouble.
T It is safer to trust nobody.	
T When someone does me a wrong, I feel I should pay him back just for the principle of the thing.	T I would never think of letting someone else be punished for my wrong doings.
T Most people are honest chiefly through fear of being caught.	F If I could get into a movie without paying for it and be sure I was not seen, I probably would do it.
T I have often had to take orders from someone who did not know as much as I did.	T When I don't know something, I don't at all mind admitting it.

[a]Listed are items from the Cook-Medley Hostility Scale and the Marlowe-Crowne Social Desirability Scale, chosen to illustrate ambivalent attitudes and intrapersonal conflict in individuals scoring high on both scales and tending to agree with items from the two scales.

hostile subjects ($p = 0.02$). These data suggest that in a social environment involving frequent interpersonal challenges and demands, hostility affects BP reactivity to work stressors as well as sustained levels and overall variability of BP during the day. Frequent exposure to highly stressful events can potentiate the negative impact on BP of an individual's disposition to hostile behavior. A defensive attitude may also contribute to a chronic elevation in BP.

A 24-hr ambulatory recording was also made in the same subjects on a day off from their work, which made it possible to examine relationships between ambulatory data and individual differences in hostility and defensiveness under presumably less stressful natural conditions. During the 24-hr period as a whole, there were no overall BP differences between the nonworkday and a workday (Goldstein, Jamner, & Shapiro, 1992). Rather than being elevated for the entire 24-hr period, work BP reflected the relatively high stress associated with specific work contexts, e.g., scene of an accident, in the ambulance going to the emergency, and hospital setting. During the day off, awake SBP was higher in high than in low hostile subjects, the same effect obtained on the workday (Fig. 4b). Moreover, this difference was almost twice as large as it was on the workday. High hostile subjects had average SBP levels that were almost the same on both days (about 135 mm Hg). In contrast, low hostile subjects

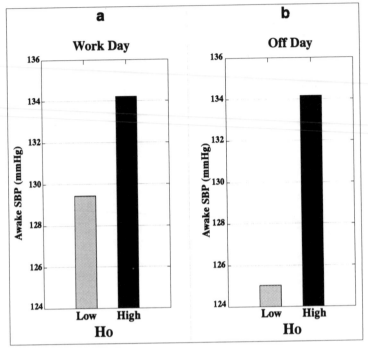

Figure 4. Effect of cynical hostility (Ho) on awake SBP. (a) Awake SBP on a workday ($p = 0.029$); (b) awake SBP on a nonworkday ($p = 0.007$). Number of subjects: Low Ho, 17; High Ho, 16.

were appreciably lower on the off day than on the workday (125 mm Hg and 130 mm Hg, respectively). As during a workday, waking ambulatory BP was higher in high defensive than in low defensive subjects (Fig. 5b). These differences were stable in the two days.

In general, interactions between behavioral disposition and ambulatory BP during a nonworkday are consistent with those obtained during a workday. Individuals who are highly hostile appear to be consistently high in BP, whether under specific conditions of work stress or during situations that obtain on a day off that typically result in reduced levels of BP for individuals who do not have a hostile disposition. The day-off BP data did not lend themselves to the analyses of location or situational context, so we are not able to determine how hostility and defensiveness interact with degree of situational stress in affecting BP reactivity during the nonworkday.

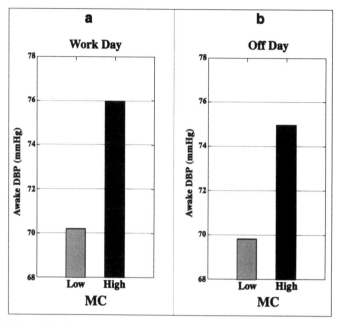

Figure 5. Effects of defensiveness (MC) on awake DBP. (a) Awake DBP on a workday ($p =$ 0.013); (b) awake DBP on a nonworkday ($p = 0.021$). Number of subjects: Low MC, 16; High MC, 17.

Clinical Implications

Finally, what are the clinical implications of this research? Despite the many advantages of ambulatory BP recording discussed earlier, ambulatory recordings have not become routine in the assessment and diagnosis of hypertension. Moreover, consensus committees have not recommended ambulatory recording as a standard in medical practice (Joint National Committee, 1988), even though ambulatory BP provides a better index of target-organ damage and of the progression and mortality of hypertension. Our findings on the significance of individual differences in hostility and defensiveness for levels and reactivity of ambulatory BP suggest that it is useful to assess these behavioral dispositions in evaluating individuals with high BP. Moreover, the fact of consistently high levels of BP in highly hostile subjects on *both* workdays and nonworkdays suggests the utility of multiple days of ambulatory recording obtained under varying degrees of social and environmental stress. It is not that individual traits of hostility are necessary features in all hypertensive patients. A subgroup of this disorder may be characterized by "behavioral" or "neurogenic" causation; other subgroups may have a different etiology (Julius, 1989).

Anger and hostility have been consistently implicated in hypertension, and the data we have presented provide solid support for this relationship based on a more extensive evaluation of BP in a natural setting. Our results are in conformity with the consensus that inhibition of anger and a hostile outlook are "toxic" in hypertension. These findings also speak to the issue of "white-coat hypertension" and whether or not one needs to take seriously the pattern of abnormal clinic BP and normal ambulatory BP. Individuals with "white-coat hypertension" appear to be comparable in a way to the subjects we have studied in a high-stress occupation who are relatively low in their ambulatory BP levels on a normal workday and clearly lower in their BP on an off day. These are individuals who are relatively low in hostility. These individuals appear to be at less risk for the complications of hypertension, as compared to individuals who are highly hostile. The latter tend to be consistently high in BP, whether in the clinic or in 24-hr recordings taken on different days.

The assessment of individual differences in defensiveness also has clinical utility, not only in helping differentiate individuals in conflict over the expression of anger or hostile feelings, but as a factor accounting directly for differences in average BP levels. In contrast to the hostility dimension, which correlates with SBP, defensiveness seems more closely correlated with DBP.

Another area of clinical application is the assessment of cardiovascular reactivity as a means of evaluating the efficacy of behavioral or drug treatments, or both, for hypertension. By and large, clinic or laboratory psychophysiological assessments using standard stressors have not been helpful in differentiating treatment effects. In the research reported herein, BP responses to natural events known to vary in degree of stressfulness appear to be sensitive to individual psychological characteristics and the nature of the events. This methodology could well be adapted as a means of comparing reactivity pre- and posttreatment. For this purpose, additional research is needed on the assessment of naturally occurring stressors in varying jobs and life situations and in the refinement of diaries and self-rating instruments. The methods may also be of value in comparing the effectiveness of different behavioral or drug treatments in terms of reactivity as well as average levels of BP occurring in everyday situations. Ambulatory BP recording is a promising method of study in applied and clinical psychophysiology.

ACKNOWLEDGMENTS.   This research was supported by NHLBI Research Grant HL-40466 and by UC-TRDRP Grant IRT205. Portions of the chapter were adapted from Shapiro *et al.* (1990), Jamner, Shapiro, Goldstein, and Hug (1991), and Goldstein *et al.* (1992).

References

Baba, S., Ozawa, H., Nakamoto, Y., Ueshima, H., & Omae, T. (1990). Enhanced blood pressure response to regular daily stress in urban hypertensive men. *Journal of Hypertension, 8*, 647–655.

Barefoot, J. C., Williams, R. B., & Dahlstrom, W. G. (1983). Hostility, CHD incidence and total mortality: A 25-yr follow-up study of 255 physicians. *Psychosomatic Medicine, 45*, 59–63.

Barefoot, J. C., Dodge, K. A., Peterson, B.L., Dahlstrom, W. G., & Williams, R. B., Jr. (1989). The Cook-Medley hostility scale item content and ability to predict survival. *Psychosomatic Medicine, 51*, 46–57.

Bevan, A. T., Honour, A. J., & Stott, F. H. (1969). Direct arterial pressure recording in unrestricted man. *Clinical Science, 36*, 329–344.

Burstyn, P., O'Donovan, B., & Charlton, I. (1981). Blood pressure variability: The effects of repeated measurement. *Postgraduate Medical Journal, 57*, 488–491.

Cheung, D., & Weber, M. A. (1988). Ambulatory blood pressure measurements: Practical considerations, methodology, feasibility, and implication in the management of hypertension. *Cardiovascular Clinics, 18*, 125–138.

Clark, L. A., Denby, L., Pregibon, D., Harshfield, G. A., Pickering, T. G., Blank, S., & Laragh, J. H. (1987). A quantitative analysis of the effects of activity and time of day on the diurnal variations of blood pressure. *Journal of Chronic Diseases, 40*, 671–681.

Clark, L. A., Denby, L., & Pregibon, D. (1989). Data analysis of ambulatory blood pressure readings before P values. In N. Schneiderman, S. M. Weiss, & P. G. Kaufmann (Eds.), *Handbook of research methods in cardiovascular behavioral medicine* (pp. 322–345). New York: Plenum Press.

Cook, W. W., & Medley, D. M. (1954). Proposed hostility and pharisaic-virtue for the MMPI. *Journal of Applied Psychology, 38*, 414–418.

Cottington, E. M., Matthews, K. A., Talbott, E., & Kuller, L. H. (1986). Occupational stress, suppressed anger, and hypertension. *Psychosomatic Medicine, 48*, 249–260.

Crowne, D., & Marlowe, D. (1960). A new scale of social desirability independent of psychopathology. *Journal of Consulting Psychology, 24*, 349–354.

Des Combes, B. J., Porchet, M., Waeber, B., & Brunner, H. R. (1984). Ambulatory blood pressure recordings: Reproducibility and unpredictability. *Hypertension, 6*, C110–C115.

Devereux, R. B., & Pickering, T. G. (1988). Relationship between ambulatory and exercise blood pressure and cardiac structure. *American Heart Journal, 116*, 1124–1133.

Dutton, L. M., Smolensky, M. H., Leach, C. S., Lorimor, R., & Hsi, B. (1978). Stress levels of ambulance paramedics and fire fighters. *Journal of Occupational Medicine, 20*, 111–115.

Ely, D. L., & Mostardi, R. A. (1986). The effect of recent life events stress, life assets, and temperament pattern on cardiovascular risk factors for Akron city police officers. *Journal of Human Stress, 12*, 77–91.

Engebretson, T. O., Matthews, K. A., & Scheier, M. F. (1989). Relations between anger expression and cardiovascular reactivity: Reconciling inconsistent findings through a matching hypothesis. *Journal of Consulting & Clinical Psychology, 57*, 513–521.

Fiedler, N., Favata, E., Goldstein, B. D., & Gochfeld, M. (1988). Utility of occupational blood pressure screening for the detection of potential hypertension. *Journal of Occupational Medicine, 30,* 943–948.

Floras, J. S., Jones, J. V., Hassan, M. O., Osikowska, B., Sever, P. S., & Sleight, P. (1981). Cuff and ambulatory blood pressure in subjects with essential hypertension. *Lancet, 2,* 107–109.

Frankenhaeuser, M., Lundberg, U., Fredrikson, M., Melin, B., Tuomisto, M., & Myrsten, A. L. (1989). Stress on and off the job as related to sex and occupational status in white-collar workers. *Journal of Organizational Behavior, 10,* 321–346.

Goldstein, I. B., Jamner, L. D., & Shapiro, D. (1992). Ambulatory blood pressure and heart rate in paramedics during a workday and a non-workday. *Health Psychology, 11,* 48–58.

Hardy, J. D., & Smith, T. W. (1988). Cynical hostility and vulnerability to disease: Social support, life stress and physiological response to conflict. *Health Psychology, 7,* 447–459.

Harenstam, A. N., & Theorell, T. P. G. (1988). Work conditions and urinary excretion of catecholamines: A study of prison staff in Sweden. *Scandinavian Journal of Work & Environmental Health, 14,* 257–264.

Harshfield, G. A., Pickering, T. G., Kleinert, H. D., Blank, S., & Laragh, J. H. (1982). Situational variations of blood pressure in ambulatory hypertensive patients. *Psychosomatic Medicine, 44,* 237–245.

Harshfield, G. A., Pickering, T. G., Blank, S. G., & Laragh, J. H. (1986). How well do casual blood pressures reflect ambulatory blood pressures? In G. Germano (Ed.), *Blood pressure recording in the clinical management of hypertension* (pp. 50–54). Rome: Edizioni L. Pozzi.

Hearn, M. D., Urray, D. M., & Leupker, R. V. (1989). Hostility coronary heart disease, and total mortality: A 33-year follow-up study of university students. *Journal of Behavioral Medicine, 12,* 105–121.

Hinman, A. T., Engel, B. T., & Bickford, A. F. (1962). Portable blood pressure recorder: Accuracy and preliminary use in evaluating intra-daily variations in pressure. *American Heart Journal, 63,* 663–668.

James, G. D., Lee, L. S., Harshfield, G. A., Blank, S. G., & Pickering, T. G. (1986). The influence of happiness, anger, and anxiety on the blood pressure on borderline hypertensives. *Psychosomatic Medicine, 48,* 502–508.

James, G. D., Pickering, T. G., Yee, L. S., Harshfield, G. A., Riva, S., & Laragh, J. H. (1988). The reproducibility of average ambulatory, home, and clinic pressures. *Hypertension, 11,* 545–549.

Jamner, L. D., Shapiro, D., Goldstein, I. B., & Hug, R. (1991). Ambulatory blood pressure and heart rate in paramedics: Effects of cynical hostility and defensiveness. *Psychosomatic Medicine, 53,* 393–406.

Joesoef, M. R., Wetterhal, S. F., DeStefano, F., Stroup, N. E., & Fronek, A. (1989). The association of peripheral arterial disease with hostility in a young, healthy veteran population. *Psychosomatic Medicine, 51,* 285–289.

Joint National Committee on Detection, Evaluation, and Treatment of High Blood Pressure (1988). The 1988 report of the Joint National Committee on Detection, Evaluation, and Treatment of High Blood Pressure. *Archives of Internal Medicine, 148,* 1024–1038.

Julius, S. (1989). Hemodynamic, pharmacologic and epidemiologic evidence for behavioral factors in human hypertension. In S. Julius & D. R. Bassett (Eds.), *Behavioral factors in hypertension* (pp. 59–74). Amsterdam: Elsevier.

Karasek, R. A., Russell, S. T., & Theorell, T. (1982). Physiology of stress and regeneration in job related cardiovascular illness. *Journal of Human Stress, 8,* 29–42.

Kawakami, N., Haratani, T., Kaneko, T., & Araki, S. (1989). Perceived job stress and blood pressure increase among Japanese blue collar workers: One year follow-up study. *Industrial Health, 27,* 71–81.

Kiecolt-Glaser, J. K., & Greenberg, B. (1981). On the use of physiological measures in assertion research. *Journal of Behavioral Assessment, 5,* 97–109.

King, A. C., Taylor, C. B., Albright, C. A., & Haskell, W. L. (1990). The relationship between repressive and defensive coping styles and blood pressure responses in healthy middle-aged men and women. *Journal of Psychosomatic Research, 34,* 461–471.

King, L. A., & Emmons, R. A. (1990). Conflict over emotional expression: Psychological and physical correlates. *Journal of Personality and Social Psychology, 58,* 864–877.

Langewitz, W., Ruddel, H., & von Eiff, A. W. (1987). Influence of perceived level of stress upon ambulatory blood pressure, heart rate, and respiratory frequency. *Journal of Clinical Hypertension, 3,* 743–748.

Leon, G. R., Finn, S. E., Murray, D., & Bailey, J. M. (1988). Inability to predict cardiovascular disease from hostility scores or MMPI items related to Type A behavior. *Journal of Consulting & Clinical Psychology, 56,* 597–600.

Mancia, G. (1990). Ambulatory blood pressure monitoring: Research and clinical applications. *Journal of Hypertension, 8,* (Suppl. 7), S1–S13.

Margolis, B. L., Kroes, W. H., & Quinn, R. P. (1974). Job stress: An unlisted occupational hazard. *Journal of Occupational Medicine, 16,* 659–661.

Matthews, K. A., Cottington, E. M., Talbott, E., Kuller, L. H., & Siegel, J. M. (1987). Stressful work conditions and diastolic blood pressure among blue collar factory workers. *American Journal of Epidemiology, 126,* 280–291.

McCranie, E. W., Watkins, L. A., Brandsma, J. M., & Sisson, B. D. (1986). Hostility, coronary heart disease (CHD) incidence, and total mortality: Lack of an association in a 25-yr follow-up study of 478 physicians. *Journal of Behavioral Medicine, 9,* 119–125.

Parati, G., Pomidossi, G., Albini, F., Malaspina, D., & Mancia, G. (1987). Relationship of 24-hour blood pressure mean and variability to severity of target-organ damage in hypertension. *Journal of Hypertension, 5,* 93–98.

Pessina, A. C., Palatini, P., Di Marco, A., Mormino, P., Fazio, G. Libardoni, M., Mos, L., Casiglia, E., & Dal, P. C. (1986). Continuous ambulatory blood pressure monitoring versus casual blood pressure in borderline hypertension. *Journal of Cardiovascular Pharmacology, 8* (Suppl. 5), S93–S97.

Pickering, T. G., & Gerin, W. (1988). Ambulatory blood pressure monitoring and cardiovascular reactivity testing for the evaluation of the role of psychosocial factors and prognosis in hypertensive patients. *American Heart Journal, 116,* 665–672.

Pickering, T. G., Harshfield, G. A., Kleinert, H. D., Blank, S., & Laragh, J. H. (1982). Blood pressure during normal daily activities, sleep, and exercise: Comparison of values in normal and hypertensive subjects. *Journal of the American Medical Association, 144,* 164–189.

Rion, R., Waeber, B., Graf, H. J., Jaussi, A., Porchet, M., & Brunner, H. R. (1985). Blood pressure response to antihypertensive therapy: Ambulatory versus office blood pressure readings. *Journal of Hypertension, 3,* 139–143.

Schlussel, Y. R., Schnall, P. L., Zimbler, M., Warren, K., & Pickering, T. G. (1990). The effect of work environments on blood pressure: Evidence from seven New York organizations. *Journal of Hypertension, 8,* 679–685.

Schnall, P. L., Pieper, C. S. J. E., Karasek, R. A., Schlussel, Y., Devereux, R. B., Ganau, A., Alderman, M., Warren, K., & Pickering, T. G. (1990). The relationship between "job strain," workplace diastolic blood pressure, and left ventricular mass index: Results of a case–control study. *Journal of the American Medical Association, 263,* 1929–1935.

Shapiro, D., & Goldstein, I. B. (1982). Biobehavioral perspectives on hypertension. *Journal of Consulting and Clinical Psychology, 50,* 841–858.

Shapiro, D., Goldstein, I. B., & Jamner, L. D. (1990). Relative contributions of trait characteristics and moods to daytime ambulatory blood pressure and HR. *Journal of Psychophysiology, 4,* 347–357.

Sokolow, M., Werdegar, D., Perloff, D. B., Cowan, R. M., & Brenenstuhl, H. (1970). Preliminary studies relating portably recorded blood pressures to daily life events in patients with essential hypertension. *Bibliotheca Psychiatrica, 144,* 164–189.

Southard, D. R., Coates, T. J., Kolodner, K., Parker, F. C., Padgett, N. E., & Kennedy, H. L. (1986). Relationship between mood and blood pressure in the natural environment: An adolescent population. *Health Psychology, 5,* 469–480.

Suarez, E. C., & Williams, R. B. (1989). Situational determinants of cardiovascular and emotional reactivity in high and low hostile men. *Psychosomatic Medicine, 51,* 404–418.

Theorell, T., Knox, S., Svensson, J., & Waller, D. (1985). Blood pressure variations during a working day at age 28: Effects of different types of work and blood pressure level at age 18. *Journal of Human Stress, 11,* 36–41.

Van Egeren, L. F., & Madarasmi, S. (1988). A computer-assisted diary (CAD) for ambulatory blood pressure monitoring. *American Journal of Hypertension, 1,* 179S–195S.

Wallace, J. M., Thornton, W. E., Kennedy, H. L., Pickering, T. G., Harshfield, G. A., Frohlich, E. D., Messerli, F. H., Gifford, R. W., Jr., & Bolen, K. (1984). Ambulatory blood pressure in 199 normal subjects, a collaborative study. In M. A. Weber & J. I. M. Drayer (Eds.), *Ambulatory blood pressure monitoring* (pp. 117–127). New York: Springer-Verlag.

Warrenburg, S., Levine, J., Schwartz, G. E., Fontana, A. F., Kerns, R. D., Delaney, R., & Mattson, R. (1989). Defensive coping and blood pressure reactivity in medical patients. *Journal of Behavioral Medicine, 12,* 407–424.

Weidner, G., Friend, R., Ficarrotto, T. J., & Mendell, N. R. (1989). Hostility and cardiovascular reactivity to stress in women and men. *Psychosomatic Medicine, 51,* 36–45.

Weinberger, D. A., Schwartz, G. E., & Davidson, R. J. (1979). Low anxious, high anxious, and repressive coping styles: Psychometric patterns and behavioral and physiological responses to stress. *Journal of Abnormal Psychology, 88,* 369–380.

Williams, R. B. (1987). Psychosocial factors in coronary artery disease: Epidemiological evidence. *Circulation, 76* (Suppl. I), I117–I123.

Williams, R. B., Haney, T. L., Lee, K. L., Kong, Y., Blumenthal, J., & Whalen, R. E. (1980). Type A behavior, hostility, and coronary atherosclerosis. *Psychosomatic Medicine, 42,* 539–550.

CHAPTER 7

Mechanisms and Treatment of Raynaud's Disease and Phenomenon

Robert R. Freedman

Introduction

Raynaud's phenomenon is characterized by episodic digital vasospasms that are provoked by cold exposure or emotional stress or both (Freedman & Ianni, 1983a). Estimates of its prevalence range from 4.3% of female respondents to a questionnaire study in North Carolina to 19% of female patients of general practitioners in the United Kingdom (Weinrich, Maricq, Keil, McGregor, & Diat, 1990; Simlan, Holligan, Brennan, & Madison, 1990). The corresponding estimates for males were 2.7% and 11%, respectively.

The term *Raynaud's disease* denotes the primary form of the disorder, in which the symptoms cannot be explained by an identifiable disease process such as scleroderma or another collagen vascular disease. When the symptoms occur secondarily to another disease, the term *Raynaud's phenomenon* is used.

Etiology

Although the etiology of Raynaud's disease is not known, two main theories have been put forth to explain it. Raynaud (1888) thought that exaggerated sympathetic nervous system activity caused an increased

ROBERT R. FREEDMAN • C. S. Mott Center, Wayne State University, Detroit, MI 48201.

Clinical Applied Psychophysiology, edited by John G. Carlson, A. Ronald Seifert, and Niels Birbaumer. Plenum Press, New York, 1994.

vasoconstrictive response to cold, whereas Lewis (1929) felt that a "local fault" rendered small peripheral blood vessels hypersensitive to local cooling. Studies of plasma catecholamine levels in Raynaud's disease patients have generally not supported Raynaud's theory. Studies of plasma epinephrine and norepinephrine in Raynaud's disease patients have found levels that in comparison with those in normal persons were higher (Peacock, 1959), lower (Surwit & Allen, 1983), or no different (Kontos & Wasserman, 1969). Moreover, microelectrode studies of skin nerve sympathetic activity found no differences between patients with primary Raynaud's disease and control subjects during cold-pressor tests or other sympathetic stimuli (Fagius & Blumberg, 1985).

Research conducted in our laboratory has supported the theory of Lewis. We found no differences between patients with primary Raynaud's disease and control subjects in their responses to a variety of sympathetic stimuli, such as reflex cooling, indirect heating, or intraarterial infusions of tyramine, a compound that causes the indirect release of norepinephrine from sympathetic nerve endings (Freedman, Mayes, & Sabharwal, 1989). In the same investigation, we demonstrated that patients had significantly greater digital vasoconstrictive responses to intraarterial phenylephrine (an α_1-adrenergic agonist) and clonidine (an α_2-adrenergic agonist) than did normal control subjects. These results suggested that patients with primary Raynaud's disease have increased peripheral vascular α_1- and α_2-adrenergic receptor sensitivity or density or both compared with normal persons. Several studies of platelet α_2-adrenergic receptors also found increased receptor density in Raynaud's disease patients relative to controls (Graafsma, Wollersheim, Draste, ten Dam, van Tits, Reyenga, et al., 1991; Keenan & Porter, 1983; Edwards, Phinney, Taylor, Keenan, & Porter, 1987).

In a subsequent investigation, we induced vasospastic attacks in 9 of 11 patients with primary Raynaud's disease and in 8 of 10 patients with scleroderma (Freedman, Mayes, & Sabharwal, 1989). The attacks were photographed using an automatic camera and scored by three independent raters. Two fingers on one hand were anesthetized by local injection of lidocaine, and the effectiveness of the nerve blocks was demonstrated by plethysmography. The frequency of vasospastic attacks in nerve-blocked fingers was not significantly different from that in the corresponding intact fingers on the contralateral hand. These findings clearly demonstrate that the vasospastic attacks of Raynaud's disease and phenomenon can occur without the involvement of efferent digital nerves and argue against the etiological role of sympathetic hyperactivity.

In vitro studies (Flavahan, Lindblad, Verebeuren, Shepherd, & Vanhoutte, 1985; Harker, Ousley, Harris, Edwards, Taylor, & Porter, 1990) have shown that cooling modulates contractile responses mediated by α-adrenergic receptors, depending on the species and blood vessels involved. We therefore sought to determine the effects of cooling on α_1- and α_2-adrenergic responses in Raynaud's disease patients, using brachial artery infusions of α_1- and α_2-adrenergic agonists (Freedman, Saharwal, Moten, Migály, & Mayes, 1993). We studied 17 primary Raynaud's disease patients and 12 female normal volunteers. Clonidine HCl and phenylephrine HCl were administered through a brachial artery catheter while blood flow was measured by venous occlusion plethysmography in cooled and uncooled fingers. Cooling potentiated α_2-adrenergic vasoconstriction in the patients ($p < 0.05$), but depressed this response in the controls ($p < 0.01$). Vasoconstrictive responses to phenylephrine were not significantly affected by cooling, but were significantly greater in the cooled and uncooled fingers of the patients than in the corresponding fingers of the controls ($p < 0.05$). These results suggest that cold-induced sensitization of peripheral vascular α_2-adrenergic receptors constitutes the "local fault" by which cooling triggers the vasospastic attacks of Raynaud's disease. Attacks that are induced by emotional stress can be explained by normal catecholamine elevations acting on hypersensitive vascular α_1- and α_2-adrenergic receptors.

Some studies have examined the physical properties of the blood in Raynaud's disease patients, but have been inconclusive. One investigation (Pringle, Walder, & Weaver, 1965) found increased blood viscosity and red blood cell aggregation in Raynaud's disease patients, although subsequent investigations failed to confirm these findings (McGrath, Peek, & Penny, 1978; Johnsen, Nielsen, & Skovborg, 1977).

In summary, the most recent evidence strongly suggests that the vasospastic attacks of Raynaud's disease are locally triggered by peripheral vascular α_2-adrenoceptors that are hypersensitive to cold. Moreover, since vascular α_1- and α_2-adrenoceptors are hypersensitive in Raynaud's disease patients in the basal state, normal catecholamine elevations produced by emotional stress or by reflex cooling can also trigger the vasospastic attacks.

Raynaud's Disease

Behavioral Treatments

Given the vasoconstrictive nature of the symptoms of Raynaud's disease and the ability of normal subjects (Freedman & Ianni, 1983b) to learn to increase peripheral blood flow using behavioral techniques, it was logical to employ behavioral procedures in the treatment of this disorder. In the first controlled study (Surwit, Pilon, & Fenton, 1978), 30 patients were randomly assigned to receive autogenic training either alone or in combination with temperature feedback. For a 1-month period, half the subjects served as a waiting list control group for the other half and then received treatment. Subjects as a whole showed significant improvement in response to a cold stress test and reported fewer attacks after treatment. However, the decline in symptom frequency reported by treated subjects (32%) did not differ significantly from that reported by the waiting list controls (10%). There were no significant differences between subjects who received autogenic training alone and those who also received biofeedback. One year later, the cold-stress responses of 19 follow-up subjects returned to pretreatment levels, although reported symptom frequency remained the same (Keefe, Surwit, & Pilon, 1979). In a subsequent study of 21 patients (Keefe, Surwit, & Pilon, 1980), no outcome differences were found among those receiving progressive relaxation, autogenic training, or a combination of autogenic training and temperature feedback; patients as a whole showed significant improvements in response to a cold-stress test and in reported symptom frequency. Another investigation (Jacobson, Manschreck, & Silverberg, 1979) treated 12 Raynaud's disease patients with 12 brief sessions of progressive relaxation alone or in combination with temperature feedback. Patients generally showed temperature elevations during training and rated themselves as improved; however, there were no outcome differences between the two groups.

Up to this point, no controlled group outcome study had been conducted in which patients were treated with temperature biofeedback alone. Therefore, we tested the relative efficacy of temperature biofeedback (TEMP), temperature feedback conducted under mild cold stress (TEMPCS), autogenic training, and electromyographic (EMG) biofeedback (Freedman, Ianni, & Wenig, 1983). For this study, 32 primary Raynaud's disease patients were assigned randomly to receive ten 32-min training sessions in one of these procedures. In addition, since emotional stress is a factor in some Raynaud's attacks (Freedman & Ianni, 1983a), cognitive stress management was employed with half the patients in each group. Patients were tested for the ability to increase temperature without feedback prior to treatment, after treatment, and 1 year later. This was done both with and without cold stress. All vasospastic attacks were recorded for 1 month before and 1 year following treatment. In addition, patients received ambulatory monitoring of finger temperature, ambient temperature, and ECG for 24 hr prior to treatment and at the 1-year follow-up evaluation.

During training, TEMP and TEMPCS subjects showed significant

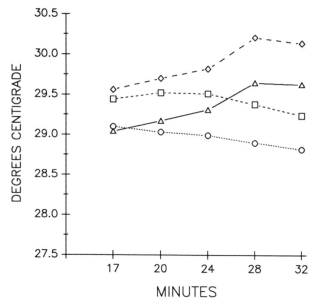

Figure 1. Finger temperatures averaged across training sessions for subjects given temperature feedback (Δ), temperature feedback under cold stress (left hand) (◇), EMG feedback (□), and autogenic training (○). From Freedman *et al.* (1983), p. 543. Copyright 1983 by the American Psychological Association. Reprinted by permission.

increases in finger temperature, whereas those receiving EMG feedback or autogenic training did not (Fig. 1). EMG and autogenic subjects showed significant declines in EMG levels and reported stress ratings and nonsignificant declines in heart rate, whereas the other groups did not. During posttraining cold-stress and voluntary control tests, the temperature elevations of the TEMP subjects were superior to those of the other three groups. At 1 year later, the TEMPCS group showed the best performance on the voluntary control test. The change shown by the TEMP group was still significant, but smaller than that shown previously. Reductions in reported symptom frequency were greatest for the TEMPCS group (Fig. 2), followed by the TEMP group, the autogenic group, and the EMG group. Differences among all four groups were statistically significant. During 1-year follow-up Medilog recordings, greater ambient finger-temperature differences were needed to produce attacks in TEMP and TEMPCS subjects compared to the EMG and autogenic subjects. The addition of cognitive stress management had no significant effects on any procedure. Data from 3-year follow-up showed that the TEMP and TEMPCS subjects

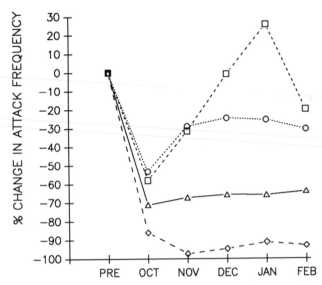

Figure 2. Reported attack frequencies during the follow-up period, expressed as percentage change from pretreatment levels, for subjects given temperature feedback (△), temperature feedback under cold stress (◇), EMG feedback (□), and autogenic training (○).

maintained their reported symptom reductions, but there were no longer significant effects on the voluntary control test (Freedman, Ianni, & Wenig, 1985). The correlation between each subject's finger temperature during voluntary control tests and the number of attacks reported during February of that year was significant ($r = -0.54$, $p < 0.05$); subjects with higher temperatures have fewer symptoms.

We have shown in normal persons (Freedman & Ianni, 1983b) and in Raynaud's patients (Freedman *et al.*, 1983) that the effects of temperature feedback are physiologically different from those of autogenic training, frontalis EMG feedback, or temperature feedback with cold stress. Temperature feedback produces digital vasodilation without bradycardia or decreased EMG levels, whereas the other techniques do produce bradycardia and lower EMG levels but not increased finger temperature. Contemporaneous research discovered a β-adrenergic vasodilating mechanism in the finger that could explain increased digital blood flow in the absence of decreased physiological arousal (Cohen & Coffman, 1981). We therefore sought to determine the involvement of this mechanism in temperature feedback using the brachial artery infusion model. In this study, 18 patients with primary Raynaud's disease were assigned to receive ten sessions of temperature feedback or autogenic training using the methods of the previous study (Freedman, Sabharwal, Ianni, Desai, Wenig, & Mayes, 1988). Following training, we showed that vasodilation during temperature biofeedback was significantly attenuated by brachial artery infusions of propranolol, whereas saline solution had no effects. There were no effects of either compound in autogenic training subjects. Using a radioisotope clearance procedure, we demonstrated that feedback-induced vasodilation occurred in the finger capillary bed in Raynaud's disease patients. This was important, because prior research (Coffman & Cohen, 1971) had shown that capillary blood flow, as opposed to arterio-venous shunt blood flow, was most depressed in primary Raynaud's patients, particularly during cooling. Patients received 1- and 2-year follow-up tests of their ability to voluntarily increase finger temperature and blood flow. The temperature-feedback subjects retained the ability to significantly increase finger temperature and isotopically measured capillary blood flow at the 1- and 2-year follow-up points. They also showed average reductions in symptom frequency of 80.5% at the 1-year follow-up and 81.3% at the 2-year follow-up. The corresponding changes shown by the autogenic training group were not statistically significant (32.3% at year 1, 26.3% at year 2).

The only known efferent vasomotor nerves in human fingers are adrenergic; neurogenic vasoconstriction is caused by the interaction of released norepinephrine with postjunctional α-adrenergic receptors (Freedman, 1989a). The findings presented above therefore raised the question of whether vasodilation achieved through temperature feedback is neurally mediated. Therefore, using selective digital nerve blocks, we showed that feedback-induced vasodilation could still be accomplished despite block-ade of the sympathetic nervous pathway. This finding was demonstrated in three separate groups of subjects (Freedman et al., 1988). We also showed that finger-skin conductance level, which is sympathetically mediated, is increased rather than decreased during temperature feedback in intact fingers (Freedman, 1989b).

These findings further questioned the role of sympathetic nervous system activity during temperature feedback. We therefore measured circulating catecholamine levels during temperature feedback and auto-genic training in 31 Raynaud's disease patients using a Cormed blood withdrawal pump (Freedman, Keegan, Migály, Galloway, & Mayes, 1991). During training, significant finger temperature and blood flow elevations were shown by temperature-feedback patients, but not by those who received autogenic training. There were no significant effects whatsoever for epinephrine or norepinephrine for either group. Small but significant elevations in heart rate, skin conductance level, and systolic and diastolic blood pressures were shown by subjects overall; there were no group differences for any measure. These findings do not support the role of decreased sympathetic activation in behavioral treatments for Raynaud's disease.

Medical Treatments

Pharmacological treatments for Raynaud's disease have been reviewed elsewhere (Coffman, 1991). Briefly, nifedipine is at present the drug of first choice for patients with primary Raynaud's disease. Nifedipine is a calcium slow channel blocker that reduces the influx of calcium into cells, thereby decreasing vasoconstriction (Nilsson, 1986). Nifedipine has been demonstrated to decrease the frequency, duration, and intensity of vasospastic attacks in about two thirds of the primary and secondary Raynaud's patients treated (Coffman, 1991).

Since serotonergic vasoconstriction is also present in human fingers, ketanserin, a serotonergic S_2 antagonist, has been used with primary and secondary Raynaud's patients. However, a very large double-blind study of primary and secondary patients produced disappointing results (Coffman, Clement, Creager, Dormandy, Janssens, McKendry, Murray, & Nielsen, 1989). The reduction in attack frequency with ketanserin was only 34%, compared with a placebo rate of 18%. There were no changes in the severity or duration of vasospastic attacks. Moreover, there were no changes in finger blood measurements during cold or warm conditions.

Surgical sympathectomies have been tried as a means of abolishing reflex sympathetic activity, but vascular tone generally recovers within a period of a few weeks (Robertson & Smithwick, 1951). Our recent finding that vasospastic attacks can be induced in primary and secondary Raynaud's patients despite digital nerve blockade raises serious questions regarding the physiological rationale for this procedure.

Secondary Raynaud's Phenomenon

Behavioral and medical treatments for Raynaud's phenomenon have been less successful than those for the primary form of the disorder. In case studies (Freedman, Lynn, Ianni, & Hale, 1981), we showed that scleroderma patients treated with finger-temperature feedback were able to increase digital temperature and show some symptomatic improvement. However, a subsequent controlled investigation produced disappointing results (Freedman, Ianni, & Wenig, 1984). In this study, 24 patients who met the classification criteria of the American Rheumatism Association (now the American College of Rheumatology) for systemic sclerosis (Freedman *et al.*, 1983) were randomly assigned to receive ten sessions of training in either finger-temperature feedback, EMG feedback, or autogenic training using the procedures of our previous study (Freedman *et al.*, 1983). Subjects who received finger-temperature feedback showed significant increases in finger temperature during training and during a posttraining voluntary control test, while those who received EMG feedback or autogenic training did not. Following treatment, however, no group showed significant reductions in the frequency of reported vasospastic attacks. There were no group differences in data obtained during ambulatory monitoring or laboratory cold-stress tests. The reasons for the failure of temperature feedback to reduce symptoms in scleroderma patients are not known. However, it is likely that the underlying pathophysiology of secondary Raynaud's phenomenon is different from that of the primary disease.

Fewer pharmacological studies have been performed on secondary than on primary Raynaud's patients. Several small-scale studies (Belch, Newman, Drury, McKenzie, Capell, & Leibermann, 1983) reported positive results of prostaglandin I2 and E1 infusions in secondary Raynaud's patients. However, it was necessary to administer the compounds by intravenous infusion. Most of the studies of the effects of nifedipine on Raynaud's disease also included secondary Raynaud's patients. Although the results were generally positive, it was not always possible to distinguish between primary and secondary patients in some published reports.

Conclusions

Thus far, the most efficacious behavioral treatment for primary Raynaud's disease appears to be temperature biofeedback without the addition of other treatments. Several controlled group outcome studies showed that primary Raynaud's patients given temperature biofeedback alone achieved reported symptom-frequency reductions ranging from 67% to 92%, which were maintained at 2- and 3-year follow-ups. The addition to temperature biofeedback of other procedures, such as autogenic training or progressive relaxation, produced less satisfactory results, as did the use of progressive relaxation and autogenic training alone. Research on the pathophysiology of Raynaud's disease indicates that the attacks are not caused by sympathetic nervous system hyperactivity, but probably by the hypersensitivity of peripheral vascular α_2-adrenergic receptors to cooling. These findings question the rationale for sympatholytic treatments for patients with primary Raynaud's disease. We have demonstrated that temperature biofeedback does not operate through the reduction of sympathetic outflow, but in part through an active β-adrenergic vasodilating mechanism. Due to the difficulty of performing invasive procedures in patients with secondary Raynaud's phenomenon, less is known regarding the pathophysiology of their vasospastic attacks. However, histological studies have shown luminal narrowing due to intimal proliferation of connective tissue, thickening of the basement membrane, and fibrosis of the adventitia in these patients (Rodnan, Myerowitz, & Justin, 1980). *In vivo* observation of skin capillaries reveals consistent abnormalities in secondary patients (Maricq, LeRoy, D'Angelo, Medsger, Rodnan, Sharpe, *et al.*, 1980), and very low levels of finger capillary blood flow have been shown (Coffman & Cohen, 1971). In light of these findings, it may be difficult to achieve consistent vasodilation in secondary Raynaud's patients, although further research on this problem should be conducted.

ACKNOWLEDGMENT.   Research conducted by the author was supported by NIH Grants HL-23828 and HL-30604.

References

Belch, J. J. F., Newman, P., Drury, J. K., McKenzie, F., Capell, H., Leiberman, P., Forbes, C. D., & Prentice, C. R. M. (1983). Intermittent epoprostenol (prostacyclin) infusion in patients with Raynaud's syndrome. *The Lancet*, 313–315.

Coffman, J. D. (1991). Raynaud's phenomenon. *Hypertension, 17*, 593–602.

Coffman, J. D., & Cohen, A. S. (1971). Total and capillary fingertip blood flow in Raynaud's phenomenon. *New England Journal of Medicine, 285*, 259–263.

Coffman, J. D., Clement, D. L., Creager, M. A., Dormandy, J. A., Janssens, M. M.-L., McKendry, R. J. R., Murray, G. D., & Nielsen, S. L. (1989). International study of ketanserin in Raynaud's phenomenon. *American Journal of Medicine, 87*, 264–268.

Cohen, R., & Coffman, J. (1981). Beta-adrenergic vasodilator mechanism in the finger. *Circulation Research, 49*, 1196–1201.

Edwards, J. M., Phinney, E. S., Taylor, L. M., Keenan, E. J., & Porter, J. M. (1987). α_2-Adrenoceptor levels in obstructive and spastic Raynaud's syndrome. *Vascular Survey, 5*, 38–45.

Fagius, J., & Blumberg, H. (1985). Sympathetic outflow to the hand in patients with Raynaud's phenomenon. *Cardiovascular Research, 19*, 249–253.

Flavahan, N. A., Lindblad, L. E., Verebeuren, T. J., Shepherd, J. T., & Vanhoutte, P. M. (1985). Cooling and α_1- and α_2-adrenergic responses in cutaneous veins: Role of receptor reserve. *American Journal of Physiology, 249*, H950– H955.

Freedman, R. R. (1989a). Raynaud's disease. In G. Turpin (Ed.), *Handbook of clinical psychophysiology* (pp. 469–495). London: John Wiley & Sons.

Freedman, R. R. (1989b). Quantitative measurements of finger blood flow during behavioral treatments for Raynaud's disease. *Psychophysiology, 26*, 437–441.

Freedman, R. R., & Ianni, P. (1983a). Role of cold and emotional stress in Raynaud's disease and scleroderma. *British Medical Journal, 287*, 1499–1502.

Freedman, R. R., & Ianni, P. (1983b). Self-control of digital temperature: Physiological factors and transfer effects. *Psychophysiology, 20*, 682–688.

Freedman, R. R., Lynn, S., Ianni, P., & Hale, P. (1981). Biofeedback treatment of Raynaud's disease and phenomenon. *Biofeedback and Self-Regulation, 6*, 355–365.

Freedman, R. R., Ianni, P., & Wenig, P. (1983). Behavioral treatment of Raynaud's disease. *Journal of Consulting and Clinical Psychology, 151*, 539–549.

Freedman, R. R., Ianni, P., & Wenig, P. (1984). Behavioral treatment of Raynaud's phenomenon in scleroderma. *Journal of Behavioral Medicine, 7*, 343–353.

Freedman, R. R., Ianni, P., & Wenig, P. (1985). Behavioral treatment of Raynaud's disease: Long-term follow-up. *Journal of Consulting and Clinical Psychology, 53*, 136.

Freedman, R. R., Sabharwal, S., Ianni, P., Desai, N., Wenig, P., & Mayes, M. (1988). Non-neural beta-adrenergic vasodilating mechanism in temperature biofeedback. *Psychosomatic Medicine, 50*, 394–401.

Freedman, R. R., Mayes, M. D., & Sabharwal, S. C. (1989). Induction of vasospastic attacks despite digital nerve block in Raynaud's disease and phenomenon. *Circulation, 80*, 859–862.

Freedman, R. R., Keegan, D., Migály, P., Galloway, M. P., & Mayes, M. (1991). Plasma catecholamines during behavioral treatments for Raynaud's disease. *Psychosomatic Medicine, 53*, 433–439.

Freedman, R. R., Moten, M., Migály, P., & Mayes, M. (1993). Cold-induced potentiation of α^2-adrenergic vasoconstriction in primary Raynaud's disease. *Arthritis & Rheumatism, 36(5)*, 685–690.

Graafsma, S. J., Wollersheim, H., Droste, H. T., ten Dam, M. A., van Tits, L. J., Reyenga, J., Rodrigues de Miranda, J. F., & Thien, T. (1991). Adrenoceptors on blood cells from patients with primary Raynaud's phenomenon. *Clin. Sci., 80(4)*, 325–331.

Harker, C. T., Ousley, P. J., Harris, E. J., Edwards, J. M., Taylor, L. M., & Porter, J. M. (1990). The effects of cooling on human saphenous vein reactivity to adrenergic agonists. *Journal of Vascular Surgery, 12*, 45–49.

Jacobson, A., Manschreck, T., & Silverberg, E. (1979). Behavioral treatment for Raynaud's disease: A comparative study with long-term follow-up. *American Journal of Psychiatry, 136*, 844–846.

Johnsen, T., Nielsen, S., & Skovborg, F. (1977). Blood viscosity and local response to cold in primary Raynaud's phenomenon. *The Lancet, 2*, 1001–1002.

Keefe, F., Surwit, R., & Pilon, R. (1979). A 1-year follow-up of Raynaud's patients treated with behavioral therapy techniques. *Journal of Behavioral Medicine, 2*, 385–391.

Keefe, F., Surwit, R., & Pilon, R. (1980). Biofeedback, autogenic training, and progressive relaxation in the treatment of Raynaud's disease: A comparative study. *Journal of Applied Behavioral Analysis, 13*, 3–11.

Keenan, E. J., & Porter, J. M. (1983). α_2-Adrenergic receptors in platelets from patients with Raynaud's syndrome. *Surgery, 94*, 204–209.

Kontos, H. A., & Wasserman, A. J. (1969). Effect of reserpine in Raynaud's phenomenon. *Circulation, 39*, 259–266.

Lewis, T. (1929). Experiments relating to the peripheral mechanism involved in spasmodic arrest of circulation in fingers, a variety of Raynaud's disease. *Heart, 15*, 7–101.

Maricq, H. R., LeRoy, E. C., D'Angelo, W. A., Medsger, T. A., Jr., Rodnan, G. P., Sharp, G. C., & Wolfe, J. (1980). Diagnostic potential of in vivo capillary microscopy in scleroderma and related disorders. *Arthritis & Rheumatism, 23(2)*, 183–189.

McGrath, M., Peek, R., & Penny, R. (1978). Raynaud's disease: Reduced hand blood flows with normal blood viscosity. *Australian and New Zealand Journal of Medicine, 8*, 126–131.

Nilsson, H. (1986). Pharmacological treatment of Raynaud's phenomenon with special reference to calcium-entry blockers. *Acta Pharmacologica et Toxicologica, 58*, 137–149.

Peacock, J. H. (1959). Peripheral venous blood concentration of epinephrine and norepinephrine in primary Raynaud's disease. *Circulation Research, 7*, 821–827.

Pringle, R., Walder, D., & Weaver, J. (1965). Blood viscosity and Raynaud's disease. *The Lancet, 3*, 1085–1088.

Raynaud, M. (1888). New research on the nature and treatment of local asphyxia of the extremities (T. Barlow, translator). London: New Syndenham Society.

Robertson, C., & Smithwick, R. (1951). The recurrence of vasoconstrictor activity after limb sympathectomy in Raynaud's disease and allied vasomotor states. *New England Journal of Medicine, 245*, 317–320.

Rodnan, G. P., Myerowitz, R. L., Justh, G. O. (1980). Morphologic changes in the digital arteries of patients with progressive sclerosis (Scleroderma) and Raynaud phenomenon. *Medicine, 59*, 393–408.

Simlan, A., Holligan, S., Brennan, P., & Maddison, P. (1990). Prevalence of symptoms of Raynaud's phenomenon in general practice. *British Medical Journal, 301*, 590–592.

Surwit, R. S., & Allen, L. M. (1983). Neuroendocrine response to cold in Raynaud's syndrome. *Life Sciences, 32*, 995–1000.

Surwit, R., Pilon, R., & Fenton, C. (1978). Behavioral treatment of Raynaud's disease. *Journal of Behavioral Medicine, 1*, 323–335.

Weinrich, M. C., Maricq, H. R., Keil, J. E., McGregor, A. R., & Diat, F. (1990). Prevalence of Raynaud's phenomenon in the adult population of South Carolina. *Journal of Clinical Epidemiology, 43*, 1343–1349.

PART **IV**

Applied Psychophysiology and Breathing

This section includes four chapters. Chapter 8, by Sonia Ancoli-Israel, Melville R. Klauber, Robert L. Fell, Linda Parker, Lynne A. Kenney, and Richard Willens, discusses inpatient sleep-disordered breathing as a predictor of mortality. Chapter 9, by Jan van Dixhoorn, examines the relative effects of exercise with and without relaxation and breathing therapy as a treatment for myocardial infarction. Chapter 10, by Robert Fried, describes the author's psychophysiological respiration profile and its application to a number of clinical cases. Finally, in Chapter 11, P. G. F. Nixon outlines his systems approach to the loss of self-regulation in breathing, specifically hyperventilation, in terms of related disorders and implications for therapy.

The chapter by Ancoli-Israel and associates provides a brief review of the literature on sleep-disordered breathing, prompting the question as to the degree to which inpatient recordings of apnea status are predictive of outpatient apnea. The authors report preliminary results on a number of male patients in a Veterans Administration Medical Center ward, yielding two major observations: (1) that inpatient sleep recordings may not be predictive of outpatient apnea status and (2) that moderate sleep-disordered breathing predicts mortality. Their results have implications both for assessment and for initiation of treatment in sleep-disordered patients.

In his chapter, van Dixhoorn summarizes a variety of research suggesting that while the treatment of choice for cardiac rehabilitation is exercise, relaxation can impact positively on risk factors for cardiovascular disease as well as related psychological factors. In van Dixhoorn's research, the relative effects of a comprehensive program of exercise, breathing awareness training, and relaxation are compared with those of exercise alone in a sample of patients recovering from myocardial infarction. Added breathing/relaxation training was found to reduce myocardial ischemia due to exercise, to enhance heart rate variability, and to reduce occurrence of cardiovascular events, as well as to impact on a number of measures of psychological improvement. One important implication of van Dixhoorn's findings is that sufficient attention to both sides of the psycho/physiology equation yields measurable benefits in clinical applications.

Fried's chapter outlines the respiration physiology that underlies his work and provides a review of his psychophysiological respiration profile—affording a comprehensive view of cardiovascular, pulmonary, temperature, and muscular reactions during rest and various activities imposed in the clinic. Fried also describes several useful case profiles, some of which demonstrate effects of clinical interventions using biofeedback and other self-regulatory methods for altering breathing. The author's work typifies the wealth of assessment strategems available for the clinician working with breathing-related disorders given the current state of readily available technology in this field.

Nixon describes in his chapter the physiology and some disorders owing to the catabolic ("downslope") stage of the performance–arousal curve when arousal reaches high levels. Nixon maintains that loss of control over breathing is common in subjects who show an inability to recover from reactions induced by stress. The clinical capnograph for assessment of exhaled carbon dioxide is described and applied to several subjects, showing the effects of hyperventilation under stress. In this chapter, Nixon provides a convenient summary of reasons for the loss of self-regulation in breathing and a fitting conclusion for this section of fine examples of applied psychophysiology in the area of breathing disorders.

CHAPTER 8

Sleep-Disordered Breathing
Preliminary Natural History and Mortality Results

Sonia Ancoli-Israel, Melville R. Klauber,
Robert L. Fell, Linda Parker, Lynne A. Kenney,
and Richard Willens

Although the description of sleep-disordered breathing (SDB) appeared as far back as 1877 (Lavie, 1984), clinicians first began recognizing it as a serious problem only some thirty years ago (Guilleminault & Dement, 1978). SDB is described as respiratory cessation (apnea) or a decrease in the amplitude of respiration (hypopnea) during sleep. Clinically, there are often hundreds of apneas and hypopneas seen during the night, accompanied by drops in oxygen saturation levels. The apneas and hypopneas are followed by brief arousals (awakenings) that allow respiration to resume. Given this pattern, many clinical patients are unable to sleep and breathe at the same time.

SDB is generally caused by obstructions of the upper airway (obstructive sleep apnea) or by failure of the respiratory centers in the central nervous system to stimulate the respiratory muscles (Stradling, 1986; Remmers, Sauerland, & Anch, 1978). Patients with SDB are frequently

SONIA ANCOLI-ISRAEL, ROBERT L. FELL, LINDA PARKER, LYNNE A. KENNEY, and RICHARD WILLENS • Department of Psychiatry, University of California, San Diego, CA 92093; Veterans Affairs Medical Center, San Diego, CA 92161.   MELVILLE R. KLAUBER • Department of Family and Preventive Medicine, University of California, San Diego, CA 92093.

Clinical Applied Psychophysiology, edited by John G. Carlson, A. Ronald Seifert, and Niels Birbaumer. Plenum Press, New York, 1994.

overweight and often have anatomical abnormalities in their upper airways (Guilleminault, 1989).

Patients with SDB complain of extreme daytime sleepiness, which results from both the hypoxemia (Orr, Martin, Imes, Rogers, & Stahl, 1979; Ancoli-Israel, Kripke, Mason, Dillon, & Fell, 1990) and the multiple awakenings that occur during the night (Weitzman, 1979; Dement, Carskadon, & Richardson, 1978). Other consequences of SDB include loud snoring (Guilleminault, 1989; Fairbanks, 1987), cardiac arrhythmias (Guilleminault, 1983; Shepard, 1989), hypertension (Kales, Bixler, Cadieux, Schneck, Shaw, Locke, Vela-Bueno, & Soldatos, 1984; Lavie, Ben-Yosef, & Rubin, 1984), neuropsychological deficits (Moldofsky, Goldstein, McNicholas, Lue, Zamel, & Phillipson, 1983; Yesavage, Bliwise, Guilleminault, Carskadon, & Dement, 1985), and perhaps early death (He, Kryger, Zorick, Conway, & Roth, 1988; Ancoli-Israel, Klauber, Kripke, Parker, & Cobarrubias, 1989; Thorpy, 1989; Partinen, Jamieson, & Guilleminault, 1988).

Treatments of SDB currently include continuous positive airway pressure (CPAP) (Sullivan & Grunstein, 1989), a variety of surgeries (Guilleminault, Riley, & Powell, 1989), mouthpieces designed with the aim of keeping the airway open (Cartwright, Stefoski, Caldarelli, Kravitz, Knight, Lloyd, & Samelson, 1988), weight loss (Smith, Gold, Meyers, Haponik, & Bleecker, 1985; Kryger, 1989), and, at times, medications (Conway, Zorick, Piccione, & Roth, 1982b; Sutton, Zwillich, Creagh, Pierson, & Weil, 1975; Conway, Roth, & Zorick, 1982a).

The true prevalence of SDB in younger adults is still being assessed. As part of an ongoing study, Kripke, Ancoli-Israel, Mason, and Mowen (1991) reported that 6 of 65 (9%) of middle-aged adults had desaturated more than 4% a total of 20 or more times per hour on each of three nights recorded, which might indicate moderate or severe breathing disturbances during sleep. In a review of the epidemiology of SDB in the elderly, Ancoli-Israel (1989b) showed that the prevalence reported has ranged from 24% to 75% in healthy older people and from 19% to 42% in older patients. In one of the most extensive studies, of 427 randomly selected, representative, community-dwelling elderly, 24% had an apnea index (number of apneas per hour of sleep), or respiratory disturbance index (RDI), greater than 5 and 62% had an RDI greater than 10. Correlates of sleep apnea in this group included nocturnal confusion, daytime sleepiness, and elevated weight. Higher RDIs were found among snorers. The strongest predictor of SDB was body mass index (Ancoli-Israel, Kripke, Klauber, Mason, Fell, & Kaplan, 1991).

In a second study of 436 hospital medical ward inpatients, the prevalence rate was even higher. In this group, 36% had 5 or more apneas per hour of sleep, and 84% had 5 or more apneas and hypopneas per hour of sleep. The increased prevalence in this group of inpatients may have been related to their acute illnesses, such as congestive heart failure (Ancoli-Israel, 1989b), which has been shown to be associated with central sleep apnea (Findley, Ancoli-Israel, Kripke, Tisi, Moser, & Zwillich, 1982a; Findley, Kreis, Ancoli-Israel, & Kripke, 1982b; Findley, Zwillich, Ancoli-Israel, Kripke, Tisi, & Moser, 1985).

This very high yield of positive findings among hospital inpatients raises the question: How predictive are inpatient recordings of the patients' apnea status when they become outpatients? Little is even known, in fact, about the longitudinal course of SDB. Bliwise, Carskadon, Carey, and Dement (1984) longitudinally followed older clinic patients and found that repeated measures over time had only modest reliability for those patients with mild SDB. Mason, Ancoli-Israel, and Kripke (1989) followed 32 volunteers more than 65 years old, over a 4.6-year period. Significant but not high correlations were found between the initial and follow-up recordings for the number of apneas ($r_s = 0.50$, $p < 0.01$) and for the number of hypopneas ($r_x = 0.58$, $p < 0.001$). There were no significant increases in the amount of SDB over the follow-up period. In fact, over time, most patients showed great variability in the amount of apnea.

We are currently restudying a subgroup of these patients to examine the predictive value of inpatient testing and the natural history of SDB. We are also conducting yearly follow-ups of the entire sample of 436 hospital patients, to determine who is still alive, in order to examine the relationship of SDB to mortality. In the following discussion, we describe preliminary mortality results as well as preliminary results on the natural history of SDB.

Methods

Subjects

The subjects were 436 males who were originally inpatients on a Veterans Affairs Medical Center medical ward. None had been admitted for symptoms of SDB or other sleep disorders, but rather for the traditional complaints such as heart disease, pulmonary disease, gastrointestinal disease, and so forth. The patients were all age 60 or older when originally studied between 1985 and 1989.

Apparatus

Each subject was studied with the modified Medilog/Respitrace portable recording system (Ancoli-Israel, 1989a) at both the initial recording session and the follow-up recording session. This system records two channels of respiration (thoracic and abdominal), one channel of tibialis electromyograph (EMG), and one channel of wrist activity, to distinguish wake from sleep (Mullaney, Kripke, & Messin, 1980; Webster, Kripke, Messin, Mullaney, & Wyborney, 1982). The data are stored on an analog tape recorder and are then played back onto a polygraph. The resulting paper record is scored for total sleep time, total wake time, number, duration, and type of apneas and hypopneas, and number of leg movements. This system has been previously validated with traditional polysomnography (Ancoli-Israel, Kripke, Mason, & Messin, 1981).

Blood oxygen saturation levels were recorded for one night with a portable finger pulse oximeter and portable computer. The oximeter samples blood oxygen saturation levels every 2 sec and stores these data in memory and on disk throughout the recording in order to minimize data loss. A special computer program, PROFOX, is used to estimate the occurrences of desaturations exceeding 4%, those lasting less than 3 min, the mean durations of each desaturation, and the percentage time at various levels of blood oxygen desaturations (Timms, Dawson, Taft, Erman, & Mitler, 1988).

Procedure

Each subject was initially randomly selected from all new admissions onto the medical wards. Once written consent had been obtained, each patient was studied for one night or, if possible, two nights, on the hospital ward. Medical records were abstracted, and each patient was given an extensive sleep interview and depression scale. Chest X rays and EKGs were also evaluated.

Patients seen in the last 2 years of the initial study were then recontacted approximately 2 years later and asked to continue participation. One of two research assistants (L.P. or L.K.) went to the subject's home to complete a sleep interview, medical history interview, depression scale, and mental status exam. Subjects were then rerecorded for one or two nights with the modified Respitrace/Medilog system and for one night with oximetry, in their own beds.

Statistical Methods

Nonparametric methods were done comparing initial visits with follow-up visits. The Mantel-Cox method was used to test statistical differences between survival curves.

Results

Natural History Results

Compliance and Demographics

Of the 143 men eligible to be recontacted, 37 (26%) agreed to be restudied, 22 (15%) refused further participation, 35 (25%) had died, and 33 (23%) are still to be contacted at a later date. There were no significant differences in amount of SDB between the patients who agreed to participate and those who refused further participation. Patients were recorded (visit 2) 2–3 years after their initial recording (visit 1). Data are available on the first 27 patients. At the time of visit 2, the mean age of the 27 men was 72.4 years (SD = 8.8, range = 64–95 years). The mean mini-mental status score was 28 (SD = 2.0), well within normal limits.

Changes in Apnea and Blood Oxygen Saturation Levels

In this group of patients, 20% showed decreases in the number of apneas, 20% showed increases, and 60% stayed the same (see Table 1). The chance of a patient having sleep apnea on visit 1 and again on visit 2 was 43%. The chance of having no sleep apnea on visit 1 or on visit 2 was 69%.

There was a significant Spearman rank order correlation between visit 1 and visit 2 in the number of apneas ($r_s = 0.47, p < 0.05$) and in body mass index (kg/m²) ($r_s = 0.66, p < 0.001$). The correlations between visit 1 and visit 2 for the number of desaturations ($r_s = 0.27$) and for the mean lowest desaturation ($r_s = 0.24$) were not significant. Means and medians are presented in Table 2.

Table 1. Percentage of Total Sample
with Sleep Apnea on Visit 1 and Visit 2

	Visit 2	
	Sleep apnea	No sleep apnea
Visit 1		
Sleep apnea	15%	20%
No sleep apnea	20%	45%

Table 2. Apnea and Saturation Values in 27 Subjects

Measure	Mean	Median	SD	Range
Number of apneas				
Visit 1	39.7	18	54.0	0–178
Visit 2	27.0	17	55.4	0–280
Number of desaturations				
Visit 1	91.2	73	74.5	16–268
Visit 2	79.2	69	71.2	5–338
Mean lowest SaO_2 (%)				
Visit 1	88.0	89.1	3.5	75.9–91.1
Visit 2	89.7	89.7	2.5	82.6–93.6
Body mass index (kg/m^2)				
Visit 1	24.6	25.0	3.5	19.3–31.1
Visit 2	26.4	26.3	3.8	19.2–33.1

Mortality Results

Mantel-Cox survival analyses were computed after the last completed follow-up of all 436 patients (i.e., 1990). At that time, 213 patients were known to be alive, 151 had died, and 72 were missing. Based on the results of the initial recordings, patients were divided into little or no SDB (RDI < 30 or apneas + hypopneas < 30) or moderate-severe SDB (RDI $\geq$ 30). There were significant differences in the survival curves ($p < 0.01$) between the groups. The group with RDIs of 30 or more had a lower survival rate (mean survival time = 1010.1 days, median = 1006 days) than the group with RDIs of 30 or less (mean survival time = 1256.5 days, median = 1699 days).

Discussion

The preliminary results of this study indicate that inpatient sleep recordings may not be predictive of patients' apnea status when they are outpatients. When these patients were initially studied, they were all acutely ill hospital inpatients. At follow-up, they were all residing at home, with no acute exacerbations. Although the amount of apnea correlated significantly over time, the reproducibility was poor. We are currently examining other factors, such as current medical history, to see which factors might be affecting the SDB. It seems, however, that acute illness may affect the amount and severity of sleep-disordered breathing.

These results support the hypothesis that there is great variability in SDB over time. It is important to note, however, that these results are preliminary. In the study of the natural history of SDB to date, only a small percentage of our total sample has been studied. While it seems that these 27 patients are representative of the entire sample, we continue to increase our sample size. With larger samples, we will be able to examine the data with multivariate regression analyses. We will also restudy all the patients every 2 years to get additional longitudinal data.

Our mortality data support the finding that moderate to severe SDB does increase the risk of death. He and colleagues (He et al., 1988) showed that younger untreated patients with sleep apnea indices greater than 20 had higher mortality rates than those who were treated. Ancoli-Israel and associates (Ancoli-Israel et al., 1989) showed that nursing home patients with RDIs greater than 50 (which is about equivalent to an apnea index of 20) had higher mortality rates than those with less severe SDB. In that nursing home study, however, we showed excess mortality for women with SDB, but not for men, partly because there were very few men in that population. In the current study of SDB and mortality in men, of the original 436 patients, 36% had SDB and only 55% of these are still alive today, compared to 63% of those with no SDB. Preliminary univariate analyses indicate that the RDI was a significant mortality predictor for these hospitalized patients; however, multivariate analyses controlling for confounding factors have not been completed.

While the natural history and definitive mortality results await further data, the current data indicate that SDB during acute illness should be remeasured immediately after the illness resolves. If patients then continue to have moderate to severe SDB, treatment should be initiated.

ACKNOWLEDGMENTS.   This research was supported by NIA AG02711, NIA AG08415, NHLBI 44915, MH 49671, and the Department of Veterans Affairs.

References

Ancoli-Israel, S. (1989a). Ambulatory cassette recording of sleep apnea. In J. S. Ebersole (Ed.), *Ambulatory EEG monitoring* (pp. 299–315). New York: Raven Press.

Ancoli-Israel, S. (1989b). Epidemiology of sleep disorders. In T. Roth & T. A. Roehrs (Eds.), *Clinics in geriatric medicine* (pp. 347–362). Philadelphia: W. B. Saunders.

Ancoli-Israel, S., Kripke, D. F., Mason, W., & Messin, S. (1981). Comparisons of home sleep recordings and polysomnograms in older adults with sleep disorders. *Sleep, 4*, 283–291.

Ancoli-Israel, S., Klauber, M. R., Kripke, D. F., Parker, L., & Cobarrubias, M. (1989). Sleep apnea in female patients in a nursing home: Increased risk of mortality. *Chest, 96*, 1054–1058.

Ancoli-Israel, S., Kripke, D. F., Mason, W. J., Dillon, K., & Fell, R. L. (1990). Daytime sleepiness, sleep fragmentation, and hypoxemia. *Sleep Research, 19*, 182.

Ancoli-Israel, S., Kripke, D. F., Klauber, M. R., Mason, W. J., Fell, R., & Kaplan, O. (1991). Sleep disordered breathing in community-dwelling elderly. *Sleep, 14(6),* 486–495.

Bliwise, D., Carskadon, M., Carey, E., & Dement, W. (1984). Longitudinal development of sleep-related respiratory disturbance in adult humans. *Journal of Gerontology, 39,* 290–293.

Cartwright, R., Stefoski, D., Caldarelli,D., Kravitz, H., Knight, S., Lloyd, S., & Samelson, C. (1988). Toward a treatment logic for sleep apnea: The place of the tongue retaining device. *Behavior Research and Therapy, 26,* 121–126.

Conway, W., Roth, T., & Zorick, F. (1982a). Protriptyline therapy for upper airway sleep apnea. *American Review of Respiratory Disorders, 125,* 102.

Conway, W. A., Zorick, F., Piccione, P., & Roth, T. (1982b). Protriptyline in the treatment of sleep apnea. *Thorax, 37,* 49–53.

Dement, W. C., Carskadon, M. A., & Richardson, G. (1978). Excessive daytime sleepiness in the sleep apnea syndrome. In C. Guilleminault & W. C. Dement (Eds.), *Sleep apnea syndromes* (pp. 23–46). New York: Alan R. Liss.

Fairbanks, D. N. F. (1987). Snoring: An overview with historical perspectives. In D. N. F. Fairbanks, S. Fujita, T. Ikematsu, & F. B. Simmons (Eds.), *Snoring and obstructive sleep apnea* (pp. 1–18). New York: Raven Press.

Findley, L., Ancoli-Israel, S., Kripke, D. F., Tisi, G., Moser, K., & Zwillich, C. (1982a). Sleep apnea in congestive heart failure. *American Review of Respiratory Disorders, 125,* 253.

Findley, L., Kreis, P., Ancoli-Israel, S., & Kripke, D. F. (1982b). Sleep apnea in hospitalized medical patients. *American Review of Respiratory Disorders, 125,* Supplement, 101.

Findley, L. J., Zwillich, C. W., Ancoli-Israel, S., Kripke, D. F., Tisi, G., & Moser, K. M. (1985). Cheyne-Stokes breathing during sleep in patients with left ventricular heart failure. *Southern Medical Journal, 78,* 11–15.

Guilleminault, C. (1983). Natural history, cardiac impact and long term follow-up of sleep apnea syndrome. In C. Guilleminault & E. Lugaresi (Eds.), *Sleep/wake disorders: Natural history, epidemiology, and long-term evolution* (pp. 107–124). New York: Raven Press.

Guilleminault, C. (1989). Clinical features and evaluation of obstructive sleep apnea. In M. H. Kryger, T. Roth, & W. C. Dement (Eds.), *Principles and practice of sleep medicine* (pp. 552–558). Philadelphia: W. B. Saunders.

Guilleminault, C., & Dement, W. C. (1978). *Sleep apnea syndromes* (pp. 1–372). New York: Alan R. Liss.

Guilleminault, C., Riley, R. W., & Powell, N. B. (1989). Surgical treatment of obstructive sleep apnea. In M. H. Kryger, T. Roth, & W. C. Dement (Eds.), *Principles and practice of sleep medicine* (pp. 571–583). Philadelphia: W. B. Saunders.

He, J., Kryger, M. H., Zorick, F. J., Conway, W., & Roth, T. (1988). Mortality and apnea index in obstructive sleep apnea: Experience in 385 male patients. *Chest, 94,* 9–14.

Kales, A., Bixler, E. O., Cadieux, R. J., Schneck, D. W., Shaw, L. C., III, Locke, T. W., Vela-Bueno, A., & Soldatos, C. R. (1984). Sleep apnoea in a hypertensive population. *The Lancet, 2,* 1005–1008.

Kripke, D. F., Ancoli-Israel, S., Mason, W. J., & Mowen, M. A. (1991). Sleep respiratory disturbances in middle-aged San Diegans. *Sleep Research, 20A,* 337.

Kryger, M. H. (1989). Management of obstructive sleep apnea: Overview. In M. H. Kryger, T. Roth, & W. C. Dement (Eds.), *Principles and practice of sleep medicine* (pp. 584–590). Philadelphia: W. B. Saunders.

Lavie, P. (1984). Nothing new under the moon: Historical accounts of sleep apnea syndrome. *Archives of Internal Medicine, 144,* 2025–2028.

Lavie, P., Ben-Yosef, R., & Rubin, A. E. (1984). Prevalence of sleep apnea syndrome among patients with essential hypertension. *American Heart Journal, 108,* 373.

Mason, W. J., Ancoli-Israel, S., & Kripke, D. F. (1989). Apnea revisited: A longitudinal follow-up. *Sleep, 12,* 423–429.

Moldofsky, H., Goldstein, R., McNicholas, W. T., Lue, F., Zamel, N., & Phillipson, E. (1983). Disordered breathing during sleep and overnight intellectual deterioration in patients with pathological aging. In C. Guilleminault & E. Lugaresi (Eds.), *Sleep/wake disorders: Natural history, epidemiology, and long-term evolution* (pp. 143–150). New York: Raven Press.

Mullaney, D. J., Kripke, D. F., & Messin, S. (1980). Wrist-actigraphic estimation of sleep time. *Sleep, 3,* 83–92.

Orr, W. C., Martin, R. J., Imes, N. K., Rogers, R. M., & Stahl, M L. (1979). Hypersomnolent and nonhypersomnolent patients with upper airway obstruction during sleep. *Chest, 75,* 418–422.

Partinen, M., Jamieson, A., & Guilleminault, C. (1988). Long-term outcome for obstructive sleep apnea syndrome patients' mortality. *Chest, 94,* 1200–1204.

Remmers, J. E., Sauerland, E. K., & Anch, A. M. (1978). Pathogenesis of upper airway occlusion during sleep. *Journal of Applied Physiology, 44,* 931–938.

Shepard, J. W., Jr. (1989). Cardiorespiratory changes in obstructive sleep apnea. In M. H. Kryger, T. Roth, & W. C. Dement (Eds.), *Principles and practice of sleep medicine* (pp. 537–551). Philadelphia: W. B. Saunders.

Smith, P. L., Gold, A. R., Meyers, D. A., Haponik, E. F., & Bleecker, E. R. (1985). Weight loss in mildly to moderately obese patients with obstructive sleep apnea. *Annals of Internal Medicine, 103,* 850–855.

Stradling, J. R. (1986). Controversies in sleep-related breathing disorders. *Lung, 164,* 1, 17–31.

Sullivan, C. E., & Grunstein, R. R. (1989). Continuous positive airways pressure in sleep-disordered breathing. In M. H. Kryger, T. Roth, & W. C. Dement (Eds.), *Principles and practice of sleep medicine* (pp. 559–570). Philadelphia: W. B. Saunders.

Sutton, F. D., Zwillich, C. W., Creagh, C. E., Pierson, D. J., & Weil, J. V. (1975). Progesterone for outpatient treatment of pickwickian syndrome. *Annals of Internal Medicine, 83,* 476–479.

Thorpy, M. J. (1989). Mortality in sleep apnea. *Chest, 95,* 1364.

Timms, R. M., Dawson, A., Taft, R., Erman, M. K., & Mitler, M. M. (1988). Oxygen saturation by oximetry: Analysis by microcomputer. *Journal of Polysomnographic Technology,* Spring, 13–21.

Webster, J. B., Kripke, D. F., Messin, S., Mullaney, D. J., & Wyborney, G. (1982). An activity-based sleep monitor system for ambulatory use. *Sleep, 5,* 389–399.

Weitzman, E. D. (1979). The syndrome of hypersomnia and sleep-induced apnea. *Chest, 75,* 414–415.

Yesavage, J., Bliwise, D., Guilleminault, C., Carskadon, M., & Dement, W. (1985). Preliminary communication: Intellectual deficit and sleep-related respiratory disturbance in the elderly. *Sleep, 8,* 30–33.

CHAPTER 9

Significance of Breathing Awareness and Exercise Training for Recovery after Myocardial Infarction

Jan van Dixhoorn

Introduction

Experts state that cardiac rehabilitation should be comprehensive and "tailored to the individual" (Kellerman, 1981; Meyer, 1985). In actual practice, the main component of rehabilitation is physical exercise (Blodgett & Pekarik, 1987). It is assumed that exercise training will improve not only the patients' physical fitness but also their morale, enhance their return to normal activities, and reduce their risk of recurring cardiac events. It is becoming clear, however, that some patients will benefit from exercise, while others will not (Uniken Venema-Van Uden, Zoeteweij, & Erdman, 1989). This difference is one of the reasons that the effectiveness of exercise-rehabilitation is limited (Barr Taylor, Houston-Miller, Ahn, Haskell, & DeBusk, 1986) and the development of cardiac rehabilitation stagnates (Hellerstein, 1986).

In this chapter, another treatment modality for cardiac patients will be examined, consisting of teaching skills for self-regulation, in particular relaxation and breathing techniques. Although it would seem obvious that stress management is important for cardiac patients and although several authors recommend its use (Fardy, 1986; Hackett & Cassem, 1982), its effectiveness is scarcely documented. There is a large literature on relax-

JAN VAN DIXHOORN • St. Joannes de Deo Hospital, Haarlem, 2003 BR The Netherlands.

Clinical Applied Psychophysiology, edited by John G. Carlson, A. Ronald Seifert, and Niels Birbaumer. Plenum Press, New York, 1994.

ation effects in stress-related disorders, but relatively few studies have dealt with its application to cardiac patients. Polackova, Bockova, and Sedivec (1982) taught autogenic training to 48 patients and found substantial psychological improvement in comparison to controls. Progressive relaxation was taught by Bohacick (1982) to 18 patients, in addition to exercise training, and resulted in lower diastolic blood pressure. Relaxation was provided by Cunningham (1980) to 15 patients in the form of tape-recorded instructions. Compared to no treatment or exercise only, there was no effect on depression. Benson's relaxation response, in addition to exercise training, was taught to 27 patients by Munro, Creamer, Haggerty, & Cooper (1988) and was found to have an effect on diastolic blood pressure. A mixed program of muscle relaxation and self-suggestion was provided to 46 patients, in addition to regular rehabilitation, by Krampen and Ohm (1984) and later to 234 patients by Ohm (1987). The researchers found a higher sense of self-awareness and of control over patients' health, a better perceived physical status, and a higher physician's rating of general and cardiovascular health status. Moreover, the rehabilitation environment was perceived more positively. Langosch, Seer, Brodner, Kallinke, Kulick, and Heim (1982) compared such a treatment in 28 patients to behavior therapy and found that both treatments were more effective than no treatment with respect to self-report data. Patel, Marmot, and Terry (1985) taught a similar program, including breathing, to 99 subjects at high cardiovascular risk. At 4-year follow-up, there were significant reductions in blood pressure and even less cardiac morbidity. Finally, relaxation and breathing techniques were included in an intensive treatment package, focusing on diet, by Ornish and associates in two studies that documented reduced cardiovascular morbidity (Ornish, Brown, & Scherwitz, 1990; Ornish Scherwitz, Doody, Kesten, & McLanahan, 1983); these techniques were included in the Type A behavior modification program of Friedman and Thoresen, which reduced the occurrence of reinfarction (Thoresen, Friedman, Powell, Gill, & Ulmer, 1985). Thus, research to date suggests that relaxation techniques may reduce cardiac risk factors and morbidity, improve psychological well-being, and enhance the effectiveness of rehabilitation.

Relaxation therapy has been part of the cardiac rehabilitation program in St. Joannes de Deo Hospital, Haarlem, The Netherlands, since 1977. A variety of techniques have been experimented with. General relaxation, in the sense of quietening mind and body, was a basic procedure, and breathing was the key element that the patients remembered and used best (van Dixhoorn, 1984). The main focus of our approach was to increase awareness of bodily signs of tension and relaxation. Thus, in 1980, a protocol for "breathing awareness" was constructed, and its effectiveness was tested in a clinical trial. The purpose of teaching breaching awareness was to enable the patient to perceive and elicit a shift in the respiratory pattern toward an easier and more relaxed way of breathing (van Dixhoorn, 1984). The patients could apply this technique both during passive rest and during daily activities, while sitting or standing.

Breathing Awareness

Respiration implies a movement of the body, which in general one is aware of only when breathing becomes difficult. Such a negative awareness occurs when the subject notices unpleasant changes: laborious, effortful, or restricted breathing. One complains of shortness of breath or dyspnea. By contrast, a positive awareness of breathing is the result of pleasant changes: easier, freer, and more effortless respiration. These changes can be elicited by way of exercises, imagery, instructions, or manual techniques. Thus, *breathing awareness*, in the context of this chapter, refers to perceptible changes in the respiratory movement, as a result of the aforementioned techniques. The procedure is as follows: The subject relaxes and notices his spontaneous breathing; he then applies a particular technique for a short while and stops the technique; again, the subject notices the spontaneous breathing movement and compares this to the experience before the technique was applied. In this way, the autonomous character of respiration is respected, yet the possibility for voluntary modification is recognized. Conscious breathing may not always result in pleasant sensations; one may also become aware of restrictions and tensions that previously remained unnoticed. Therefore, the patient is advised to practice when he or she is feeling relatively calm.

General relaxation is a precondition for breathing awareness, since relaxation of the body is necessary to breathe more easily and mental relaxation is necessary for passive attention and the perception of spontaneous breathing. Usually, the subject who practices some form of breathing technique tries to breathe in a particular way—for instance, slowly and abdominally. It is pointed out, however, that one should at first try not to do anything and simply focus attention on the actual tension state and breathing pattern of the body. Also, the subject is asked to do the technique in a "lazy" or indifferent, almost careless way. Afterward, one simply notices how the body responded to the particular technique. In time, the habitual breathing pattern may change, without the conscious effort of the subject to breathe "better." This attitude toward the body differs sharply from the usual view, as well as from the way the body is treated during exercise training. The point was made that one should respect and listen to physical signs and signals, and try to understand their meaning, rather than suppress unpleasant self-perceptions. This metacommunication seems to be important (Peper & Sandler, 1987). In order to relax, one must inevitably become aware of tension.

One of the techniques is to make the passage of air audible by slightly compressing the lips. As a result, one receives audible feedback on the actual breathing pattern. The increased resistance at the lips during exhalation, or during inhalation and exhalation, puts a load on the respiratory muscles. As a result, respiration tends to become slower and fuller, tidal volume increases, and respiratory excursion becomes more expansive and more clearly perceptible. One stops this after about five respiratory cycles and then notices how one's breathing continues by itself. This pattern is to be repeated two times or so, after which the changes in breathing pattern and in one's body sensations can be evaluated.

Another technique consists of coupling or uncoupling a body movement and respiration. For instance, in the supine position, the subject flexes the feet during exhalation and stops flexing during inhalation. This combination is unusual, since one tends to inhale while making effort. In this exercise, inhaling while relaxing the feet and exhaling while pulling them up associates inhalation with relaxation and passivity. Moreover, the movement of the feet is related mechanically to the exhalation movement: The pelvis is tilted backward slightly, the abdomen flattens, and the spine is pushed up a little bit, which implies a relative downward motion of the ribs. After some time, the combination becomes easy and almost natural. When the movement is stopped, spontaneous respiration may be perceived as easier and more effortless.

An example of a manual technique is as follows: The subject is seated on a stool and the therapist sits (squats) behind and places a hand at either side of the lumbar spine. The subject is asked to pay attention to the hands and to notice whether any movement is perceptible with respiration. If one sits and breathes easily, one feels the hands spreading during inhalation and thereby perceives a sideways movement. Conversely, when one mentally follows the sideways spreading and contracting movement in the lumbar region, one tends to sit more relaxed and comfortable and to breathe more slowly, fully, and easily.

There are a number of such techniques to gradually involve the whole body in the respiratory movement, which enhances its efficiency. The perception of such "whole-body breathing" is an unmistakable and very pleasant experience.

Research Questions

In order to assess the effect of breathing awareness, a program of exercise training was compared to a more comprehensive treatment, consisting of the same exercise training combined with individual relaxation and breathing therapy. Since myocardial infarction patients were randomly assigned to either of the two treatments, differences in outcome can be attributed to the difference in treatment. The significance of exercise training was assessed in another way. Since patients were referred for exercise-rehabilitation, they could not be assigned to a control group that received no exercise training. Therefore, a composite criterion, developed to determine the success of the exercise training, was used to stratify the patients into two groups: those for whom exercise training had been successful and those for whom training had not resulted in physical improvement. Rehabilitation outcome was compared between these two groups.

The questions to be answered were: (1) What is the effect of breathing awareness on the rehabilitation outcome? (2) Is training success associated with a positive rehabilitation outcome?

Patients and Methods

Patients

After discharge, cardiac patients from various hospitals were referred to the regional rehabilitation center at St. Joannes de Deo Hospital. A total of 156 myocardial infarction patients were admitted to the study and were randomly assigned to one of two treatment protocols. There were 147 men and 9 women. The median age was 56, the range from 36 to 76. Baseline characteristics of the study population have been described elsewhere (van Dixhoorn, Duivenvoorden, Staal, & Pool, 1989; van Dixhoorn, Duivenvoorden, Pool, & Verhage, 1990b) and are summarized in Table 1.

Procedure

Clinical baseline data and medical history were obtained from the referring cardiologist. On entry, patients were interviewed to obtain psychosocial information and were asked to participate in the study. After providing informed consent, they completed additional psychological questionnaires on a separate occasion, when measurements of respiratory variables were also taken. These tests were repeated after rehabilitation and at a 3-month follow-up interview. On that occasion, roughly half a year after hospital discharge, data on daily activities and work were acquired. All patients participated in a 5-week daily physical conditioning program, starting approximately 4–5 weeks after hospital discharge. Graded exercise testing was performed on a bicycle ergometer before and after physi-

Table 1. Baseline Clinical Data for the Two Treatments[a]

	Relaxation + exercise	Exercise only
Number of cases	76	80
Age (years)	55 ± 8	56 ± 8
Number of men (%)	71 (93)	76 (95)
Working (%)	50 (66)	51 (64)
Preinfarction angina pectoris (%)	14 (18)	12 (15)
Infarction		
Large (%)	25 (33)	27 (34)
Anterior (%)	29 (38)	24 (30)
Complications (%)	14 (18)	13 (16)
Postinfarction		
Start of training[b]	4.8 ± 2.8	5.2 ± 2.1
Work capacity[c]	90 ± 15	87 ± 20
Heart rate	80 ± 16	80 ± 17
Resting Watts = 60	103 ± 18	101 ± 18

[a]Data are reported as number of cases (percentages) or as means ± SD.
[b]Weeks after hospital discharge.
[c]Maximal work load (% of normal).

cal training, supervised by the cardiologist. Half the patients were randomly assigned to six sessions of individual breathing and relaxation therapy, additional to the exercise training. Long-term follow-up data on cardiac events were collected as follows: Patients received a postal questionnaire after 2 years, and the general practitioner was contacted in case of nonresponders. Medical records were searched in case of death or hospital readmission. Patients who were admitted in the early part of the study were invited for an interview.

Measurements

Exercise testing was submaximal, with increasing workloads of 30 watts every 2 min until symptoms prevented the patient from continuing or until the physician terminated the test. The occurrence of angina pectoris, ST abnormalities, and arrhythmias was noted. ST abnormalities consisted mostly of ST depressions greater than 2 mm, horizontal or downsloping, occurring during or immediately after the test. A bipolar ECG (CM5) was taken during the last half minute before the work load was increased, and heart rate was read from this. Blood pressure was taken before the test and at maximum work load. The outcome of exercise training was assessed on the basis of changes in exercise testing. In order to obtain a single measure indicating the efficacy of physical training, these changes were integrated into a composite criterion for training benefit. The procedure is discussed in detail elsewhere (van Dixhoorn *et al.*, 1989; van Dixhoorn, Duivenvoorden, & Pool, 1990a). In short, the following measurements were ranked according to their clinical relevance: (1) exercise-induced signs of cardiac dysfunction (ST-abnormalities, angina pectoris, complex ventricular arrhythmias), (2) maximal work load, (3) heart rate, and (4) systolic blood pressure response. At each level, a patient could be assigned to success or failure when a substantial change in a particular measurement had taken place. Dropouts were classified on the basis of the reason for not completing the program. Thus, physical outcome could be assessed for all subjects as follows: (1) patients who experienced little or no change, (2) patients who improved (success), or (3) patients who deteriorated (failure). The criterion was an operationalization of the primary purpose of exercise training to improve physical fitness and lower the threshold for myocardial ischemia.

Psychological questionnaires included: (1) Heart Patients Psychological Questionnaire, for measuring the well-being of cardiac patients, consisting of four scales: (a) well-being, (b) feelings of invalidity, (c) displeasure, (d) social inhibition); (2) anxiety, measured by the State and Trait Anxiety Index in two modes: state and trait anxiety; (3) sleeping habits, consisting of questions about hours of sleep, daytime nap, and quality of sleep; (4) functional symptoms, consisting of physical complaints not typical of angina pectoris. In addition, two questionnaires referred to the preinfarction period: (5) the Jenkins Activity Scale for Type A behavior and (6) the Maastricht Questionnaire for vital exhaustion and depression (van Dixhoorn *et al.*, 1990b). At a 3-month follow-up, the patients' activity compared to preinfarction situation was rated by an interviewer, with respect to physical activity, daily affairs, and work, as a measure of social recovery.

Respiratory variables were measured during a physiological test, which was presented to the patient as a test of the resting condition (van Dixhoorn & Duivenvoorden, 1989). Recordings were made of respiratory movement, using stretch-sensitive bands around the thorax and abdomen, and of beat-to-beat variation of the heart rate (Psychophysiograph, ZAK). Capnographic and spirometric recordings were taken, after which the patient was asked to remain quiet for 6 min. The patient's perception of the body's state was then assessed.

Treatments

Physical exercise training consisted of 5 weeks of interval training on a bicycle ergometer, once a day, for half an hour. Training was given in groups of four patients, supervised by two physical therapists. Each patient was exercised up to 70–80% of the maximal heart rate (Karvonen method) attained at the pretraining exercise test. Relaxation therapy was given once a week in six individual 1-hr sessions. The therapy was provided by five experts and is discussed in the Introduction. The rehabilitation program did not have a structured form of patient education. At the patients' request, information was given and questions were answered by the rehabilitation staff.

Results

Training Outcome

In 139 patients, exercise testing results were available before and after training (van Dixhoorn et al., 1989). Both treatments showed a clear but modest training response: Maximal work load increased and heart rate at a given work load decreased. Heart rate reduction was more pronounced for patients who participated in relaxation therapy. Exercise-induced signs of cardiac dysfunction remained relatively stable, except for a remarkable decrease in ST depression in patients who underwent relaxation therapy. The difference between treatments was statistically significant ($p < 0.02$). Seventeen patients (making a total of 156) did not complete their training, 9 of whom were classified as unsuccessful because of dropping out for cardiac problems and 6 of whom stopped for noncardiac reasons and were classified as unchanged. The other 2 patients stopped rehabilitation because they became fully active again; they were classified as successful. There was no significant change in medication during rehabilitation, probably because the program covered only a short period of time.

The results on the composite criterion are shown in Fig. 1. For 79 of the 156 patients (51%), training was successful, whereas for 42 patients (28%), the outcome was negative. There was a shift to a more positive outcome in the combined treatment. The difference in training failure was significant: The odds for failure were higher for exercise as a sole treatment (odds ratio: 2.07; 95% confidence interval 1.002–4.28; $p < 0.05$).

Psychological Changes

Measurements were available for 137 patients (van Dixhoorn et al., 1990b). Figure 2 summarizes the changes in four scales. The pre–post differences are expressed in Cohen's d (Cohen, 1969). As a rule of thumb, d less than 0.20 means no effect and d equals 0.5 means a medium effect.

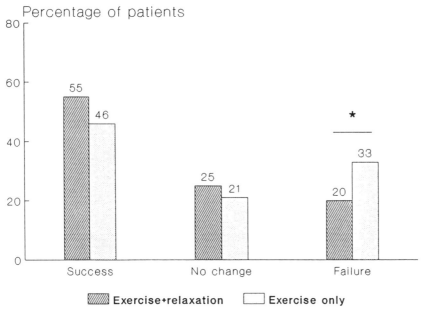

Figure 1. Success and failure of exercise training for two treatments. (*) $p < 0.05$.

It appeared that exercise training did not result in any psychological change, on the average. After relaxation therapy, patients improved in state-anxiety, well-being, and invalidity feelings. The difference between treatments was significant for well-being ($p < 0.001$).

The psychological significance of exercise training was further investigated by differentiating patients with and without psychological improvement, according to training outcome. Two composite scores were constructed on the basis of changes in six questionnaires: psychic improvement, reflecting changes in state- and trait-anxiety and depression; somatic improvement, reflecting changes in sleeping quality, feelings of invalidity, and functional complaints (van Dixhoorn *et al.*, 1990b). Since some patients did not complete all the questionnaires, the composite scores were available for a smaller number of patients. Improvement on the scale "well-being" was considered separately. Table 2 shows the results. The odds ratios in the rightmost column indicate the effect of relaxation therapy; the odds ratios in the two middle columns indicate the effect of training success for the two treatments separately.

Psychic improvement occurred in 89 patients (69%), whereas 40

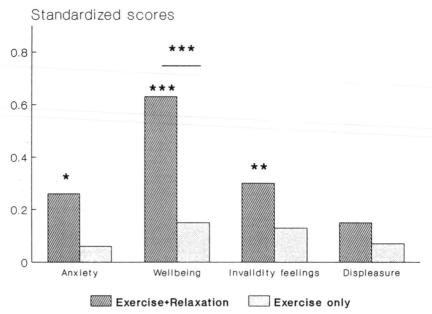

Figure 2. Psychological changes after rehabilitation for two treatments. (*) $p < 0.05$; (**) $p <$ 0.01; (***) $p < 0.001$.

patients did not improve. Thus, the odds for improvement were greater than 2 in both treatments (odds ratio: 1.03). They were slightly lower for patients whose training was successful, particularly after relaxation therapy, compared to the odds of patients without training success (odds ratio: 0.64 and 0.83, respectively), although statistically not significant. Thus, the composite score for psychic improvement was not influenced by breathing and relaxation therapy or by training outcome.

Somatic improvement occurred in 80 patients (64%), whereas 46 patients did not improve. The odds for somatic benefit were slightly higher after relaxation therapy than after exercise training only (odds ratio: 1.37). Interestingly, the association between training success and somatic benefit showed a different pattern for the two treatments: For exercise as the sole treatment, the odds for improvement were *higher* for successful patients than for unsuccessful patients, although statistically not significant (odds ratio: 2.07). For the combined treatment, the odds for somatic improvement were significant *lower* in patients with training success than in unsuccessful patients (odds ratio: 0.32).

Consequently, in unsuccessful patients, the odds for improvement

Table 2. *Psychological Benefit for the Two Treatments,*
in Relation to Training Success (TS)

Question	Exercise + relaxation therapy			Exercise training only			Odds ratio	
	Yes	No	Odds	Yes	No	Odds	(95% CI)[a]	
Psychic improvement?								
Total	43	19	2.26	46	21	2.19	1.03	(0.49–2.2)
TS +	25	13	1.92	22	11	2.0	0.96	(0.36–2.6)
TS −	18	6	3.0	24	10	2.40	1.25	(0.38–4.1)
Odds ratio (TS +/−)	0.64	(0.20–2.0)		0.83	(0.30–2.34)			
Somatic improvement?								
Total	41	20	2.05	39	26	1.50	1.37	(0.66–2.8)
TS +	20	15	1.3	22	10	2.20	0.61	(0.22–1.7)
TS −	21	5	4.2	17	16	1.06	4.0	(1.2–13.0)
Odds ratio (TS +/−)	0.32	(0.10–1.0)		2.07	(0.75–5.7)			
Well-being improved?								
Total	57	9	6.3	47	24	1.96	3.2	(1.4–7.6)
TS +	34	4	8.5	19	16	1.2	7.2	(2.1–24.5)
TS −	23	5	4.6	28	8	3.5	1.3	(0.38–4.6)
Odds ratio (TS +/−)	1.85	(0.45–7.6)		0.34	(0.12–0.95)			

[a](CI) confidence interval.

were significantly higher after relaxation therapy compared to exercise only (odds ratio: 4.0). Thus, relaxation and breathing therapy had a beneficial effect on the score for somatic improvement for patients who did not benefit physically from training.

Improvement in "well-being" occurred in 104 of 137 patients (76%). The odds for improvement were significantly higher for patients who had followed breathing and relaxation therapy (odds ratio: 3.2). Remarkably, the pattern of association with training success differed again between the treatments, but contrary to the association of somatic benefit. Training success tended to be positively associated with increased feelings of well-being for the combined treatment (odds ratio: 1.85), but was negatively associated for exercise as a sole treatment (odds ratio: 0.34). As a result, the effect of relaxation therapy was particularly clear for patients with training success (odds ratio: 7.2), whereas for unsuccessful patients, the addition of relaxation therapy did not make a difference (odds ratio: 1.3).

Respiration and Body Sensation

The average respiration frequency before rehabilitation was 14.7 cycles/min for the combined treatment and 15.2 cycles/min for exercise

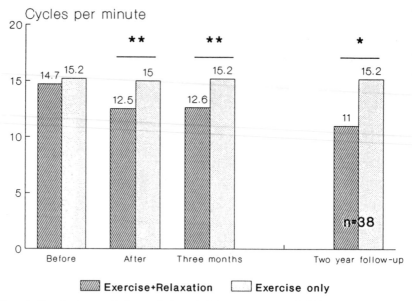

Figure 3. Respiration rate before and after rehabilitation, at 3-month follow-up, and at 2-year follow-up for two treatments. (*) $p < 0.01$; (**) $p < 0.001$.

training only (van Dixhoorn & Duivenvoorden, 1989). Figure 3 shows that after rehabilitation, and at the 3-month follow-up, respiration rate remained the same for the single treatment (15.0 and 15.2, respectively), but dropped significantly for the combined treatment (12.5 and 12.6, respectively). The difference between treatments was highly significant ($p < 0.0001$). A fine-grain analysis on a subset of the population ($N = 48$) confirmed the idea that a lower respiration rate implied a larger tidal volume (van Dixhoorn & Duivenvoorden, 1989). Thus, after relaxation and breathing therapy, patients were breathing more slowly and more fully, but minute volume was unchanged. After exercise training, tidal volume decreased slightly, implying that patients tended to breathe more superficially. The fine-grain analysis also revealed that heart rate variability during breathing at a fixed rate of 6 cycles/min, an indicator of cardiac vagal tone, increased after relaxation therapy, but remained the same after exercise training only. The differences between treatments were significant for both tidal volume ($p < 0.05$) and heart rate variability ($p < 0.05$). At 2-year follow-up, respiratory measurements were taken in 38 patients. It appeared that patients who had participated in relaxation and breathing therapy were still breathing more slowly (see Fig. 3). The difference between treatments was even greater and highly significant ($p < 0.01$).

Before rehabilitation, 28% of the patients in both treatments had a pleasant body sensation after resting supine during the physiological test. For exercise as a sole treatment, this percentage remained stable after rehabilitation and at the 3-month follow-up (33% and 28%, respectively). The majority felt nothing in particular, and a minority had unpleasant sensations (7%, 12%, and 12%, respectively, before rehabilitation, after rehabilitation, and at the 3-month follow-up). After rehabilitation through exercise and relaxation therapy, 60% had a pleasant sensation during rest, and 59% reported this at follow-up as well. The increase in pleasant sensations was highly significant ($p < 0.001$), and the difference between treatments was significant as well ($p < 0.01$). A minority felt physically uncomfortable during rest before and after rehabilitation and at follow-up (10%, 8%, and 9%, respectively).

Social Recovery Three Months Later

Data on physical activity level at the 3-month follow-up were available for 130 patients, 53 of whom (41%) had become physically more active and only 25 of whom (19%) had become less active than they were before infarction. Information on daily activities was elicited at a later phase of the study and was available for 82 patients. Half of them (51%) had become as busy in daily life as they were before infarction, whereas only 3 (4%) had become busier. Almost half of them (45%) had become less busy than before. Coping style had changed for 44%, usually meaning that they said "No" to requests more easily and were taking things more lightly. Thus, compared to preinfarction, the most common changes were that patients became less busy but physically more active. Before infarction, 101 patients had been working and an additional 2 patients had been on sick leave. Of the 103 patients, 68 had returned to work about 6 months after hospital discharge (66%), either part-time (47%) or full-time (19%). Information on changes in behavioral style at the workplace was available on 60 patients who had resumed work, 48% of whom said they were doing things differently now. Again, this usually meant they took things easier and delegated responsibility more than had been their habit previously.

The effect of relaxation therapy can be deduced from the odds ratios in the rightmost column of Table 3. It appeared that the odds for increased physical activity did not differ between the treatments (odds ratio: 0.96), whereas the odds for fewer daily activities were higher in the combined treatment (odds ratio: 2.16), although statistically not significant. Also, the odds for a changed coping style in daily life were more than twice as high

Table 3. *Resumption of Activities, Three Months after Rehabilitation, for the Two Treatments and in Relation to Training Success (TS)*

Question	Exercise + relaxation therapy			Exercise training only			Odds ratio	
	Yes	No	Odds	Yes	No	Odds	(95% CI)[a]	
More physical activity?								
Total	27	40	0.68	26	37	0.70	0.96	(0.48–1.9)
TS +	17	21	0.80	16	16	1.0	0.81	(0.32–2.1)
TS −	10	19	0.52	10	21	0.48	1.10	(0.38–3.2)
Odds ratio (TS +/−)	1.5	(0.57–4.2)		2.1	(0.76–5.8)			
Less daily activities?								
Total	21	17	1.24	16	28	0.57	2.16	(0.89–5.3)
TS +	12	10	1.20	8	15	0.53	2.25	(0.68–7.5)
TS −	9	7	1.26	8	13	0.62	2.10	(0.56–7.9)
Odds ratio (TS +/−)	0.93	(0.26–3.4)		0.87	(0.25–2.97)			
Coping differently (daily life)?								
Total	21	17	1.24	15	28	0.54	2.30	(0.94–5.6)
TS +	12	10	1.20	7	15	0.46	2.57	(0.75–8.8)
TS −	9	7	1.26	8	13	0.62	2.10	(0.56–7.9)
Odds ratio (TS +/−)	0.93	(0.26–3.4)		0.76	(0.22–2.67)			
Return to work?								
Total	37	13	2.85	31	21	1.48	1.79	(0.78–4.1)
TS +	21	12	1.75	18	10	1.8	0.97	(0.34–2.8)
TS −	16	2	8.0	13	11	1.18	6.78	(1.3–36.1)
Odds ratio (TS +/−)	0.22	(0.04–1.12)		1.5	(0.5–4.6)			
Coping differently (work)?								
Total	20	11	1.82	9	20	0.45	4.04	(1.4–11.9)
TS +	13	7	1.86	6	11	0.55	3.4	(0.88–13.2)
TS −	7	4	1.75	3	9	0.33	5.3	(0.87–31.6)
Odds ratio (TS +/−)	1.06	(0.23–4.9)		1.64	(0.32–8.45)			

[a](CI) Confidence interval.

(odds ratio: 2.3) in the combined treatment, approaching significance. The odds for work resumption were greater than 1 in both treatments, but tended to be higher in the combined treatment (odds ratio: 1.79). There was a significant difference with respect to coping style at work. The odds for such a change were almost 2 in the combined treatment, but less than 0.5 in the single treatment. Thus, patients in the combined treatment changed their behavior 4 times more often than patients in the single treatment (odds ratio: 4.04).

The significance of training success can be seen from the odds ratios in the two middle columns of Table 3. The odds for increased physical activity were greater than 1 for both treatments, implying that patients with training success tended to be physically more active. However, the association was statistically not significant in either of the treatments or for the total population. The odds for fewer daily activities did not differ between patients with and without training success, in either of the treatments, nor was there a difference in the odds for changed behavior in daily life. Thus, training outcome did not affect daily life at all. Interestingly, the association of training outcome with work resumption showed an opposite pattern for the two treatments. In the combined treatment, the odds for work resumption were much lower for successful patients then for unsuccessful patients, largely because almost all patients without training success returned to work (odds ratio: 0.22). In the single treatment, the odds for work resumption were somewhat higher in successful patients (odds ratio: 1.5). Neither of the two associations was statistically significant, but their opposite direction resulted in the fact that relaxation therapy significantly enhanced return to work among unsuccessful patients (odds ratio: 6.78). By contrast, relaxation therapy had no effect at all among patients who benefited physically from training (odds ratio: 0.97). Finally, the odds for an easier coping style at the workplace were not greater in successful patients compared to unsuccessful patients. Thus, training outcome did not influence coping behavior.

Cardiac Events

Data on cardiac events during 2 years after infarction were available for the patients admitted in the first years of the study, 43 in the combined and 47 in the single treatment (van Dixhoorn, Duivenvoorden, Staal, Pool, & Verhage, 1987). Of these 90 patients, 2 were lost to follow-up, 1 in each treatment. Further, 2 patients had died for cardiac reasons, both in the single treatment, and 9 had a recurrent infarction, 4 in the combined and 5 in the single treatment. Coronary bypass graft surgery was undergone by 6 patients, only 1 of whom was in the combined treatment. There were 15 readmissions to hospital for cardiac reasons, mostly unstable angina pectoris, 3 in the combined treatment and 12 in the single treatment. Thus, there was a total of 8 events in 7 patients (17%) after relaxation therapy, and there were 24 events in 17 patients (37%) after exercise training only. The odds for an event were higher for exercise as a single treatment than for relaxation therapy (odds ratio: 2.9; 95% confidence interval: 1.07–8.04).

Discussion

Effect of Breathing Awareness

The study had been designed primarily as a clinical trial of breathing and relaxation therapy in cardiac rehabilitation. It turned out that the outcome of rehabilitation was positively influenced by the addition of this therapy individually to a regular exercise program. It resulted in a stable effect on respiratory pattern, which became more efficient, slower, and fuller, even after 2 years. Also, more patients felt pleasant after taking a rest. These effects may be taken as the direct result of the techniques for breathing and body awareness and indicate that, on average, the therapy had been successful. More important, however, are the wider effects on traditional rehabilitation-outcome measures. The literature, reviewed in the Introduction, indicated that physical, psychological, and behavioral effects could be expected. It turned out that effects were found in each of these dimensions, but the physical effects were the most striking. Breathing and relaxation therapy reduced the incidence of deterioration after training (training failure), reduced the occurrence of exercise-induced signs of myocardial ischemia (ST depressions), increased cardiac vagal tone (heart rate variability), and reduced the occurrence of cardiac events in a 2-year follow-up period. Thus, the conclusion of Ohm (1987), that relaxation therapy enhances the general effectiveness of rehabilitation, is supported by this study.

Obviously, teaching awareness of respiration and of bodily tension is quite different from exercise training. It involves a learning process and skills training, rather than physical conditioning. Also, the attitude toward the body is one of respecting and listening to bodily signs with receptive attention. When a subject actually adopts this attitude and applies the techniques, it can be expected that behavioral patterns (habits) will be influenced and show lasting effects. The available data suggest that behavioral changes did indeed take place. On the physiological level, breathing habits were changed even 2 years later. Coping style had changed 3 months after rehabilitation, almost exclusively in the combined treatment. An interesting phenomenon was that breathing awareness influenced the effect of the exercise sessions. The association of training success with psychological and social outcome measures differed between the two treatments. As a result, breathing and relaxation therapy were particularly beneficial for patients who did not benefit physically from exercise training: It improved somatic aspects of psychological benefit (feelings of invalidity, sleeping quality, and functional complaints), and it promoted return to work.

Training Outcome

Although the value of exercise-rehabilitation depends to a large degree on its contribution to social recovery and secondary prevention, the immediate purpose is to improve the patients' physical fitness and morale. The composite criterion for physical outcome, integrating the major measurements of exercise testing, was meant as an operationalization of the primary purpose of exercise training, to improve fitness and raise the threshold for myocardial ischemia. The fact that only half the patients actually reached this aim and benefited from exercise training is therefore most remarkable. Even more important is the fact that about one quarter had a negative outcome. Only a few authors evaluated the outcome of training in terms of success and failure instead of average changes in exercise testing parameters. Hammond, Kelly, Froelicher, and Pewen (1985) found that the percentage of patients showing at least 5% improvement in a training response, after 1 year of training, three times a week, was 44% for resting heart rate and thallium ischemia, 58% for heart rate at low work level, and 52% for measured maximal oxygen uptake. Uniken Venema-Van Uden and associates (Uniken Venema-Van Uden et al., 1989) used a composite criterion derived from the one used in this study on 370 cardiac patients, rehabilitated in three centers with programs of differing length (6–12 weeks) and intensity (2–5 times a week) of training. On the whole, 54% improved after training and 16% deteriorated. Unlike the criterion in this study, dropouts (13%) were not included in the outcome, which may be a reason there were fewer failures. Thus, it seems realistic to say that exercise training is really appropriate only for about half of cardiac patients referred for rehabilitation. This questions the very basis of present-day rehabilitation, in which exercise is the main component (Blodgett & Pekarik, 1987; Hellerstein, 1986).

The significance of exercise training for recovery is unclear. In general, postinfarction patients are very enthusiastic about exercise, and the majority are convinced that it is extremely helpful in convalescence. The results of this study do not support this idea and confirm the conclusion of one recent review (Langosch, 1988), that the evidence of a psychological effect of exercise is weak. We did not find an improvement on any psychological questionnaire after exercise training was given. Moreover, patients with a positive training outcome did not improve psychologically any more than patients without physical benefit. With respect to social recovery, at 3 months follow-up, there was a weak association of training success with an increased level of physical activity. Daily activity level, return to work, and coping style were not associated. Thus, there was little evidence for the assumed significance of exercise training for the recovery and well-being of cardiac patients.

Rehabilitation Policy

These results question the one-sided reliance of rehabilitation on physical exercise as well as the idea of increasing fitness as a main purpose of exercise sessions. Cardiac rehabilitation should indeed be comprehensive and tailored to the individual. It means that more than one treatment modality should be employed and that subjects should be assigned to the treatment or treatment combination that seems to be best. This study indicates that such a differentiated program will have a higher overall effect than exercise training alone.

It should be noted that the results do not necessarily invalidate the utility of all physical exercise. Increasing aerobic power may be important for some patients, while for others the context of exercise sessions may be more meaningful. For some, increasing work loads may even be detrimental, and training is therefore not appropriate. It appears that if the staff were to take a more comprehensive attitude, rather than urge the "dogged repetition of mindless exercise," as Nixon, Al-Abbasi, King, and Freeman (1986) put it, the program would become an "arena for interchange and education" (Fletcher, Lloyd, & Fletcher, 1988) and probably more effective, physically, mentally, and socially.

Several authors stated that integration of relaxation exercises and body awareness into the exercise sessions would make them more interesting and more effective (Fardy, 1986; Sime, 1980). It should be emphasized, however, that group sessions may not be sufficient to actually learn self-regulation skills and to acquire awareness of personally relevant strategies for relaxation and tension control. In this study, therefore, individual sessions were utilized. At present, in our hospital, relaxation and breathing therapy are still implemented individually in about 40% of the rehabilitation patients. All the patients receive group instruction in addition to the exercise program. The individual treatments are retained for two reasons: A substantial number of patients require personal contact and guidance, verbally or manually, to be able to sense concrete differences in bodily tension, which is necessary for practice at home and in the group. For some of them, the sessions also have a counseling nature, and for a few they are the main treatment. Second, the individual therapy requires fine-tuning of skill and sensitivity on the therapists' part. Since the therapists are mainly physiotherapists who conduct the group sessions as well, this attitude will carry over into the style and quality of the group sessions. Actually, incorporating the individual therapy appears to influence the attitude of the entire rehabilitation staff.

To conclude, individual breathing and relaxation therapy is a treatment modality on its own, and its addition to a rehabilitation program is a worthwhile effort that will enhance the effect of cardiac rehabilitation in a number of ways.

ACKNOWLEDGMENT.   This study was supported by a grant from the Dutch Heart Foundation, The Hague.

References

Barr Taylor, C., Houston-Miller, N., Ahn, D., Haskell, W., & DeBusk, R. (1986). The effects of exercise training programs on psychosocial improvement in uncomplicated postmyocardial infarction patients. *Journal of Psychosomatic Research, 30*, 581–587.

Blodgett, C., & Pekarik, G. (1987). Program evaluation in cardiac rehabilitation I–IV. *Journal of Cardiopulmonary Rehabilitation, 7*, 316–323, 374–382, 410–414, 466–474.

Bohachick, P. A. (1982). Progressive relaxation training in cardiac rehabilitation: Effect on physiological and psychological variables. *Dissertation Abstracts International, 42*, 3191.

Cohen, J. (1969). *Statistical power analysis for behavioral sciences.* New York: Academic Press.

Cunningham, J. (1980). The effects of exercise and relaxation training upon psychological variables in coronary heart patients. *Dissertation Abstracts International, 41*, 2313–2314.

Fardy, P. (1986). Cardiac rehabilitation for the outpatient: A hospital-based program. In M. L. Pollock, D. H. Schmidt, & D. T. Mason (Eds.), *Heart disease and rehabilitation* (pp. 423–435). New York: John Wiley.

Fletcher, B. J., Lloyd, A., & Fletcher, G. F. (1988). Outpatient rehabilitative training in patients with cardiovascular disease: Emphasis on training method. *Heart and Lung, 17*, 199–205.

Hackett, T. P., & Cassem, N. H. (1982). Coping with cardiac disease. In J. J. Kellerman (Ed.), *Comprehensive cardiac rehabilitation* (pp. 212–217). Basel: Karger.

Hammond, H., Kelly, T., Froelicher, V., & Pewen, W. (1985). Use of clinical data in predicting improvement in exercise capacity after cardiac rehabilitation. *Journal of the American College of Cardiology, 6*, 19–26.

Hellerstein, H. K. (1986). Cardiac rehabilitation: A retrospective view. In M. L. Pollock & D. H. Schmidt (Eds.), *Heart disease and rehabilitation* (pp. 701–711). New York: John Wiley.

Kellerman, J. J. (1981). *Comprehensive cardiac rehabilitation.* Basel: Karger.

Krampen, G., & Ohm, D. (1984). Effects of relaxation training during rehabilitation of myocardial infarction patients. *International Journal of Rehabilitation Research, 7*, 68–69.

Langosch, W. (1988). Psychological effects of training in coronary patients: A critical review of the literature. *European Heart Journal, 9*, 37–42.

Langosch, W., Seer, P., Brodner, G., Kallinke, D., Kulick, B., & Heim, F. (1982). Behavior therapy with coronary heart disease patients: Results of a comparative study. *Journal of Psychosomatic Research, 24*, 475–484.

Meyer, G. C. (1985). Cardiovascular rehabilitation: A discipline in need of a new direction? *Journal of Cardiopulmonary Rehabilitation, 5*, 507–509.

Munro, B. H., Creamer, A. M., Haggerty, M. R., & Cooper, F. S. (1988). Effect of relaxation therapy on post-myocardial infarction patients' rehabilitation. *Nursing Research, 37*, 231–235.

Nixon, P. G. F., Al-Abbasi, A. H., King, J., & Freeman, L. J. (1986). Hyperventilation in cardiac rehabilitation. *Holistic Medicine, 1*, 5–13.

Ohm, D. (1987). *Entspannungstraining und Hypnose bei Patienten mit koronaren Herzkrankheit in der stationären Rehabilitation.* Regensburg: Roderer Verlag.

Ornish, D., Scherwitz, L. W., Doody, R. S., Kesten, D., & McLanahan, S. M. (1983). Effects of stress management training and dietary changes in treating ischemic heart disease. *Journal of the American Medical Association, 249*, 54–59.

Ornish, D., Brown, S. E., & Scherwitz, L. W. (1990). Can lifestyle changes reverse coronary heart disease? *The Lancet, 336*, 129–133.

Patel, C., Marmot, M., & Terry, D. (1985). Trial of relaxation in reducing coronary risk: Four year follow up. *British Medical Journal, 290*, 1103–1106.

Peper, E., & Sandler, L. S. (1987). The metacommunications underlying biofeedback training. *Clinical Biofeedback and Health, 10*, 37–42.

Polackova, J., Bockova, E., & Sedivec, V. (1982). Autogenic training: Application in secondary prevention of myocardial infarction. *Active Nerve Supplement, 24*, 178–180.

Sime, W. E. (1980). Emotional stress testing and relaxation in cardiac rehabilitation. In F. J. McGuigan, W. E. Sime, & J. Macdonald Wallace (Eds.), *Stress and tension control* (pp. 41–48). New York: Plenum Press.

Thoresen, C., Friedman, M., Powell, L., Gill, J., & Ulmer, D. (1985). Altering the Type A behavior pattern in postinfarction patients. *Journal of Cardiopulmonary Rehabilitation, 5*, 258–266.

Uniken Venema-Van Uden, M. M. A. T., Zoeteweij, M, W., & Erdman, R. A. M. (1989). Medical, social and psychological recovery after cardiac rehabilitation. *Journal of Psychosomatic Research, 33*, 651–656.

van Dixhoorn, J. (1984). Body awareness: The proper application of relaxation and breathing technique. *Gedrag, 12*, 31–45.

van Dixhoorn, J., & Duivenvoorden, H. J. (1989). Breathing awareness as a relaxation method in cardiac rehabilitation. In F. J. McGuigan, W. E. Sime, & J. M. Wallace (Eds.), *Stress and tension control 3*, (pp. 19–36). New York: Plenum Press.

van Dixhoorn, J., Duivenvoorden, H. J., Staal, J. A., Pool, J., & Verhage, F. (1987). Cardiac events after myocardial infarction: Possible effect of relaxation therapy. *European Heart Journal, 8*, 1210–1214.

van Dixhoorn, J., Duivenvoorden, H. J., Staal, H. A., & Pool, J. (1989). Physical training and relaxation therapy in cardiac rehabilitation assessed through a composite criterion for training outcome. *American Heart Journal, 118*, 545–552.

van Dixhoorn, J., Duivenvoorden, H. J., & Pool, J. (1990a). Success and failure of exercise training after myocardial infarction: Is the outcome predictable? *Journal of the American College of Cardiology, 15*, 974–982.

van Dixhoorn, J., Duivenvoorden, H. J., Pool, J., & Verhage, F. (1990b). Psychic effects of physical training and relaxation therapy after myocardial infarction. *Journal of Psychosomatic Research, 34*, 327–337.

CHAPTER **10**

Respiration in Clinical Psychophysiology
How to Assess Critical Parameters and Their Change with Treatment

Robert Fried

Introduction

Clinical psychophysiology is concerned, for the most part, with psychological, psychophysiological, and neuromuscular disorders that cause pain, or impair health or function, or are likely to do so in the future. It is not uncommon to find that their etiology is vague, and they may span an astonishing range of disorders, such as cardiovascular (e.g., angina, hypertension), cardiac (e.g., arrhythmias), digestive (e.g., gastritis, ulcers, colitis), pulmonary (e.g., hyperventilation, asthma), psychiatric (e.g., depression, anxiety, panic, phobias, sexual dysfunction), neurological (e.g., migraine, poststroke or other trauma), insomnia, and many more.

Many of these disorders, with notable exceptions, are attributed to stress, which Selye (1974) defines as the "nonspecific response of the body to any demand made upon it." But, this does not explain stress; it merely describes what follows chronic exposure to *stressors*.

What is the nonspecific response? No one knows, but I agree with the Pavlovians (Gantt, 1970) that all nonspecific reactions begin with an *orienting response* (OR), in which activity, especially breathing, is inhibited,

ROBERT FRIED • Hunter College, City University of New York, New York, NY 10021; Institute for Rational Emotive Therapy, New York, NY 10021.

Clinical Applied Psychophysiology, edited by John G. Carlson, A. Ronald Seifert, and Niels Birbaumer. Plenum Press, New York, 1994.

this inhibition being followed by an excitatory increased metabolic demand for oxygen (O_2). Based on an extensive review of the relevant physiological research literature, I have come to suspect that the body cannot *sustain* intermittent OR, and sympathetic arousal, for any considerable length of time and still meet increased metabolic demand for O_2. If this suspicion is correct, then the "nonspecific response" is not so nonspecific after all; it is the consequence of increased tissue air hunger.

When metabolic rate rises, it dictates a concomitant increase in O_2, by increasing blood circulation and raising pressure (favoring diffusion) and by adjusting the O_2 transport system [favoring O_2 release from hemoglobin (Hb) in the red blood cells]. But prolonged homeostatic adjustment to these arousal mechanisms results in lower tissue O_2, i.e., *graded* hypoxia, a state that may compromise many physiological processes including neurotransmitter biosynthesis (Blass & Gibson, 1979; Katz, 1982).

Hypoxia is not fatal (unlike anoxia, which leads to asphyxiation in minutes). Among other effects, however, it does raise blood lactate levels (Cohen & Woods, 1976; Huckabee, 1961; Kreisberg, 1980; Park & Arief, 1980), causing metabolic acidosis. Metabolic acidosis, in turn, must be compensated, typically by increased lung ventilation, which often leads to hyperventilation (HV) (Edwards & Clode, 1970; Gamble, 1982; Shapiro, Harrison, & Walton, 1982). Most behavioral scientists are unaware that a "functional" breathing disorder such as HV may be homeostatic, and homeostasis is not without physiological cost. In order to better understand metabolic arousal and homeostatic mechanisms, it is essential to become more knowledgeable about respiration, ventilation, and the O_2 and CO_2 transport systems.

Respiration involves dynamic and static lung air volumes: The dynamic volume is the volume of air that moves into the lungs (inspiratory tidal volume) or out of the lungs (expiratory end-tidal volume). Static volume is the volume that remains as *dead space* in the lungs. Inspiration fills the lungs with air, and O_2 diffuses into the bloodstream in the alveoli, because its pressure there is greater than that in blood. Conversely, in expiration, CO_2 pressure, greater in blood, diffuses from blood into the alveoli, for expulsion. When O_2 diffuses into the blood, most of it passes through the membrane of the red cells, where it binds to Hb to form oxyhemoglobin (OHb). The degree of affinity of Hb for O_2 is a function of blood pH, which is controlled by *buffering* of the major blood acid, hydrogen ion (H^+), the blood concentration of which is related to CO_2 concentration in the body. The pH of blood is thus principally controlled by breathing.

The CO_2 transport system involves an enzyme [from the kidneys and the red blood cells (RBCs)], carbonic anhydrase, and the formation in the blood of bicarbonate and volatile carbonic acid. Carbonic anhydrase helps CO_2 to hydrolyze, forming carbonic acid (H_2CO_3) which readily breaks down to H^+ and bicarbonate (HCO_3)—a more efficient way to expel CO_2. Normal blood pH is about 7.4—slightly alkaline. Decreased alkalinity favors OHb dissociation, while its increase, alkalosis, favors OHb retention. Maintenance of acid–base balance usually involves the lungs (about 85%), which expel CO_2, and the kidneys (15%), which expel "base excess," i.e., bicarbonate. Thus, regulation of the acid–base balance of the body occurs breath-by-breath, and O_2 available from each breath depends on the outcome of only a few of the breaths preceding it.

Bohr, Hasselbach, and Krogh (1904) were the first to show that O_2–Hb affinity depends on CO_2 availability, i.e., the *partial pressure* of CO_2 in arterial blood (Pa_{CO_2}), which in the average normal person is about 5.00%, or 38 torr. Body cells have a lower pH because local metabolism raises CO_2 concentration. The greater acidity favors OHb *dissociation*, and O_2 diffuses into the cells, while CO_2 diffuses back into the blood, where the concentration is initially lower. Most of the CO_2 is transported away by Hb. Figure 1 shows the OHb dissociation curve (ODC) at different values of pH, at normal body temperature. When pH is normal, 7.4 (center curve), 50% blood saturation occurs at $Po_2 = 27$ mm Hg (torr). If pH rises (alkalosis) to 7.6, 50% saturation occurs at about 21 torr; if it drops to 7.2, Po_2 will be about 33 torr.

The shift of the OHb curve to the left (Bohr effect) is usually momentary and compensated by the homeostatic lung–kidney system. But as Kerr, Dalton, and Gliebe (1937) detailed, it may be profound in some

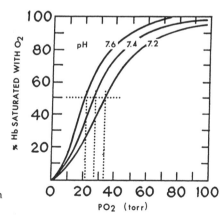

Figure 1. Blood oxyhemoglobin dissociation curve (7.4 is the normal blood pH).

persons and may lead to an astonishing array of symptoms, though in the long run, blood pH will be compensated to near-normal and respiratory alkalosis is indicated only by excretion of bicarbonate. Thus, the critical variable in respiratory psychophysiology is not O_2, but CO_2.

Tidal-volume norms, for any individual, are given by a *nomograph* (see Radford, 1955), a graph that gives equivalence among body weight, tidal volume (V_t), and breathing rate for men and women. V_t *times* breathing rate is minute volume (V_{min}): An average 150-lb man at rest with a breathing frequency of 12 breaths/min, would be expected to have a V_t of 500 ml ($\times$ 12 = V_{min} of 6000 ml).

In an average normal person at rest, alveolar Pco_2 below 38 torr (hypocapnia) is the commonly accepted criterion for HV (Comroe, 1974), which is often erroneously defined simply as rapid, shallow breathing. Correlation between Pco_2 and $Paco_2$ is about +0.93 (Comroe, 1974). Many of the sequelae of HV are the symptoms we observe. That is why I deplore the use of the *hyperventilation challenge* (Hardonk & Beumer, 1979)—fast breathing for about 2 min to induce HV-related symptoms. Sustained HV causes peripheral and cerebral arterial vasoconstriction, and by reducing blood flow to the brain, and the heart, it may lead to angina, stroke, and seizures (Darrow & Graf, 1945; Kety & Schmidt, 1948; Penfield & Jasper, 1954; Yu & Yim, 1958; Yu, Yim, & Stansfield, 1959). It has been my experience that symptoms will emerge below about 30 torr.

Most persons with psychiatric, psychosomatic, and stress disorders have HV-related complaints—"I can't seem to catch my breath." "I can't seem to get enough air" (dyspnea), "I huff and puff"—and they may show frequent sighing, swallowing, and chest heaving. Alternately, they may show little breathing movement (Fried, 1987, 1990).

More recently, Hirsch and Bishop (1981) and Grossman (1983) also linked HV to stress. According to Grossman, alteration in ventilatory parameters may result in lowered parasympathetic cardiac controls, leading to inadequate myocardial and cerebral oxygenation. Nixon's "patient-specific *Think Test*" also demonstrates that when patients recall unpleasant or stressful events they have experienced, they hyperventilate (Nixon & Freeman, 1988).

It cannot be coincidence that HV symptoms are indistinguishable from many psychiatric, psychosomatic, and stress disorders (Lowry, 1967). Only the physiology of graded hypoxia with chronic lacticacidemia accounts for this observation. That is why I have focused much of my clinical and research efforts over the past ten years on developing breathing-assessment techniques and protocols and therapeutic strategies based in large part on the numerous published reports of (1) the crucial effect of respiration on brain function, (2) breathing-related symptoms in stress and anxiety, and (3) the reportedly successful treatment of these conditions with strategies centering on breathing.

Assessment: The Psychophysiological Respiration Profile

The Psychophysiological Respiration Profile (PRP) was updated from an earlier HV profile (Fried, Fox, Carlton, & Rubin, 1984). The PRP and $PETCO_2$ biofeedback methods (Fried, Rubin, Carlton, & Fox, 1984) were tested on clients of the Stress and Biofeedback Clinic of the Institute for Rational Emotive Therapy (IRET) in New York. They were from all walks of life, though predominantly professionals who ranged in age between 19 and 81 years. About two thirds were women. With few exceptions, they reported various combinations of the symptoms common to those of the HV syndrome:

- Tension—a "feeling of tension"; muscle ache;
- Irritability; low frustration tolerance;
- Anxiety—apprehension, heightened vigilance;
- Dyspnea—inability to catch one's breath; choking sensation; feeling of suffocation; frequent sighing; chest heaving; lump in throat;
- Fatigue, tiredness, burnout;
- Insomnia;
- Heart palpitations—pounding in chest, seemingly accelerated pulse rate; heaviness on the chest—like a weight; diffuse chest pain;
- Depression, restlessness, nervousness;
- Dizzy spells, shakiness, trembling;
- Coldness of the hands and feet and, occasionally, tingling sensations;
- Inability to concentrate;
- Bloating;
- Others.

In most cases, they reported symptoms of allergies, anemia, angina, arthritis, asthma, cardiac arrhythmia, colitis, constipation, diabetes, gastritis, headache/migraine, heart disease, hypertension, irritable bowel, musculoskeletal and temporomandibular trauma and pain, Raynaud's disease, seizures (idiopathic and organic), joint pain, bruxism, and many more. The procedures were also applied to those with psychological disorders, including anxiety, panic, simple phobia and agoraphobia, depression, and obsessive compulsive disorder.

Method

Percentage of Alveolar CO₂ (PETCO₂). End-tidal breath is sampled by nasal catheter (⅛ × 1/32 in., 6 in. long) inserted about ¼ in. into a nostril and taped to the upper lip. The proximal segment is connected to a fitting in the tubing that leads to the capnometer. The client is protected from infection with precut Latex sterile surgical tubing used for the nasal segment and immediately discarded after use.

An Ohmeda OxiCap 4700 is coupled to a computer (PC-compatible, VGA monitor, Epson LQ 850 printer) with a J & J Instruments I-330 Physiological Monitoring Systems isolation amplifier (ISA).[1] Screen duration is 30 sec.

Arterial Blood Oxyhemoglobin Saturation (Sao₂). The oximeter (sensor over the left index finger) is coupled to a J & J ISA. The readout is whole-integer percentage, but the analog output is to 0.1%.

Chest vs. Abdominal Mode and Breathing Pattern. A pneumograph module (J & J) renders trace analogs of the magnitude of the displacement of the chest and abdomen derived from Velcro-fastened strain gauges.

Pulse Rate and Respiratory Sinus Arrhythmia (RSA). The J & J plethysmograph (sensor over the right index finger) renders interbeat rate variation over time, indicating RSA over the breathing cycle (Angelone & Coulter, 1964; Davies & Neilson, 1967; Fried, 1987; Melcher, 1976; Porges, McCabe, & Yongue, 1982).

Hand and Head-Apex Temperature. Two J & J thermal units are used: One sensor taped to the little finger of the nondominant hand (for norms, see Blanchard, Morrill, Wittrock, Scharff, & Jaccard, 1989) and another attached to the scalp apex record "local" temperature (Tachibana, Kuramoto, Inanaga, & Ikemi, 1967). I take scalp-apex temperature to reflect blood flow through the brain below because there are no vasoconstrictor reflexes in the scalp and forehead circulation (Fox, Goldsmith, & Kidd, 1962; Hertzman & Roth, 1942; Royer, 1965). Since sympathetic arousal cannot cause scalp vasoconstriction, which would lower its temperature, parasympathetic inhibition cannot reverse it.

---

[1]For information about the J & J I-330 Physiological Monitoring System or the Ohmeda OxiCap 4700 CO₂ monitor, please write the author at 1040 Park Avenue, New York, NY 10028.

Blood Pressure (BP).   BP decreases with deep-diaphragmatic breathing (Fried, 1987), but is seldom included unless hypertension is a treatment consideration.

Muscle Tension (EMG).   Electromyography (EMG) may be used to monitor muscle tension in the upper chest during diaphragmatic breathing training to assess the extent of ancillary breathing muscle involvement. Figure 2 illustrates this application: EMG and P_{ETCO_2} are slightly out of phase because EMG is instantaneous, while there is a delay of about 1.0 sec in the CO_2 trace. Electrodes were placed at the right and left upper pectorals (pectoralis major), just below the collar bone (clavicula).

The Profile.   The PRP (Fig. 3A) is obtained on the first visit, before training begins:

- Breathing
- Rate (BR)
- Mode (chest vs. abdomen)
- Pattern or rhythm (inspiration/expiration ratio)
- End-tidal CO_2 (P_{ETCO_2})

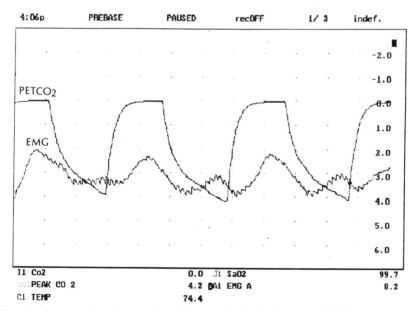

Figure 2. Correspondence between breathing, as reflected by P_{ETCO_2}, and EMG changes with upper thoracic (pectoralis) movement.

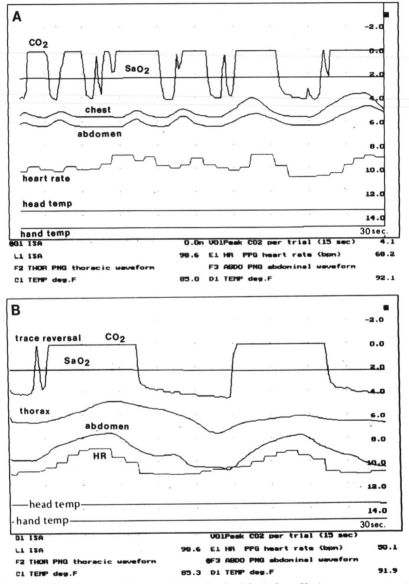

Figure 3. (A) A 30-sec multiparametric psychophysiological profile in a person at rest, showing $P_{ET}CO_2$, Sao_2, thoracic and abdominal pneumographs, pulse rate, and head and hand temperature. (B) Profile in the same person during deep-diaphragmatic breathing training.

- Arterial blood O_2 saturation (SaO_2)
- Heart
- Pulse rate (PR)
- Interbeat interval distribution—RSA
- Circulation
- Hand temperature (HT) and scalp-apex temperature (ST)

A second PRP (Fig. 3B) is obtained during or after training.

Figure 4A is a modified PRP preceding breathing training in a 32-year-old woman reporting stress: BR is 18 breaths/min; $PETCO_2$, 4.3% (33 torr); SaO_2, 97.9%; PR, 68; HT, 79.5°F; ST, 92.8°F (76°F is room temperature). Figure 4B shows the PRP during breathing training. At first, BR is rapid (tachypnea). The PCO_2 and HT are low; ST is normal—showing peripheral vasoconstriction. PR is low—she is a runner. After 10 min of deep-diaphragmatic breathing training, the breathing rate drops to 6 breaths/min. But respiration has not adjusted yet, and though breathing is "deeper," there is still chest movement and loss of CO_2 continues: $PETCO_2$ is 3.7%, or about 28 torr. HT and ST drop somewhat with lower PCO_2, and SaO_2 rises about 1% with increased alkalosis, so training is discontinued

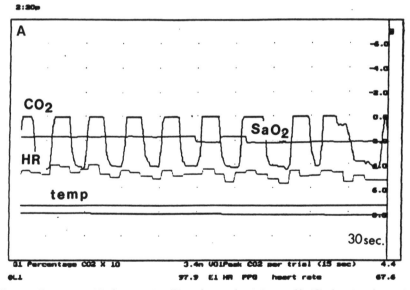

Figure 4. Pretraining (A), first training (B), and second training profile (C), showing change in $PETCO_2$, SaO_2, HR, and head and hand temperature. The breathing rate drops from 18 (A) to 3 breaths/min (C).

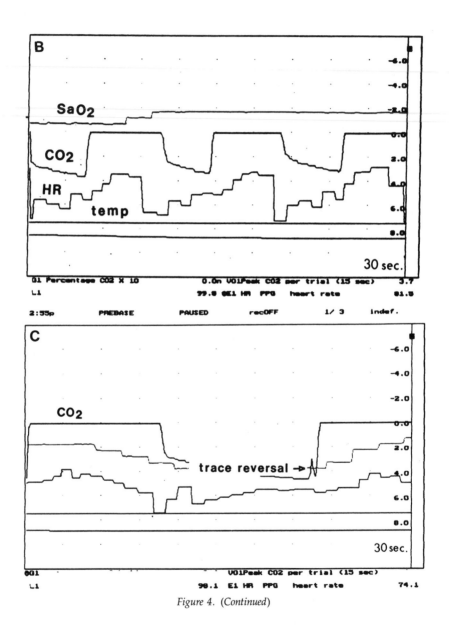

Figure 4. (*Continued*)

until P_{CO_2} stabilizes at the higher value. Then it is reinstituted. Breathing training procedures are detailed in Fried (1990, 1993). A reversal at the beginning of the P_{CO_2} trace, as exemplified in Figure 3B, shows diaphragmatic fatigue and usually disappears as the trainee becomes accustomed to sustained deep-diaphragmatic breathing.

The P_{ETCO_2} tracing itself may also indicate momentary anxiety: Figure 5 shows the P_{ETCO_2} tracing, during deep-diaphragmatic breathing, of a 47-year-old man imagining the object of his phobia. Or P_{ETCO_2} may reflect deep-diaphragmatic breathing: Figure 6 shows a CO_2 tracing (capnogram) with *cardiac oscillation* during expiration. This pattern is produced when the abdomen pushes the diaphragm up and the heart against the lungs. As the heart beats against the lungs, it expels a small amount of air. Each oscillation therefore reflects a heartbeat.

Typical Findings

Combining elements of the PRP helps to assess patterns of treatment-related changes:

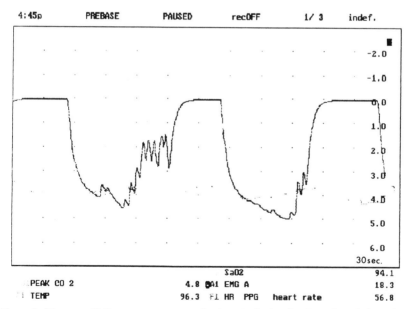

Figure 5. Hyperventilation consequent on the imaginal visualization of a phobia object during counterarousal self-regulation by deep-diaphragmatic breathing.

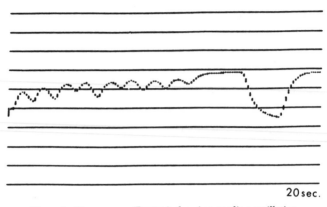

Figure 6. Capnogram (PETCO$_2$) showing cardiac oscillation.

- Breathing rate (BR) drops, and PCO$_2$ may rise, at first; when training stabilizes (in 5–10 training sessions), BR may be between 3 and 5 breaths/min (often below 3 b/min).
- Tidal volume (V_t) monitoring is too invasive for the typical clinical application, but the Radford monograph gives an accurate estimate based on BR and weight.
- Breathing mode becomes predominantly abdominal and rhythmic, with inspiration/expiration ratio = 1.00; upper thoracic EMG attenuates.
- SaO$_2$ normalizes between 95% and 98%, though it may increase, despite PCO$_2$ increase, during the inspiration phase of diaphragmatic breathing due to increased perfusion with increased intrapulmonary air pressure (it does not reflect left-shifted ODC, since there is no alkalosis).
- Hand (HT) and head temperature (ST) both rise, in many cases to within 0.5°F of the pretraining values.
- Pulse rate (PR) typically drops, except that it rises slightly where there is bradycardia (50 beats/min or less).
- Respiratory sinus arrhythmia (RSA), typically absent before training, may become pronounced—up to 10 beats or more over the breathing cycle.
- Blood pressure (BP) may rise slightly at first, if diastolic BP drops. After a few sessions, systolic BP also drops if diastolic BP remains down.

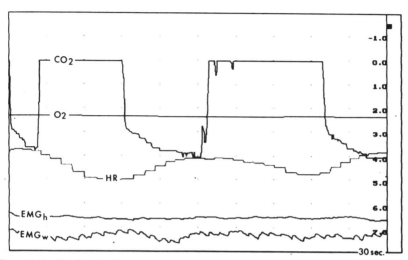

Figure 7. Profile showing P_{ETCO_2}, Sa_{O_2}, pulse rate, and frontalis (h) and wrist-to-wrist (w) EMG. Note that at the same filter values, EMG_w has a greater cardiac component than EMG_h.

- Frontalis, wrist-to-wrist, and other EMG measures attenuate [Fig. 7 shows a modified PRP with EMG_h (frontalis) and EMG_w (wrist-to-wrist)].
- The EEG may show elevation of the *theta* band before training: During training, *theta* will drop, as *alpha* frequency becomes more coherent at a lower frequency in the band and increases in amplitude (such changes may be accompanied by reported experience of "thoughtless consciousness," i.e., *samadhi*, an "altered state of consciousness").

Sample Clinical Case Profiles

Case 1. Comparison of a modified PRP (30-sec screen duration) in a 31-year-old woman with exercise-induced asthma, on the 5th training session, before (Fig. 8A) and after 4 min of breathing training (Fig. 8B). Breathing normalizes at 4 breaths/min. The P_{CO_2} and Sa_{O_2} both rise. PR drops.

Case 2. EEG power spectrum before and during breathing training in a 42-year-old woman with severe stress, fatigue, depression, and pulmon-

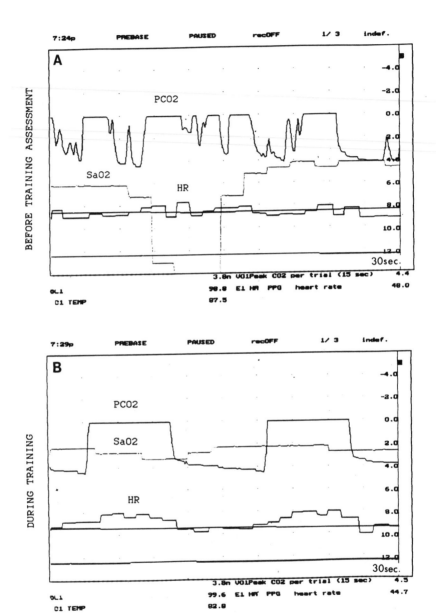

Figure 8. Pretraining (A) and posttraining (B) profiles. Sao₂ rises and a distinct ECG/RSA emerges as breathing slows and normalizes.

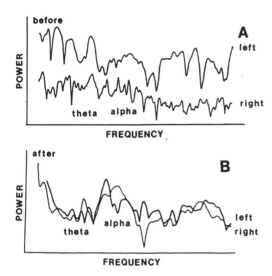

Figure 9. Pretraining (A) and posttraining (B) right- and left-hemisphere EEG power spectra. *Theta* is prominent in the right and left pretraining EEG, with left-hemisphere dominance. *Theta* attenuates, *alpha* increases, right and left, and hemispheric dominance disappears during deep-diaphragmatic breathing training.

ary ventilatory deficiency ($PETCO_2 = 5.9$). Before training (Fig. 9A), the left-side voltage was elevated over the right, and both right and left showed *theta* elevation with no coherent *alpha*. During training (Fig. 9B), voltage equalized, right and left, and average *theta* decreased, with coherent *alpha* on both sides, though more prominently on the right.

The effect of breathing on the EEG is rapid and profound: HV causes cerebral arterial vasoconstriction and impairs brain blood flow and metabolism. Lennox, Gibbs, and Gibbs (1938) reported a near-linear relationship between brain blood CO_2 content and EEG fundamental frequency; i.e., low CO_2 correlates with low frequency. Subsequently, Kety and Schmidt (1948) showed that a decrease in CO_2 level, from normal (38 torr, or 5.00%) to 30 torr (3.95%), results in a 20% decrease in cerebral blood flow. Also, Engel, Ferris, and Logan (1947) plotted the effect of sustained HV on EEG fundamental frequency and subjective measures of awareness (see Fig. 10).

Case 3.   This 47-year-old professional woman reported stress, anxiety, and chest symptoms that were vague (and that she had been told were "functional"). Figure 11A shows poor ventilation ($PETCO_2$ ranged between 5.1 and 5.9), a slow BR, and a strange pulse interbeat interval pattern. She was referred for a clinical ECG, and it showed ventricular premature contractions (VPCs) (see Fig. 11B). After about 10 min of breathing training,

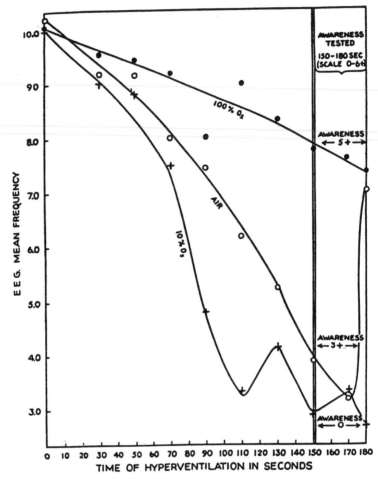

Figure 10. Effect of sustained HV on EEG fundamental frequency and subjective level of consciousness. From Engel *et al.* (1947).

BR dropped to 1½ beats/min, and P_{ETCO_2} normalized at 4.7. There was also a significantly reduced incidence of VPCs (Fig. 11C).

Case 4. This 29-year-old professional man reported work-related stress, fatigue, anxiety, mild depression, and mild allergies. Medical and social history held nothing of significance. Breathing training showed a paradoxical increase in P_{ETCO_2} to 5.9, with Sa_{O_2} slightly below normal, at 94.1% (see Fig. 12A). Uneven expiration suggested asthma, a fact that he had failed to reveal—his allergies were acting up. Deep-diaphragmatic breathing improved his ventilation: PETCO$_2$ dropped to 5.2, SaO$_2$ rose to 95.4%, and he reported feeing better (see Fig. 12B). Here is a case in which organic conditions, asthma and allergies, underlie the stress.

Case 5. This 42-year-old woman reported stress and moderate hypertension, 146/94 mm Hg, nothing else of note in her medical history, and no psychological disorders. At the initial profile (see Fig. 13A), BR was elevated (22/min), PETCO$_2$ was depressed at 4.10, SaO$_2$ was normal (97.4), and PR (52/min) was low—typical in a runner, though there was no RSA. After several rounds of breathing training (3 breaths/round) over a 22-min period, BR dropped to a little over 2/min, PETCO$_2$ rose to 4.5, SaO$_2$ to 98.5, PR to 63, and her BP was 153/90 (Fig. 13B).

Case 6. This 39-year-old man suffered an industrial accident resulting in severe back injury (L. sacrospinalis) that causes him to suffer constant pain. Although EMG biofeedback to reduce the differential tension was helpful (see Fig. 14A), he did not achieve a significant reduction of the pain until the following procedure was initiated: After several sessions of deep-diaphragmatic breathing training, when he attained a

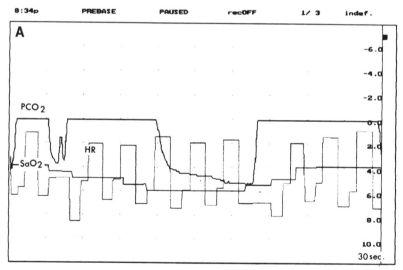

Figure 11. (A) Pretraining profile with cardiac interbeat interval pattern showing VPCs; (B) clinical ECG tracing of the VPCs; (C) disappearance of VPCs with deep-diaphragmatic breathing.

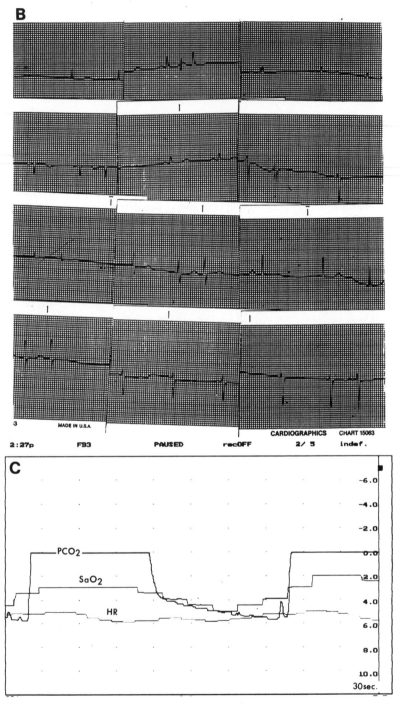

B

2:27p   F93   PAUSED   recOFF   2/ 5   indef.

C

Figure 11. (Continued)

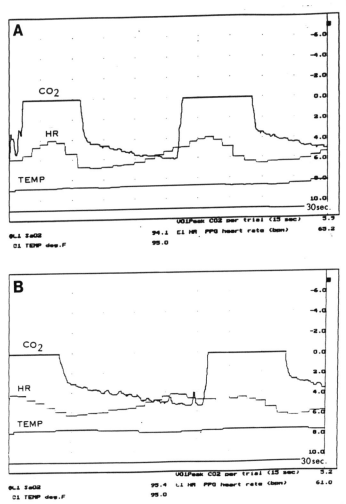

Figure 12. Pretraining (A) and posttraining (B) profiles. Typically, $P_{ET}CO_2$ rises with slower breathing; the decrease from 5.9 to 5.2 is not paradoxical, but is common in poor lung ventilation.

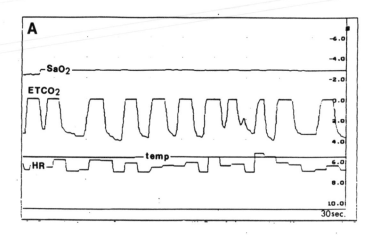

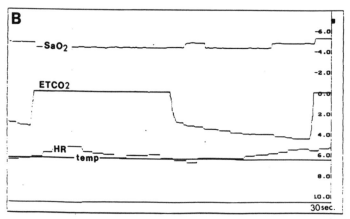

Figure 13. Pretraining (A) and posttraining (B) profiles. Breathing drops from 22 to 2+ beats/min, with RSA, as BP drops in this hypertensive woman.

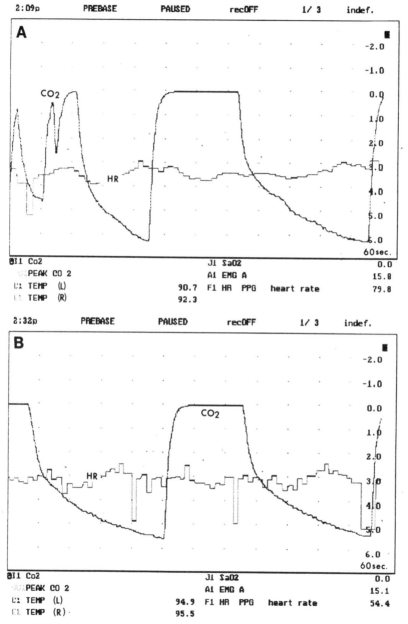

Figure 14. Pretraining (A) and posttraining (B) profiles showing change in local temperature in injured (left) and intact (right) sacrospinalis muscle, using breathing and local-warming imagery.

1½–2 beats/min rate, thermistors were taped to the corresponding right and left side, over the sacrospinalis, and he was instructed as follows:

> Imagine yourself, in your mind's eye, to be in your back. Look at the injured muscles. See them twisted and taut. Can you see it? Good. Feel the energy in your breath as you breathe in and allow it to splash all over the injured muscles. See the muscles relax. Can you feel them warming? Good. And let the tension in your muscles flow out with your breath as you exhale.

After several breaths, he reported that he felt his back warming and that the muscles seemed to loosen up. The profile corroborated the subjective report (see Fig. 14B): The injured left side rose from 90.7° to 94.9°F and the noninjured right side from 92.3° to 95.5°F. The EMG, parenthetically, dropped only slightly. Thus, the rise in local temperature seemed to be a greater determinant of pain reduction than the change in EMG, which was negligible. It is interesting to note that there was about a 1.5°F difference in the temperature of the muscles before training began.

Summary

All psychophysiological modalities are influenced by the momentary availability of O_2, dissipation of CO_2, and the resultant acid–base balance of the cellular and extracellular milieu. Vascular caliber and blood flow to the body tissues and the brain, neuronal excitability, and muscle tone are dependent, on a breath-by-breath basis, on the mechanics and physiology of breathing behavior.

Physiological monitoring of common modalities, such as temperature, ECG, EMG, and EEG, reveals patterns in psychological, psychophysiological, and stress-related disorders that strongly suggest an underlying tissue O_2 deficit, i.e., graded hypoxia. Successful biofeedback and self-regulation treatment strategies suggest a correction of that deficit, based on the hypothetical mechanisms currently thought to underlie the processes in these modalities.

References

Angelone, A., & Coulter, N. A. (1964). Respiratory sinus arrhythmia: A frequency dependent phenomenon. *Journal of Applied Physiology, 3*, 479–482.

Blanchard, E. B., Morill, B., Wittrock, D. A., Scharff, L., & Jaccard, J. (1989). Hand temperature norms for headache, hypertension, and irritable bowel syndrome. *Biofeedback & Self-Regulation, 14*, 319–331.

Blass, J. P., & Gibson, G. E. (1979). Consequences of mild, graded hypoxia. In S. Fahn and Hasselbach, K. A. (Eds.), *Advances in neurology*. New York: Raven Press.

Bohr, C., Hasselbach, K. A., & & Krogh, A. (1904). Ueber einen in biologischer Beziehung wichtigen Einfluss, den die Kohlensaurespannung des Blutes auf dessen Sauerstoffbindung übt. *Scandinavian Archives of Physiology, 16,* 402–412.

Cohen, R. D., & Woods, H. F. (1976). *Clinical and biochemical aspects of lactic acidosis.* Oxford: Blackwell.

Comroe, J. H. (1974). *Physiology of respiration.* 2nd ed. Chicago: Yearbook Medical Publications.

Darrow, C. W., & Graf, C. C. (1945). Relation of electroencephalogram to photometrically observed vasomotor changes in the brain. *Journal of Neurophysiology, 8,* 449–461.

Davies, C. T. M., & Neilson, J. M. M. (1967). Sinus arrhythmia in man at rest. *Journal of Applied Physiology, 22,* 947–955.

Edwards, R. H. T., & Clode, M. (1970). The effect of hyperventilation on lacticacidemia of muscular exercise. *Clinical Science, 38,* 269–276.

Engel, G. L., Ferris, E. G., & Logan, M. (1947). Hyperventilation: Analysis of clinical symptomatology. *Annals of Internal Medicine, 27,* 683–704.

Fox, R. H., Goldsmith, R., & Kidd, D. J. (1962). Cutaneous vasomotor control in the human head, neck and upper chest. *Journal of Physiology, 161,* 298–312.

Fried, R. (1987). *The hyperventilation syndrome—Research and clinical treatment.* Baltimore: Johns Hopkins University Press.

Fried, R. (1990). *The breath connection.* New York: Insight/Plenum Press.

Fried, R. (1993). *The psychology and physiology of breathing in behavioral medicine, clinical psychology, and psychiatry.* New York: Plenum Press.

Fried, R., Fox, M. C., Carlton, R. M., & Rubin, S. R. (1984). Method and protocols for assessing hyperventilation and its treatment. *Journal of Drug Research and Therapy, 9,* 280–288.

Fried, R., Rubin, S. R., Carlton, R. M., & Fox, M. C. (1984). Behavioral control of intractable idiopathic seizures: I. Self-regulation of end-tidal carbon dioxide. *Psychosomatic Medicine 46,* 315–332.

Fried, R., Fox, M. C., & Carlton, R. M. (1990). Effect of diaphragmatic respiration with end-tidal CO_2 biofeedback on respiration, EEG, and seizure frequency in idiopathic epilepsy. *Annals of the New York Academy of Sciences, 602,* 67–96.

Gamble, J. L. (1982). *Acid–base physiology.* Baltimore: Johns Hopkins University Press.

Gantt, W. H. (1970). *Pavlovian approaches to psychopathology.* New York: Pergamon Press.

Grossman, P. (1983). Respiration, stress, and cardiovascular function. *Psychophysiology, 20,* 284–300.

Hardonk, H. J., & Beumer, H. M. (1979). Hyperventilation syndrome. In *Handbook of clinical neurology,* Vol. 38. Amsterdam: North Holland.

Hertzman, A. B., & Roth, L. W. (1942). The absence of vasoconstrictor reflexes in the forehead circulation: Effect of cold. *American Journal of Physiology, 136,* 692–697.

Hirsch, J. A., & Bishop, B. (1981). Respiratory sinus arrhythmia in humans: How breathing patterns modulate heart rate. *American Journal of Physiology, 241,* 179–180.

Huckabee, W. E. (1961). Abnormal resting blood lactate. *American Journal of Medicine, 30,* 833–840.

Katz, I. R. (1982). Is there a hypoxic affective syndrome? *Psychosomatics, 23,* 846–853.

Kerr, W. J., Dalton, J. W., & Gliebe, P. A. (1937). Some physical phenomena associated with anxiety states and their relationship to hyperventilation. *Annals of Internal Medicine, 11,* 961–992.

Kety, S. S., & Schmidt, C. F. (1948). The effects of altered arterial tensions of carbon dioxide and oxygen on cerebral blood flow and cerebral oxygen consumption in normal young men. *Journal of Clinical Investigation, 27,* 484–492.

Kreisberg, R. A. (1980). Lactate homeostasis and lactic acidosis. *Annals of Internal Medicine,* *92,* 227.

Lennox, W. G., Gibbs, F. A., & Gibbs, E. L. (1938). The relationship in man of cerebral activity to blood flow and blood constituents. *Journal of Neurological Psychiatry, 1,* 221–225.

Lowry, T. P. (1967). *Hyperventilation and hysteria.* Springfield, IL: Charles C. Thomas.

Melcher, A. (1976). Respiratory sinus arrhythmia in man. *Acta Physiologica Scandinavica,* Suppl., *435,* 7–31.

Nixon, P. G. F., & Freeman, L. J. (1988). The "think test": A further technique to elicit hyperventilation. *Journal of the Royal Society of Medicine, 81,* 277–279.

Park, R., & Arief, A. I. (1980). Lactic acidosis. *Advances in Internal Medicine, 25,* 33.

Penfield, W., & Jasper, H. (1954). *Epilepsy and the functional anatomy of the brain.* Boston: Little Brown.

Porges, S. W., McCabe, P. M., & Yongue, B. G. (1982). Respiratory heart-rate interactions: Psychophysiology—implications for pathophysiology and behavior. In J. T. Cacioppo & R. E. Petty (Eds.), *Perspectives in cardiovascular psychophysiology.* New York: Guilford Press.

Radford, E. P., Jr. (1955). *Journal of Applied Physiology, 7,* 451.

Royer, F. L. (1965). Cutaneous vasomotor components of the orienting reflex. *Behavior Research & Therapy, 3,* 161–170.

Selye, H. (1974). *Stress without distress.* Philadelphia: Lippincott.

Shapiro, B. A., Harrison, R. A., & Walton, J. R. (1982). *Clinical application of blood gases.* Chicago: Yearbook Medical Publications.

Tachibana, S., Kuramoto, S., Inanaga, K., & Ikemi, Y. (1967). Local cerebrovascular response in man. *Confina Neurologica, 29,* 289–298.

Yu, P. N., & Yim, B. J. (1958). Electrocardiographic changes in hyperventilation syndrome: Possible mechanisms and clinical applications. *Transactions of the American Association of Physicians, 71,* 129–141.

Yu, P. N., Yim, B. J., & Stansfield, C. A. (1959). Hyperventilation syndrome. *Archives of Internal Medicine, 103,* 902–913.

CHAPTER **11**

Breathing
Physiological Reasons for Loss of Self-Control

P. G. F. Nixon

Survival and health depend on the ability of the organism to maintain its internal environment in an orderly, stable, and controlled condition. This axiom (Dubos, 1980) is the basis of the author's approach to the failures of homoeostatic regulation of the breathing that are called "hyperventilation"; he does not include the overbreathing that is secondary to organic conditions such as pulmonary embolism or metabolic disorders (e.g., aspirin intoxication). Respiratory disregulation does not appear on its own, but as one element of the multiple systems disturbances that occur in people who are stretched beyond the boundaries of their physiological tolerance by effort and distress. The loss of order and stability and control of the internal milieu is the result of inability to deal successfully with environmental stressors and adapt to change. In civilian life, these challenges to human performance may be so low in profile and so long drawn out as to be well-nigh invisible, but in wartime they are prominent, and excellent descriptions have been written (e.g., T. Lewis, Cotton, Barcroft, Milroy, Drifton, & Parsons, 1916; T. Lewis, 1918).

Human performance in the face of effort and distress depends chiefly on two factors: (1) the unconscious homoeostatic competence of the individual and (2) cognitive responses to the challenges of the external environment. Those with high and enduring performance are regarded as

P. G. F. NIXON • 43 Weymouth Street, London WIN3LD, England.

Clinical Applied Psychophysiology, edited by John G. Carlson, A. Ronald Seifert, and Niels Birbaumer. Plenum Press, New York, 1994.

"hardy" (Kobasa, Maddi, & Kahn, 1982) or "coherent" (Antonovski, 1985). Those who fall easily into loss of performance and health are vulnerable, often through poverty and deprivation in childhood (e.g., Barker, 1991).

The chief enemy of order and stability is arousal. At one end of its spectrum, arousal can provide for wakefulness, vigilance, and well-fitting responses to environmental challenges. At higher levels, beyond the physiological tolerance of the individual, it can produce homeostatic degradation, catabolic disorders, and acceleration of entropy. It is unfortunate that arousal cannot be measured as an entity, but we can be thankful that Frankenhaeuser (1989) and Henry (1982) are helping us to picture the relationships between the various emotions involved and their neuroendocrine expression.

The relationships between performance and arousal have long been acknowledged, but not previously employed in health care as a model for diagnosis, management, prevention, and rehabilitation (Nixon, 1989). The performance–arousal curve appears to be a much more useful model for solving the riddles of failure of respiratory self-control than a binary or reductionist approach.

Such a curve is illustrated in Fig. 1. Healthy function of the internal milieu is one of the rewards for living on the upslope in a well-balanced fashion. The hardy have high curves. The vulnerable have low curves and

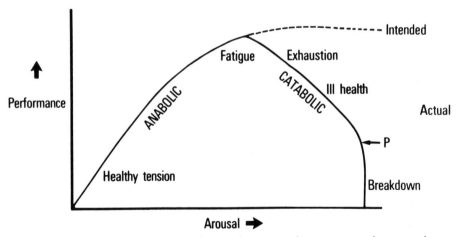

Figure 1. Human function curve. This diagram depicts a performance–arousal curve used as a model for a systems or biopsychosocial approach to clinical problems (e.g., the hyperventilation-related disorders). (P) Point of instability, at which little extra arousal is required to produce the catastrophe of breakdown.

"go over the top" into downslope incompetence at lower levels of stimulation and effort.

The top of this curve is not drawn with the traditional plateau because most patients can see a watershed in an event, a change of relationship, a loss or trauma that took them from order to disorder. Alexithymics have difficulties in perceiving this watershed, and carry on struggling until their freedom is interrupted by one or more of the somatic downslope disorders. Their being unaware of movement beyond the boundaries of physiological tolerance makes it difficult for them to learn how to maintain order and stability, and many cardiovascular patients are drawn from their ranks (King, 1991).

In this context, "fatigue" refers to a healthy condition of tiredness readily relieved by rest and sleep, while "exhaustion" refers to a self-defeating, morbid condition in which vicious cycles are set up, for example, by hyperventilation and anxiety, and the sleep loss they cause. These vicious cycles can carry the individual downward as he struggles furiously but fruitlessly to close the gap between his diminishing performance and health and the higher level of performance he believes to be intended of him. It is useful to regard the gap as the breeding ground of hyperventilation.

The principal feature of life on the downslope is that the struggle to improve performance causes it to deteriorate, and this deterioration generates further arousal. It is for this reason that a struggle to improve and control breathing behavior is defeated under tuition when pupil and therapist try too hard. Downslope life is accompanied in its earlier or lighter phases by hypersensitivity to stimulation and increased reactivity, a phenomenon probably responsible for "neurasthenia" and other pejorative labels. In the later and deeper phases, there is a depression of sensitivity and responsivity. These two phases correspond with and are probably caused by the biphasic neuronal responses to hypocapnia (Lum, 1981). The earlier phase generates anxiety and stimulates the breathing, and its adrenergic effect increases the breathing response to any given level of carbon dioxide in the blood (Schaefer, 1958). It is probable that hyperventilation-related cardiac disorders are generated in the first phase and the fatigue syndromes in the second.

Downslope life is impaired by a variety of physiological and behavioral alterations collectively called the "downslope disorders" (see Table 1). The inappropriate breathing or hyperventilation is both the marker of a downslope position and the trigger of other disorders. For example, the chronic loss of carbonic acid by expiration is balanced by the increased secretion of alkalis into the urine. When severe, the depletion of the alkaline reserves in the muscles, for example, causes fatigue and loss of the

Table 1. Downslope Disorders

Functions impaired on the downslope[a]	
Performance	Emotionalism
Information processing	Behavior
Adaptation	Social support
Habituation	Internal milieu:
Alexithymia	Neuroendocrine
Respiration	Immune
Sleep	Sex steroid
	K, Mg
AUTONOMY	

[a]The factors listed are those that impair human performance when arousal extends beyond physiological tolerance and carries the individual onto the downslope of his or her performance–arousal curve. K and Mg refer to the excessive loss of potassium and magnesium ions. AUTONOMY denotes the quality lost when freedom is removed by illness or surrendered to control and surveillance by medical authorities.

capacity for physical effort through diminution of the anaerobic threshold (effort syndrome). Common symptoms are fatigue and aching limbs, the major elements of many chronic fatigue syndromes. The unbuffered acid is carried centrally and stimulates further overbreathing, another self-injurious respiratory vicious cycle.

In highly aroused subjects, there is diuresis of magnesium ions (Seelig, 1989). This loss of "nature's own calcium blocker" reduces opposition to the rise of intracellular calcium ionization that is induced by the respiratory alkalosis of hyperventilation and thereby promotes vasoconstriction. The intracranial vessels are highly sensitive to this type of vasoconstriction, and cerebral ischaemia might be one reason the hyperventilator is unaware of his disorder and often aggressively opposed to the very notion that his illness can be related to overbreathing (B. I. Lewis, 1959; King, Rosen, & Nixon, 1990). The effects of this ischemia can be aggravated by the Bohr effect, namely, the reduced release of oxygen from the blood in respiratory alkalosis.

The catabolic shifts that take place in high-arousal states and increase with the loosening of homoeostatic and cognitive controls in exhaustion (Sterling & Eyer, 1988) add to the burdens of effort and distress and, consequently, encourage further hyperventilation. By producing arousal-induced disorders of self-regulation, such as hypertension and hypercholesterolemia, these shifts can divert diagnostic and therapeutic attention away from the prime mover, which might be the vicious cycle of hyperventilation's amplifying arousal and arousal's increasing the over-breathing (see Table 2).

Sleep provides the opportunity for anabolism, a powerful promoter of order and stability in the internal systems. Unfortunately, its value is reduced by chronic hyperventilation. The chronic depletion of the alkaline buffering systems that is produced by prolonged excessive loss of carbonic acid causes the pH regulation to be sensitive to small changes of breathing behavior. When the breathing is reduced during the first 2 or 3 hr of sleep, an acidosis develops. At a critical point, this reduction triggers an over-breathing response and wakens the subject with hypocapnia (Ley, 1988). The consequences can include anxiety, panic, sleepwalking, nausea, muscular pains or cramps, and cardiac pain or arrhythmia or both. These symptoms are commonly attributed to depressive illness, but the nocturnal awakening from depression occurs later in the night. The sleep disturbance due to hyperventilation-induced pH instability aggravates the exhaustion and the catabolic disorders and provides one more reason for failure of self-control of breathing. The daytime counterpart of the sleep disorder is an urge to activity that defeats attempts to rest in even the most exhausted of hyperventilators.

Table 2. Metabolic Shifts Found in High-Arousal Conditions[a]

Catabolic hormones increased	Anabolic hormones decreased
Cortisol (glucocorticoids)	Insulin
Epinephrine	Calcitonin
Norepinephrine	Testosterone
Glucagon	Estrogen
Growth hormone	Prolactin
Antidiuretic hormone (vasopressin)	Luteinizing hormone
Renin	Follicle-stimulating hormone
Angiotensin	Gonadotropin-releasing hormone (GnRH)
Aldosterone (mineralocorticoids)	Prolactin-releasing hormone (PRH)
Erythropoietin	Atriopeptin
Thyroxine	Thymosins
Parathormone	Lymphokines
Melatonin	Cytokines
Thyroid-releasing hormone (TRH)	
Adrenocorticotropic hormone (ACTH)	
Opiates	
Enkephalin	
Dynorphin	
Endorphin	

[a]Based on Sterling and Eyer (1988).

Diagnosis and Clinical Testing

The most important step is to think of loss of control of breathing behavior in subjects who present failure to make and to sustain effort as they ought and get worse when they try harder. Features of the downslope position will be present, as well as a variety of symptoms from the list of B. I. Lewis (1959) (see Table 3). The respiration is likely to be unobtrusive, but increase of rate, upper chest movement, and sighing, particularly when emotionally charged subjects are discussed, provides clues for the observant.

Until the late 1980s, many clinicians relied on a forced hyperventilation provocation test to elicit the symptoms of the patient's complaint. This test fails more often than it succeeds because the important determinants of symptomatology, namely, arousal and chronicity (buffer base depletion), are not replicable. On the other hand, the discussion of an emotionally charged topic or personally relevant stressor might trigger a bout of severe and prolonged hypocapnia (B. I. Lewis, 1954, 1959; Nixon & Freeman, 1988). It is not suggested that the population can be divided into

Table 3. Common Presenting Symptoms in Hyperventilation-Related Illness[a]

1. Neurological
  A. Central
    Disturbances of consciousness—
    faintness, dizziness, unsteadiness,
    impairment of concentration and
    memory, feelings of unreality,
    "losing mind," complete loss of
    consciousness (infrequent)
  B. Peripheral
    Paraesthesias—numbness, tingling
    and coldness of fingers, face, and
    feet
2. Musculoskeletal
  Diffuse and/or localized myalgia and
  arthralgia, tremors and coarse twitching
  movements, carpopedal spasm and
  generalized tetany (infrequent)
3. Respiratory
  Cough, chronic throat "tickle,"
  shortness of breath, atypical "asthma,"
  tightness in or about the chest, sighing
  respiration, excessive yawning
	4. Cardiovascaular
	  Palpitations, "skipped beats,"
	  tachycardia, atypical chest pains—
	  sharp precordial twinges, dull
	  precordial or lower costal ache—
	  variable features of vasomotor
	  instability
	5. Gastrointestinal
	  Oral dryness, globus, dysphagia, left
	  upper quadrant or epigastric distress,
	  aerophagia, belching, bloating, and
	  flatulence
	6. Psychic
	  Variable anxiety, tension, and
	  apprehension, inappropriate pseudo-
	  calmness (hysterical subjects)
	7. General
	  Easy fatigability, generalized weakness,
	  irritability and chronic exhaustion,
	  frightening dreams, sleep disturbances

[a]Based on B. I. Lewis (1959).

hyperventilators and nonhyperventilators, but that the reduction of self-control of breathing in patients with hyperventilation-related illness permits them to breathe more deeply and to go on longer than others in response to imagery.

Physiological Testing

For physiological testing, the author uses a clinical capnograph, an instrument that continuously records the partial pressure of the carbon dioxide in the exhaled air drawn through a fine plastic tube held by a light headband in one nostril (Nixon & Freeman, 1988). It can be used to seek evidence of loss of homoeostatic self-correction, loss of cognitive self-control, vulnerability to the imagery of personally relevant stressors, and depletion of alkaline buffering systems. These features can be seen in the capnograms presented below.

Capnogram 1.   Capnogram 1 (Fig. 2) is taken from a 30-year-old man informed 10 days earlier that he had aortic incompetence (AI) and needed open-heart surgery. He is extremely anxious but shows no signs of hyperventilation. The upper level, the end-expiratory level known as the P_{ETCO_2}, is normal and stable in the control period and not altered by a minute of reading aloud. The 3-min forced hyperventilation test is followed by a return to the same level as in the control period. This level is maintained during the imagery of his predicament. [Note that alexithymics are expected to be unresponsive to imagery (King, 1991).]

Capnogram 2.   Capnogram 2 (Fig. 3) is a tracing from a middle-aged businessman with an alcohol problem. The upper-level (P_{ETCO_2}) is not constant, but falls from 38 to 30 mm Hg during the control period and

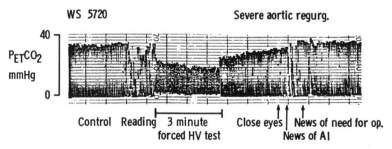

Figure 2. Capnogram 1.

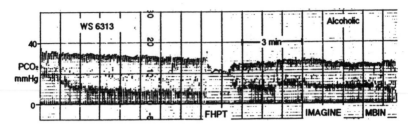

Figure 3. Capnogram 2.

remains at 26 mm Hg for 2 min after the 1-min forced hyperventilation provocation test (FHPT). These two features indicate failure of homeostatic self-regulation. During the imagery of a personally relevant stressor, his P_{ETCO_2} falls again, indicating vulnerability. At MBIN (his statement "My breathing is normal"), he is convinced that his breathing is normal but the P_{ETCO_2} is now extremely low, 25 mm Hg, revealing gross error of perception.

Capnogram 3.   Capnogram 3 (Fig. 4) is from a middle-aged man with pseudoangina due to hyperventilation. Before pedaling on a lightly loaded bicycle ergometer, the P_{ETCO_2} falls from 34 to 26 mm Hg from failure of homoeostatic self-regulation. Cycling brings him to his anaerobic threshold at 5 min (a), and the P_{ETCO_2} starts to fall. The legs ache at (a). At (b) he has chest pain, and at (c) he is compelled to stop by feelings of exhaustion.

Conclusions

The reductionist approaches of conventional medicine to hyperventilation have yielded little of value for everyday diagnosis and manage-

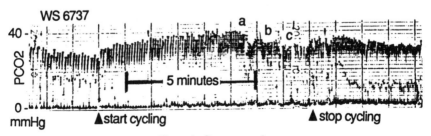

Figure 4. Capnogram 3.

ment, probably because this inappropriate breathing behavior does not stand as an entity. A systems approach, using a modified performance–arousal curve as a model, enables hyperventilation to be seen as a marker of loss of order and stability of the internal systems through failure of homoeostatic and cognitive control—when individuals are thrust beyond the boundaries of physiological tolerance onto the downslope of their performance–arousal curves. After this point the overbreathing is accompanied by other downslope disorders, a shift from anabolic to catabolic metabolism, and a startling diversity of somatic symptoms of the internal disarray. The hyperventilation is not only a marker of position but also an author of further deterioration.

There are five major reasons for loss of self-regulation of the breathing. The first is the excessive loss of carbonic acid (CO_2 + HO_2) from the system. The body responds by dumping alkalis, magnesium, and potassium into the urine. In severe and prolonged cases, the consequence is depletion of the body's alkaline buffering systems and gross reduction of the anaerobic threshold. The skeletal muscles weaken and ache, and the unbuffered lactic acid reaches the brain, where it increases the respiratory overdrive. The difficulty of making and sustaining effort also increases the arousal level, which in turn further simulates the breathing. In buffer depletion, the pH regulation becomes sensitive to variations of breathing and effort. The most common clinical footprints of this condition, apart from the growing difficulty of making effort, are wakening with hypocapnic symptoms 2–3 hr after falling asleep, inability to relax the muscles or the breathing, and difficulties of standing still in a line after hurrying to the queue.

The second reason is that the breathing-control system is but one facet of the whole body's failure of homoeostatic control in the exhaustion and disarray of the downslope.

The third reason is the failure of cognitive self-correction: The individual cannot correct his hypercapnia if he is unaware of it. This lack of perception may reflect cerebral ischemia caused by hypocapnic vasoconstriction and hypoxia caused by the Bohr effect.

The fourth reason is the vulnerability of some individuals to hyperventilation when they encounter or imagine personally relevant stressors. The hypocapnia can be severe and prolonged, and remain uncorrected by homoeostatic and cognitive mechanisms.

A fifth reason is vulnerability to the vicious cycles of arousal and hyperventilation. Arousal stimulates the breathing, which in turn amplifies the arousal. A point is reached at which the individual becomes hypersensitive and hyperreactive to stimuli and produces somatic symptoms. These increase the anxious arousal and thereby aggravate the hyperventilation.

It would be a naïve therapist who took the simplistic view that hyperventilation is an entity requiring no more than a breathing drill for its correction. Much more is required (King, 1988). The subject is easily exhausted and in homoeostatic disarray. The problems of adapting and coping with the psychosocial environment require help. The recovery of an anabolic upslope position is essential. Adequate sleep and the ability to modulate arousal must be achieved. It is axiomatic that too hard a struggle to succeed guarantees failure of recovery.

Finally, it is helpful to the therapist to think of uncoupling the breathing from its liaison with arousal and recoupling it to the body's needs for making and sustaining effort.

Summary

Hyperventilation is considered to be a part of human failure to maintain an orderly and stable internal milieu in the face of adversity. This chapter describes its associated disorders and the physiological reasons for failure of self-regulation, together with therapeutic implications.

References

Antonovski, A. (1985). *Health, stress and coping.* San Francisco: Jossey-Bass.

Barker, A. (1991). *The childhood environment and adult disease.* Chichester: John Wiley.

Dubos, R. (1980). *Man adapting.* New Haven: Yale University Press.

Frankenhaeuser, M. (1989). A biopsychosocial approach to work life issues. *International Journal of Health Services, 19,* 747–758.

Henry, J. P. (1982). The relation of social to biological processes in disease. *Social Sciences Medicine, 16,* 369–380.

King, J. C. (1988). Hyperventilation—A therapist's point of view. *Journal of the Royal Society of Medicine, 81,* 532–536.

King, J. C. (1991). *Sympathetic and hypocapnic pathways between the brain and the heart: Implications for healthcare.* Master's thesis. University of Surrey (Roehampton Institute).

King, J. C., Rosen, S. D., & Nixon, P. G. F. (1990). Failure of perception of hypocapnia: Physiological and clinical implications. *Journal of the Royal Society of Medicine, 83,* 765–767.

Kobasa, S. C., Maddi, S. R., & Kahn, S. (1982). Hardiness and health: A prospective study. *Journal of Personality and Social Psychology, 42,* 168–177.

Lewis, B. I. (1954). Chronic hyperventilation syndrome. *Journal of the American Medical Association, 155,* 1204–1209.

Lewis, B. I. (1959). Hyperventilation syndrome: A clinical and physiological evaluation. *California Medicine, 91,* 121–126.

Lewis, T. (1918). *The soldier's heart and the effort syndrome.* London: Shaw & Sons.

Lewis, T., Cotton, C. A., Barcroft, J., Milroy, T. R., Drifton, D., & Parsons, T. R. (1916).

Breathlessness in soldiers suffering from irritable heart. *British Medical Journal, 2*, 517–519.

Ley, R. (1988). Chronic hyperventilation and panic attacks during sleep. C. Von Euler & Katz-Salomon (Eds.), *Respiratory psychophysiology*. London: Macmillan Press.

Lum, L. C. (1981). Hyperventilation and anxiety state. *Journal of the Royal Society of Medicine, 74*, 1–4.

Nixon, P. G. F. (1989). Human functions and the heart. In D. Seedhouse & A. Cribb (Eds.), *Changing ideas in health care*. Chichester: John Wiley.

Nixon, P. F. G., & Freeman, L. F. (1988). The "think test"—A further technique to elicit hyperventilation. *Journal of the Royal Society of Medicine, 81*, 277–279.

Schaefer, K. E. (1958). Respiratory pattern and respiratory response to CO_2. *Journal of Applied Physiology, 13*, 1–14.

Seelig, S. (1989). Cardiovascular consequences of magnesium deficiency and loss: Pathogenesis and manifestations—Magnesium and chloride loss in refractory potassium repletion. *American Journal of Cardiology, 63*, 4G–12G.

Sterling, P., & Eyer, J. (1988). Allostasis: A new paradigm to explain arousal pathology. In S. Fisher & J. Reason (Eds.), *Handbook of life stress, cognition and health*. Chichester: John Wiley.

PART **V**

Neuromuscular Disorders

The two chapters in this neuromuscular section apply clinical psycho-physiology to two quite distinct categories of disorders. Chapter 12, by Herta Flor and Niels Birbaumer, looks at chronic back and temporoman-dibular pain from the standpoint of assessment and treatment. By contrast, Chapter 13, by Edward Taub, examines the problem of "learned nonuse" of a limb from the perspective of the development of the disorder and rehabilitation in both monkeys and humans.

In their chapter, Flor and Birbaumer review a number of studies in their laboratory showing that maximum electromyographic (EMG) levels occur at the site of chronic pain (in the back or jaw). These and other studies support their "diathesis–stress" model of musculoskeletal pain. The authors also summarize three of their treatment studies in which the effectiveness of EMG feedback training was assessed relative to cognitive behavior therapy and standard medical treatment for pain. Their results generally support the use of biofeedback and even suggest some negative effects of combining biofeedback with cognitive treatment. The careful and systematic work by these researchers helps document the psycho-physiological nature of neuromuscular pain syndromes and the usefulness of applied psychophysiology with biofeedback in clinical interventions.

Taub's chapter provides a detailed review of work in his and others' laboratories relating to the problem of a failure of recovery from a loss of motor ability owing to a period of nonuse of a limb—learned nonuse. Taub reviews extensive research with monkeys deafferented to produce a loss of motor ability in one arm. His hypothesis is that following deafferentation, the animals do not use the affected limb for a considerable period of time, and when initial attempts are made to use the limb, the animal fails and is punished; thereby it learns not to use it (learned nonuse). Taub's research shows that such techniques as (1) deafferentation of the other arm, (2) training (shaping) of the deafferented arm, and, most important, (3) restraint of the other (intact) limb will all lead to an increased ability to use the deafferented limb. Presumably, immobilizing the intact arm increases motivation for use of the deafferented arm. Outside the animal laboratory, in his own research with small groups of stroke victims, Taub has demonstrated considerable improvement in a group restrained from using their nonaffected arms. Taub's procedures present physical therapists and others in the field of rehabilitation with simple but elegant options for treating a wide variety of cases of impaired motor ability, including such problems as spinal cord injury, incontinence, nonuse of a prosthetic limb, and others.

CHAPTER **12**

Psychophysiological Methods in the Assessment and Treatment of Chronic Musculoskeletal Pain

Herta Flor and Niels Birbaumer

Theoretical Background

Psychophysiological assessments of chronic musculoskeletal pain—specifically chronic back pain—have become very popular over the last decade (cf. Cram, 1988; Dolce & Raczynski, 1985; Flor, Miltner, & Birbaumer, 1992b). Bilateral asymmetries, abnormal resting tension levels, abnormal movement patterns, and abnormal reactivity to stressors have all been targets of assessment. However, there have been few attempts to apply psychophysiological theories to the study of chronic musculoskeletal pain and to establish a program of research based on hypotheses regarding psychophysiological specificities that may contribute to the development or maintenance of chronic pain, or to both processes. Moreover, grave methodological problems [e.g., inadequate sample selection, inadequate recording sites, lack of stressor definition (for a review, see Flor & Turk, 1989)] have led to very inconsistent results in the published literature.

Two theoretical concepts are of value in the study of the psychophysiology of chronic musculoskeletal pain. First, the respondent condi-

HERTA FLOR • Institute of Medical Psychology and Behavioral Neurobiology, University of Tübingen, D-72074 Tübingen, Germany.   *NIELS BIRBAUMER* • Department of Clinical and Physiological Psychology, University of Tübingen, D-72074 Tübingen, Germany, and Department of General Psychology, Universitá degli Studi, I-35122 Padova, Italy.

Clinical Applied Psychophysiology, edited by John G. Carlson, A. Ronald Seifert, and Niels Birbaumer. Plenum Press, New York, 1994.

tioning of tension and pain has been postulated as a basic mechanism to account for the development of chronic musculoskeletal pain syndromes (cf. Flor, Birbaumer, & Turk, 1990; Gentry & Bernal, 1977; Linton, Melin, & Götestam, 1985). It is assumed that pain leads to reflex muscle spasm and sympathetic activation that may become conditioned to innocuous stimuli present in the pain-eliciting situation. Over time—provided the increases in muscle tension are frequent and of sufficient magnitude and duration— these physiological processes may eventually lead to persistent pain and suffering. This newly acquired pain is often unrelated to the original source of pain, although patients may attribute it to the original pain- eliciting event.

Based on this model, it is important to demonstrate that (1) muscle tension levels can be classically conditioned, (2) the muscle tension levels attained induce pain, and (3) chronic pain patients overreact physio- logically to stimuli associated with the original pain episode.

A second important theoretical concept is that of response stereotypy and—in the case of a physical disorder—symptom specificity. The term "response specificity" was introduced by the Laceys (cf. Lacey & Lacey, 1958; Lacey, 1967) and refers to the observation that in addition to stimulus- specific responses, individuals display a stereotypical physiological reac- tion to a variety of stimuli—namely, a temporally consistent hierarchy of physiological responses. Malmo and his co-workers (e.g., Malmo, Sha- gass, & Davis, 1949) suggested that pain patients are prone to show maximum physiological reactivity—so-called "symptom specificity"—in the muscular system and that this overutilization might induce musculo- skeletal pain syndromes. This concept was extended by Sternbach (1966), who noted that the prolonged return to baseline levels following the response to a stressor might be more indicative of physiological dysregula- tion than the amplitude of the response. Thus, the demonstration of a musculoskeletal response specificity (increased response amplitude or duration or both) would be of considerable value in understanding the pathophysiology of chronic musculoskeletal pain.

We have included these concepts in a diathesis–stress model of chronic musculoskeletal pain (cf. Flor et al., 1990). Specifically, we pro- posed that once a diathesis to respond with a specific body site and system has been established, e.g., through learning, trauma, or genetic differ- ences, frequent and intense life stress that is not adequately coped with may lead to a hyperreactivity of a specific muscle group to stress (see Fig. 1). Over time, this overutilization of a muscle group may lead to pain that may later be maintained by additional instrumental learning as described by Fordyce (1976).

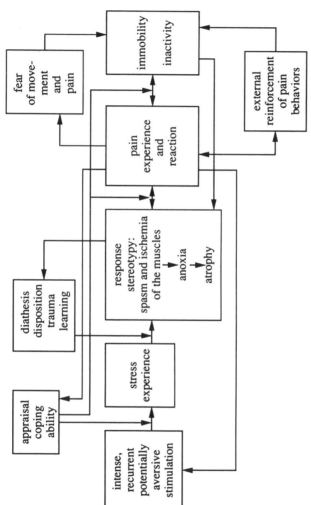

Figure 1. Diathesis–stress model of chronic musculoskeletal pain.

Response Specificity in Chronic Musculoskeletal Pain

In a series of studies (Flor, 1991; Flor, Birbaumer, & Turk, 1987; Flor, Birbaumer, Schugens, & Lutzenberger, 1992a; Flor, Birbaumer, Schulte, & Roos, 1991a; Flor, Turk, & Birbaumer, 1985), we examined the diathesis–stress model in patients with chronic back pain (CBP), patients with heterogeneous types of pain [general pain group (GP)], and patients with chronic temporomandibular pain and dysfunction (TMPD), using adequate methodology. Study 1 included 17 CBP patients, 17 patients who suffered from a diverse array of chronic but not musculoskeletal pain syndromes, and 17 healthy controls (HC). Mental math, recitation of the alphabet, and discussion of stress and pain episodes were used as stressful and neutral situations. Electromyography (EMG) was recorded from the lower and upper back and from the frontalis muscle. Heart rate and skin conductance were utilized as general measures of arousal. The data from this study showed that (1) CBP patients displayed a maximum response in the back musculature, whereas frontalis, heart rate, and skin conductance responses did not differ from those of the HC or the GP group (see Fig. 2); (2) the CBP patients also showed a prolonged return to baseline levels in the back musculature; and (3) they responded in a manner different from the HC group and the GP group only in the personally relevant (discussion of life events), but not during the general stress situation (mental math) or while reciting the alphabet (neutral control). Depression, as well as cognitive and affective pain components, explained most of the variance in physiological reactivity.

In a second study, we set out to replicate these findings using patients with TMPD (cf. Flor *et al.*, 1991a). Again, a maximum response at the site of pain (here the masseter muscles) was obtained. There were no differences between patients with muscular or articular dysfunctions. In order to assess the extent to which this response was site-specific or generalized, a third study included both TMPD and CBP patients and used imagery of personally relevant stressful and neutral events in order to reduce talking-related artifacts (Flor *et al.*, 1992a). The results of the previous studies were virtually replicated. Again, we found a maximum EMG response of the back pain patients in the back musculature as compared to the masseter and biceps muscles that served as controls. In addition, we observed that the TMPD patients were maximally responsive in the masseter muscle. However, using imagery, the response was much more pronounced on the left than on the right side of the body. We also replicated the prolonged return to baseline data for the lower back. (This was not possible at the masseter because the subjects were engaged in reports of the image

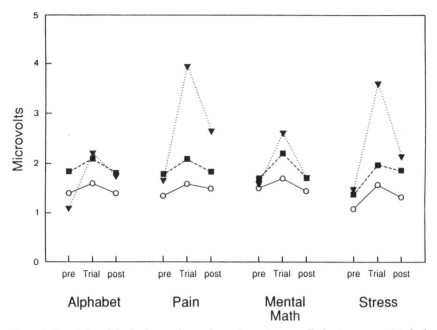

Figure 2. Reactivity of the back muscles to the various stressors. Each stressor consisted of 1 min prebaseline, 1 min discussion, and 1 min postbaseline. Healthy controls, ———; chronic back pain group, ⋯⋯; general pain group, – – – –.

content after the imagery.) Skin conductance levels and the EMG at the nonaffected muscles behaved identically in all three groups.

Using imagery, we obtained a different heart rate response pattern. Whereas the healthy controls displayed their maximum response in heart rate, the back pain patients had only a nonsignificant heart rate change. Lacey and Lacey (1958) have interpreted heart rate acceleration as some type of perceptual defense, and deceleration as increased attending to the environment. The observed dissociation of heart rate and EMG in the patients might also be interpreted as reflecting active coping, the lack of heart rate reactivity as passive coping sensu Obrist (1976). The significant negative correlation ($r = -0.38$) between heart rate reactivity and helplessness toward the pain might reflect this circumstance. Arntz, Merckelbach, Peters, and Schmidt (1991) also observed lower heart rate reactivity in CBP patients during a cold-pressor test and put forth a similar interpretation.

In order to obtain a comparable scale of the physiological measures across all subjects, we standardized the stressor-related responses of all

Z–Score

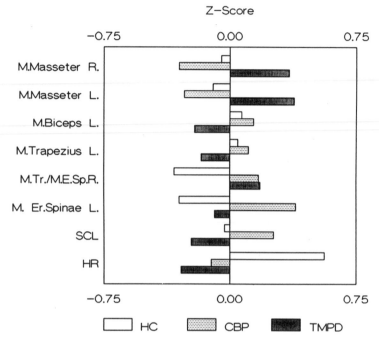

Figure 3. Standardized z-scores for the psychophysiological reactivity (stress phase minus baseline). (HC) Healthy controls; (CBP) chronic back pain group; (TMPD) temporomandibular pain and dysfunction group; (M) musculus; (SCL) skin conductance level; (HR) heart rate; (L) left; (R) right; Tr = trapezius; M.E.Sp. = muscular erector spinae; Er = erector spinae.

groups by using z-scores. This display (see Fig. 3) shows that the healthy controls are maximally responsive in their heart rate, whereas the CBP patients and the TMPD patients responded most with their affected muscles. These data clearly support the muscular response stereotypy notion of our diathesis–stress formulation.

In addition to these reactivity measures, we assessed how well the patients were able to discriminate and control the muscle-tension levels they produced. Lack of discrimination, and hence lack of control of muscle tension, might explain why these patients maintain their elevated muscle-tension levels over prolonged periods of time. In order to assess discrimination, we presented the subjects—again 20 CBP, 20 TMPD, and 20 HC— with bars of varying height on a video monitor (cf. Flor, Schugens, & Birbaumer, 1992c). Subjects were instructed to tense their back or their jaw musculature to the degree that matched the height of the bar presented to them. Analysis of these data revealed that all three groups of subjects were able to achieve comparable muscle-tension levels overall. Neither the mean nor the maximum values differed, thus making a pain-related inability of the patients to tense their muscles highly unlikely. Both the average correlation coefficients and the slopes of the EMG–subjective rating relationship were significantly lower in the pain patients as compared to the healthy controls. This was true for both the masseter and the back muscles (see Fig. 4).

Thus, these patients do not have a localized deficit in tension discrimination that might be explained by changes in proprioception at the site of pain; rather, they display a generalized central proprioceptive defect. We are currently investigating whether this lack of discrimination is restricted to the somatosensory system or whether it extends to other modalities (e.g., the auditory).

Finally, we have begun a program of research to determine the extent to which classically conditioned EMG responses may contribute to the development and maintenance of chronic musculoskeletal pain syndromes. So far, we have found that EMG responses of the forearm musculature may be quite easily conditioned to neutral tones (cf, Fig. 5), as well as to slides of human faces, and that the conditioned responses are of substantial magnitude. Moreover, we have noted generalized increases in muscle tension over the course of an experimental session (Flor, Fürst, Hermann, Schugens, Lutzenberger, & Birbaumer, 1991b).

However, we also found very large individual differences in the condi-

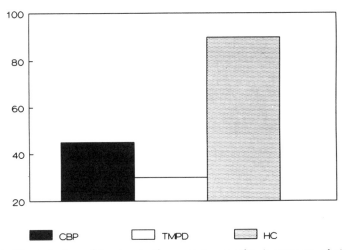

Figure 4. Discrimination of tension in the masseter muscles (percentage of significant correlations). (CBP) Chronic back pain group; (TMPD) temporomandibular pain and dysfunction group; (HC) healthy controls.

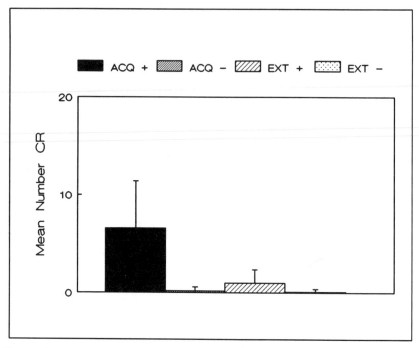

Figure 5. Mean number of conditioned responses (CRs) to the neutral tone stimulus. CRs are defined as deviations from the baseline that exceed 3 standard deviations. (ACQ+) Acquisition for CS+; (ACQ−) acquisition for CS−; (EXT+) extinction for CS+; (EXT−) extinction for CS−.

tionability of the EMG and sizable differences in the amount of generalization to unrelated muscles such as the trapezius. We are currently studying this phenomenon with analog pain patients (students who suffer from episodic pain) and also plan to investigate these differences in clinical samples.

Behavioral Treatment of Chronic Musculoskeletal Pain

Based on these psychophysiological findings, a reduction of EMG reactivity and an improvement of the perception of muscle tension would seem to constitute specific treatments for chronic musculoskeletal pain syndromes—pain syndromes that have traditionally been resistant to medical interventions. A treatment method that ideally meets these goals is EMG biofeedback. In three successive studies, we assessed the efficacy of EMG biofeedback for chronic back pain and chronic temporomandibular pain and dysfunction. Study 1 compared EMG biofeedback to a pseudotherapy (playback of the stored feedback from another patient) and a medically treated control group. Auditory, criterion-oriented biofeedback was provided from the site of pain, complemented by perception and tension-reduction exercises. The training lasted for 12 sessions and was provided on an inpatient basis. Follow-up data were collected 4 months and 2 years posttreatment.

This study showed that EMG biofeedback is very effective in reducing pain in CBP patients (see Fig. 6). Its effects clearly exceed those of the placebo treatment. In addition, significant changes were observed in pain-related cognitions, EMG levels, and use of the health care system (Flor, Haag, Turk, & Köhler, 1983). These positive results were maintained at the 2-year follow-up (Flor, Haag, & Turk, 1986).

Study 2 examined both CBP and TMPD patients and compared biofeedback (BFB) to cognitive–behavior therapy (CBT) and traditional medical treatment (MED). CBT was chosen as a control because it also includes a relaxation and stress-management component and has yielded positive results with chronic pain patients. The protocol followed the

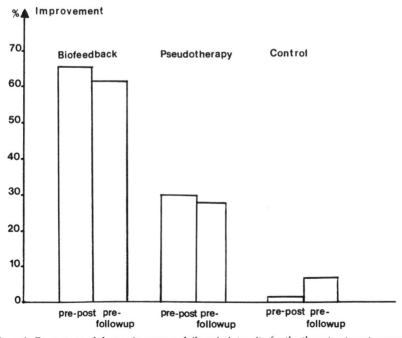

Figure 6. Percentage of change in average daily pain intensity for the three treatment groups.

suggestions by Turk, Meichenbaum, and Genest (1983) and Holzman, Turk, and Kerns (1986). Both treatments consisted of eight 60-minute individual therapy sessions. The biofeedback was structured as in study 1. In addition, stress phases during which patients were required to reduce tension levels while assuming a stressful body position or while imaging a stressful life event were interspersed with feedback-free phases. Tension-perception and relaxation exercises performed at home complemented the program.

Assessment of treatment-related changes was undertaken on the medical–somatic, the psychophysiological, the behavioral, and the verbal–subjective level (cf. Birbaumer, 1984). In addition, process-oriented measures and credibility ratings for the treatments were obtained.

This study again yielded a superior effect of the EMG biofeedback treatment compared to both the cognitive–behavioral and the medical treatments (Flor & Birbaumer, 1991; Flor & Birbaumer, 1993). These positive effects were most marked on the verbal–subjective levels. Pain severity and interference related to the pain [as measured with the MPI (Kerns, Turk, & Rudy, 1985)] were reduced by 40–60% in the BFB group only, whereas the CBT and the MED group exhibited marginal changes in these variables. Cognitive and affective variables such as life control and affective distress were also most significantly improved in the BFB group. These changes were maintained at the 15-month follow-up (see Fig. 7). Although

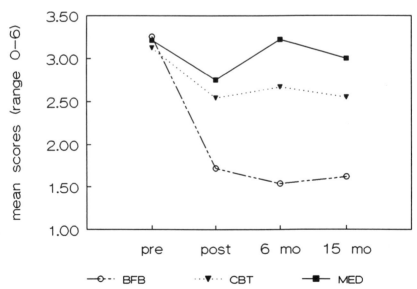

Figure 7. Treatment-related changes in pain severity (MPI). (BFB) Biofeedback; (CBT) cognitive behavior therapy; (MED) medical treatment; (mo) months.

these patients displayed a few pain behaviors, they were typical doctor shoppers overutilizing the health care system. The number of doctor visits was reduced in all treated groups, but this reduction was significant only in the BFB group. EMG baseline levels were unchanged compared to pretreatment; stress reactivity was most reduced in the BFB group, with the reduction becoming marginally significant at the follow-up. The success of the BFB treatment group was highly related to initial stress-related reactivity ($r = -0.55$, $p < 0.01$) and to the amount of practice the patients undertook during the course of the treatment ($r = 0.54$, $p < 0.01$), whereas the success of CBT was predicted by cognitive variables such as catastrophizing ($r = -0.45$, $p < 0.01$). There was no specific predictor for the success of the medical treatment; however, chronicity was a significant negative predictor for all therapies. In contrast to most of the studies reviewed by Turk and Rudy (1990), this study did not use treatment-specific exclusion criteria; moreover, the results of the patients who dropped out of treatment were considered in the analysis.

We suspected that the lack of success of the CBP treatment might have been related to the inadequate duration of the treatment. In addition, we thought that a combination of EMG biofeedback and CBT might yield even better results and that it might also be more cost-effective than CBT by itself. We therefore conducted a third study in which four 30-min sessions of EMG–BFB combined with eight 60-min sessions of group CBT were compared with ten 60-min sessions of group CBT. A third group received an equal amount of conservative medical treatment. The assessment instruments were identical and the patient sample comprised 90 patients.

The still preliminary results of this study suggest that the combination of BFB and CBT is less effective than each treatment delivered separately. Compared to the previous studies, the results are also positive for the psychological treatments—but more modest: The BFB–CBT combination and the extended CBT both yielded greater reduction in pain severity than the MED group, but less than the BFB treatment in studies 1 and 2.

Interference underwent a far greater change in the CBT group than in the BFB and MED groups. Both life control and affective distress changed most markedly in the CBT group, but at follow-up, both psychologically treated groups were more changed than the MED group in life control, and only the BFB group maintained its change in affective distress.

If the results of study 2 and study 3 are compared, it becomes quite clear that the BFB treatment by itself leads to the most significant improvements in all subjective variables. The combination of BFB with CBT lowers the efficacy of BFB. BFB used by itself is an easily understood and easily learned procedure that yields immediate reinforcement, whereas the CBT approach is more difficult for the patients to follow and probably needs extended treatment times. This assumption is supported if one compares the results of the 8-session individual treatment from study 2 with the extended 12-session group CBT of study 3. The change obtained through the CBT is consistently higher in study 2 compared to study 3. In both studies, the conservatively treated groups did not make any significant treatment gains (see Fig. 8).

Conclusions

The results of these studies suggest that chronic musculoskeletal pain syndromes such as chronic back pain (CBP) and temporomandibular pain and dysfunction (TMPD) are truly psychophysiological disorders. It has been shown that both CBP and TMPD patients respond with muscular hyperreactivity to stress and possess deficits in self-perception and self-regulatory abilities. Treatments such as EMG biofeedback that are geared toward the removal of these deficits may thus be most effective. Psychophysiological assessments that are based on a sound theoretical rationale are useful tools in selecting patients for psychophysiological treatments and are themselves valuable predictors of treatment outcome.

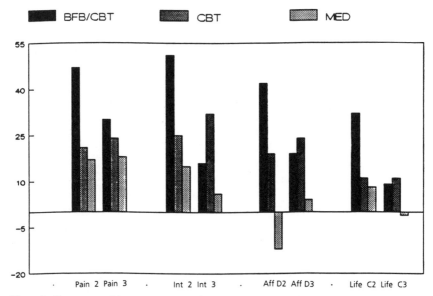

Figure 8. Percentage of improvement on the MPI Scales in study 2 and study 3. (BFB/CBT) Biofeedback treatment in study 2, combined biofeedback and cognitive behavior therapy in study 3; (CBT) cognitive behavior therapy (eight sessions in study 2, ten sessions in study 3); (MED) medical treatment; (Pain) MPI pain intensity; (Int) interference; (AffD) affective distress; (Life C) life control.

ACKNOWLEDGMENTS. This study was supported by the DFG Fl 156/1-6, 8-1) and the Bundesministerium für Forschung und Technologie (Grant 0701503).

References

Arntz, A., Merckelbach, H., Peters, M. C., & Schmidt, A. J. M. (1991). Chronic low back pain, response specificity and habituation to painful stimuli. *Journal of Psychophysiology, 5,* 177–188.

Birbaumer, N. (1984). Psychologische Analyse und Behandlung von Schmerzzuständen [Psychological analysis and treatment of pain]. In M. Zimmermann & H. O. Handwerker (Eds.), *Schmerz, Konzepte und ärztliches Handeln [Pain concepts and clinical treatment],* (1st ed.) (pp. 114–153). Heidelberg: Springer.

Cram, J. R. (1988). Surface EMG recordings and pain-related disorders: A diagnostic framework. *Biofeedback & Self-Regulation, 13,* 123–138.

Dolce, J. J., & Raczynski, J. M. (1985). Neuromuscular activity and electromyography in painful backs: Psychological and biomechanical models in assessment and treatment. *Psychological Bulletin, 97,* 502–520.

Flor, H. (1991). *Psychobiologie des Schmerzes [Psychobiology of pain].* Bern: Huber Verlag.

Flor, H., & Birbaumer, N. (1991). Comprehensive assessment and treatment of chronic back pain patients without physical disabilities. In M. R. Bond, J. E. Carlton, & C. J. Woolf (Eds.), *Proceedings of the VIth World Congress on Pain* (pp. 229–234). Amsterdam: Elsevier.

Flor, H., & Birbaumer, N. (1993). Verhaltensmedizinische Grundlagen [Principles of behavioral medicine]. In M. Zenz & I. Jurna (Eds.), *Lehrbuch der Schmerztherapie [Handbook of Pain Treatment]* (pp. 95–106). Stuttgart: Wissenschaftliche Verlagsgesellschaft.

Flor, H., & Turk, D. C. (1989). Psychophysiology of chronic pain: Do chronic pain patients exhibit symptom-specific psychophysiological responses? *Psychological Bulletin, 105,* 215–259.

Flor, H., Haag, G., Turk, D. C., Köhler, H. (1983). Efficacy of EMG-biofeedback, pseudotherapy, and conventional medical treatment for chronic rheumatic back pain. *Pain, 17,* 21–31.

Flor, H., Turk, D. C., & Birbaumer, N. (1985). Assessment of stress-related psychophysiological reactions in chronic back pain patients. *Journal of Consulting and Clinical Psychology, 53,* 354–364.

Flor, H., Haag, G., & Turk, D. C. (1986). Long-term efficacy of EMG-biofeedback for chronic rheumatic back pain. *Pain, 27,* 195–202.

Flor, H., Birbaumer, N., & Turk, D. C. (1987). Ein Diathese–Stress-Modell chronischer Rückenschmerzen: Empirische Überprüfung und therapeutische Implikationen [A diathesis–stress model of chronic back pain: Empirical evaluation and therapeutic implications]. In W. D. Gerber, W. Miltner, K. Mayer (Eds.), *Verhaltensmedizin: Ergebnisse und Perspektiven empirischer Forschung [Behavioral medicine: Results and perspectives of empirical research]* (pp. 37–54). Weinheim: Edition Medizin.

Flor, H., Birbaumer, N., & Turk, D. C. (1990). The psychobiology of chronic pain. *Advances in Behaviour Research and Therapy, 12,* 47–84.

Flor, H., Birbaumer, N., Schulte, W., & Roos, R. (1991a). Stress-related EMG responses in patients with chronic temporomandibular pain. *Pain, 46,* 145–152.

Flor, H., Fürst, M., Hermann, C., Schugens, M. M., Lutzenberger, W., & Birbaumer, N. (1991b). Central and peripheral components of classically conditioned responses. *Psychophysiology, 28,* S22.

Flor, H., Birbaumer, N., Schugens, M. M., & Lutzenberger, W. (1992a). Symptom-specific responding in chronic pain patients and healthy controls. *Psychophysiology, 29*, 452–460.

Flor, H., Miltner, W., & Birbaumer, N. (1992b). Psychophysiological recording methods. In D. C. Turk & R. Melzack (Eds.), *Handbook of pain assessment*. New York: Guilford.

Flor, H., Schugens, M. M., & Birbaumer, N. (1992c). Discrimination of EMG-levels in chronic pain patients and healthy controls. *Biofeedback and Self-Regulation, 17*, 165–177.

Fordyce, W. E. (1976). *Behavioral methods in chronic pain and illness*. St. Louis: Mosby.

Gentry, W. D., & Bernal, G. A. A. (1977). Chronic pain. In R. Williams & W. D. Gentry (Eds.), *Behavioral approaches to medical treatment* (pp. 173–182). Cambridge, MA: Ballinger.

Holzman, A. D., Turk, D. C., & Kerns, R. D. (1986). The cognitive-behavioral approach to the management of chronic pain. In A. D. Holzman & D. C. Turk (Eds.), *Pain management* (pp. 31–50). New York: Pergamon Press.

Kerns, R. D., Turk, D. C., & Rudy, T. E. (1985). The West-Haven Multidimensional Pain Inventory (WHYMPI). *Pain, 23*, 345–356.

Lacey, J. I. (1967). Somatic response patterning and stress: Some revisions of activation theory. In M. H. Apley & R. Trumball (Eds.), *Psychological stress*. New York: Appleton-Century-Crofts.

Lacey, J. I., & Lacey, B. C. (1958). Verification and extension of the principle of autonomic response stereotypy. *American Journal of Psychology, 71*, 50–73.

Linton, S. J., Melin, L., & Götestam, K. G. (1985). Behavioral analysis of chronic pain and its management. *Progress in Behavior Modification*, Vol. 18. New York: Academic Press.

Malmo, R. B., Shagass, C., & Davis, F. H. (1949). Specificity of bodily reactions under stress. *Journal of the Association of Research in Nervous and Mental Disorders, 29*, 231–261.

Obrist, P. A. (1976). The cardiovascular–behavioral interaction—as it appears today. *Psychophysiology, 13*, 95–107.

Sternbach, R. A. (1966). *Principles of psychophysiology*. New York: Academic Press.

Turk, D. C., & Rudy, T. E. (1990). Neglected factors in chronic pain treatment outcome studies—referral patterns, failure to enter treatment, and attrition. *Pain, 43*, 7–26.

Turk, D. C., Meichenbaum, D. H., & Genest, M. (1983). *Pain and behavioral medicine: A cognitive–behavioral approach*. New York: Guilford.

CHAPTER 13

Overcoming Learned Nonuse
A New Approach to Treatment in Physical Medicine

Edward Taub

When an injury to the nervous system or other part of the body results in an initial loss of motor ability, the long-term result is generally considered to involve one of two possible outcomes: (1) The injury permanently destroyed an anatomical substrate or structure on which the lost movement was based; thus, motor function will never return. (2) The injured substrate will recover or heal, either entirely or in part, and motor function will then return to the maximum extent permitted by the underlying restitution of the anatomical substrate. The assumption that these are the two main possible outcomes is sufficiently strong that alternate outcomes are rarely considered. The purpose of this chapter is to suggest a third possibility related to the existence of a new mechanism, termed "learned nonuse." This mechanism is behavioral in nature. It is proposed here that the mechanism often prevents the return of motor function following a number of different types of injury to a level consistent with the recovery of the substrate, thereby making an initial motor deficit permanent. However, the mechanism can be overcome or reversed by behavioral means so that all or much of the lost capability can be reinstated.

The plan of this chapter is to first describe the learned nonuse mechanism and the techniques for overcoming it. They were unexpectedly

EDWARD TAUB • Department of Psychology, University of Alabama at Birmingham, Birmingham, AL 35294.

Clinical Applied Psychophysiology, edited by John G. Carlson, A. Ronald Seifert, and Niels Birbaumer. Plenum Press, New York, 1994.

discovered in the course of research on the effects of somatosensory deafferentation in monkeys. Next, there will be a description of the manner in which this work led to the development of a new approach to the rehabilitation of chronic motor deficit after stroke in humans. A clear symmetry was found between the results from the basic research laboratory following deafferentation in monkeys and the results from the clinic following stroke in humans, and it was also found that this symmetry could be used for therapeutic purposes. In the next section of the chapter, it will be suggested that the learned nonuse mechanism also operates to produce excess motor disability in a variety of other conditions, including neurological injury other than that produced by stroke, and possibly during periods of remission in arthritis and after fracture of the pelvis and fracture of other bones, especially in the elderly. If so, then the techniques developed for overcoming learned nonuse following deafferentation in monkeys and stroke in man might have general applicability to other situations in which the motor deficit appears to be in excess of that warranted by the organic condition. Finally, it will be suggested that overcoming learned nonuse is one of the major reasons that biofeedback is effective in many cases in which it results in functional improvement in physical medicine. Education or reeducation of muscles is important, but so is overcoming learned nonuse.

Somatosensory Deafferentation in Monkeys

Background

The spinal nerves emerge from the spinal cord in two roots. The dorsal root is sensory, and by severing all the dorsal roots that innervate a limb, one can eliminate all sensation from that limb capable of supporting ongoing sequences of behavior; however, the motor innervation through the ventral roots remains intact. The general problem originally addressed in a series of somatosensory deafferentation experiments with monkeys that I began with Harriet Knapp and A. J. Berman was whether or not somatosensory feedback and spinal reflexes are necessary for the performance of different categories of movement and for various types of learning.

The classic experiment in the area was carried out by Mott and Sherrington (1895), who deafferented a single upper extremity in a series of monkeys and found that the animals did not make use of it in the free situation. Mott and Sherrington recognized that severing dorsal roots abolishes spinal reflexes by interrupting their sensory component. On the basis of their data and this consideration, they concluded that spinal reflexes are necessary for the performance of purposive or (in their terms) voluntary movement, and further that they are the basic building blocks from which the behavior of organisms is constructed. This contention became the cornerstone of the Sherringtonian reflexological position. It was the dominant view in neurophysiology for approximately 70 years, and also strongly influenced some of the major learning theories of behavior that were the hallmark of behaviorism in the late 1920s and 1930s (for additional discussion of this topic, see Taub, 1977).

The basic observation that monkeys do not use a single deafferented upper extremity was replicated in a number of neurophysiologically oriented studies [Sherrington & Denny-Brown (cited in Sherrington, 1931); Lassek, 1953; Twitchell, 1954]. However, given the theoretically important nature of this finding, our laboratory decided to reevaluate it through the use of behavioral techniques; this had not yet been done in a consistent fashion.

We found, contrary to the accepted view, that there were a variety of techniques that could lead monkeys to exhibit purposive movement of the affected extremity following somatosensory deafferentation (summarized in Taub, 1977). These results indicated that chained stretch reflexes were not necessary for the learning and performance of most types of movement in monkeys.

Because of the basic orientation of the research, the main effort was directed at uncovering the nature of the mechanisms responsible for the phenomena we were observing. It did not become apparent for some time that some of our findings had potential therapeutic relevance for the human case.

Behavioral Methods for Overcoming Motor Deficit following Unilateral Forelimb Deafferentation in Monkeys

There are two general behavioral methods and one surgical method that can be used to induce a monkey to use a single deafferented forelimb. The first behavioral method involves preventing use of the intact limb by means of a restraining device that immobilizes the intact limb but leaves the deafferented extremity free. While in the restraining device, our animals were observed to use the deafferented limb extensively for postural support, ambulation, climbing, and even prehension (Knapp, Taub, & Berman, 1963). This finding was confirmed by Stein and Carpenter (1965). A similar observation had been made in the early part of the century by Munk (1909), but, perhaps because of the immense authority of Sherrington, it had been ignored and was consequently unknown in the 1960s. In our work, we found that when restraint was imposed for only 1 or 2 days, there was a striking immediate reversion to nonuse of the deafferented extremity as soon as the restraining device was removed. However, if the device was allowed to remain in place for a longer period, the ability to use the affected extremity transferred from the restraint condition to the life situation and became permanent (Taub, 1976, 1977, 1980). A useless limb was thereby converted into a limb capable of extensive movement. We have obtained a permanent motor improvement with a restraint period as brief as 3 days, but never shorter.

A second behavioral method for overcoming the inability to use a single deafferented limb is the application of techniques for training that limb. In our early work, we employed conditioned response techniques for enabling the animals to make a variety of movements, including phasic forelimb flexion (Knapp, Taub, & Berman, 1958, 1963; Taub & Berman, 1963, 1968; Taub, Bacon, & Berman, 1965), grasp (Taub, Ellman, & Berman, 1966), forelimb flexion on a fixed-ratio schedule of reinforcement (Taub, Williams, Barro, & Steiner, 1978), and sustained limb flexion and compensation for progressively increasing loads on the arm (Taub, 1976, 1977; Wylie & Tyner, 1981, 1989). However, transfer never occurred between the experimental and life situations (Taub, 1976, 1977). The movements that were trained in the conditioning chamber were never observed to be performed in the colony environment.

The situation was different when we used shaping techniques (Skinner, 1938). A shaping technique is a type of training method in which a desired motor or behavioral objective is approached in small steps, by "successive approximations." The amount of improvement required for successful performance at each step is always small. With shaping techniques, the animals not only learned to employ a single deafferented limb in the training situation but also its use transferred to the life situation. This result was in contrast to the case for conditioned response training. Shaping appeared to provide a bridge from the training situation, enabling extensive movement in the animals' normal environment.

The behaviors shaped included (1) reaching toward visual targets (Taub, Goldberg, & Taub, 1975a) and (2) prehension in juveniles deafferented on day of birth (Taub, Perrella, & Barro, 1973) and prenatally (Taub, Perrella, Miller, & Barro, 1975b), who had never exhibited any prehension previously. In both cases, shaping permitted an almost complete reversal of motor capacity, which progressed from total absence of the target behavior to very good (though not normal) performance.

Bilateral Forelimb Deafferentation

A third technique that leads to use of a deafferented forelimb in the free situation is, paradoxically, surgical deafferentation of the contralateral intact extremity (Knapp *et al.*, 1963; Taub & Berman, 1968). This observation has been confirmed by a number of investigators (Bossom, 1972; Bossom & Ommaya, 1968; Denny-Brown, 1966; Eidelberg & Davis, 1976; Gilman, Carr, & Hollenberg, 1976; Liu & Chambers, 1971; Wylie & Tyner, 1981, 1989). Thus, doubling the size of the lesion does not make the motor deficit greater, as might be expected, but rather enables the animal to make extensive use of a limb that was not previously employed at all in the free situation. This observation is of primary interest with respect to theoretical considerations concerning the Sherringtonian reflexological position (Taub & Berman, 1968; Taub, 1977). However, it is also relevant to the issues of interest in this chapter, in two ways: (1) The work uncovered the fact that spinal shock supervenes (and then diminishes) following limb deafferentation, thereby preventing use of the extremity in the early postoperative period. (2) The work made even more salient the question of why a monkey does not use a single deafferented limb in the free situation.

Spinal Shock

Several months after operation, a *unilaterally deafferented forelimb* is not paralyzed. The affected limb either has normal tone or is mildly hypotonic, and it is often kept flexed at the elbow and adducted at the shoulder in the so-called "paretic posture." The limb engages in movement; Mott and Sherrington referred to these movements as "associated movements" because they often occur when the other limbs, especially the contralateral intact forelimb, are moved. However, the limb is never used.

Following *bilateral forelimb deafferentation*, the forelimbs are also useless in the immediate postoperative period. They exhibit little movement and typically hang limply, almost without tone. However, in contrast to the chronic unilateral case, there is subsequently recovery of function that is characterized by its gradual character. After the restitution process has gone to completion, the bilaterally deafferented animals are capable of the same wide range of movement as is exhibited by unilaterally deafferented monkeys after restraint of the intact forelimb. For most classes of movement, the recovery process requires from 2 to 6 months. For prehension, increases in dexterity have been noted on occasion well into the second year after surgery (Taub, 1976, 1977; Taub & Berman, 1968).

The absence of movement and tone in the forelimbs following bilateral deafferentation is the result of a shocklike phenomenon that follows substantial neurological injury, whether at the level of the spinal cord (spinal shock) or brain (diaschisis). With regard to deafferentation, the elimination of somatosensory input results initially in a reduction within the spinal cord in the background level of excitation that maintains neurons in a subliminal state of readiness to respond. This effect is most marked in the deafferented segments of the spinal cord, where the depressed condition of the motoneurons greatly elevates the threshold for incoming excitation necessary to produce movement. The early postsurgical spinal shock may also be partly due to active inhibitory processes. As time elapses following bilateral deafferentation, recovery processes raise the background level of excitability of motoneurons so that movements can once again be expressed.

The nature of these recovery processes is at present not clearly understood. Sprouting of collaterals from intact neural elements in the vicinity of synaptic spaces denuded by the degeneration of severed afferent axons was observed some time ago (Liu & Chambers, 1958; Goldberger, 1974; Goldberger & Murray, 1974). This mechanism has never been conclusively shown to be involved in the recovery from bilateral forelimb deafferentation; however, it remains a clear logical candidate for at least part of the effect.

The Central Question: Difference in the Results for Bilateral and Unilateral Deafferentation

As noted, deafferentation of a contralateral intact forelimb results in a monkey being able to use a single deafferented forelimb that had never been employed in the free situation. Why, then, did monkeys not use that extremity before the deafferentation was rendered more extensive? This question became one of the central enigmas of the primate deafferentation literature. A second question also emerged. There were now three procedures that led to the ability to use a single deafferented forelimb: deafferentation of the contralateral limb, restraint of the intact extremity, and training of the deafferented limb. Was the mechanism of recovery of use the same in the three cases? If so, what was it?

Learned Nonuse

The search for the answer to these questions required the conduct of a number of experiments over approximately 15 years. The work took place intermittently, different studies being done when new ideas presented themselves as an explanation for the puzzling experimental phenomena. False starts were made with regard to the first two hypotheses considered. [For a more complete account, see Taub (1977, 1980) and Taub and Berman (1968).]

The Learned Nonuse Formulation

The final hypothesis considered, based on several converging lines of evidence, suggested that the nonuse of a single deafferented limb in the free situation is a learning phenomenon involving a conditioned suppression of movement. The mechanism was said to operate in the following manner: Immediately after operation, monkeys cannot use a deafferented limb; recovery of function requires considerable time, as data from animals with bilateral forelimb deafferentation had shown. An animal with one deafferented limb tries to use that extremity in the immediate postoperative situation, but finds that it cannot. It gets along quite well in the laboratory environment on three limbs and is therefore rewarded for this pattern of behavior. Moreover, continued attempts to use the deafferented limb often lead to aversive consequences, such as incoordination and falling and, in general, failure in any activity attempted with the deafferented limb. Many learning experiments have demonstrated that aversive consequences or punishment results in the suppression of behavior (e.g., see Kimble, 1961). This habit persists, and consequently the monkeys never learn that several months after operation, the limb has become potentially useful. In contrast, animals with both limbs deafferented (and incapacitated) do not get along very well in the laboratory environment. Motivation remains very high to use the deafferented extremities (in contrast to the unilateral case), and as soon as utility begins to return, the limbs are used to the extent possible.

When the intact limb is immobilized several months after unilateral deafferentation, motivation to use the deafferented limb increases sharply. The animal either uses the limb or it cannot with any degree of efficiency feed itself, locomote, or carry out a large proportion of its normal activities of daily life. This increase in motivation overcomes the learned nonuse of the deafferented limb, and consequently the animal uses it. However, if the straitjacket is removed a short while after the early display of purposive movement, as was the case in our initial experiment, the newly learned use of the deafferented limb acquires little strength and is therefore quickly overwhelmed by the well-learned habit of nonuse. If the straitjacket is left on for several days, however, use of the deafferented limb acquires strength and is then able to compete successfully with the learned nonuse of that limb in the free situation.

The learned nonuse mechanism is depicted schematically in Fig. 1, and the method by which techniques that overcome learned nonuse operate is presented in Fig. 2. The models shown in the figures explain the phenomena that follow forelimb deafferentation in monkeys. However, they are meant as more general formulations that also apply to other

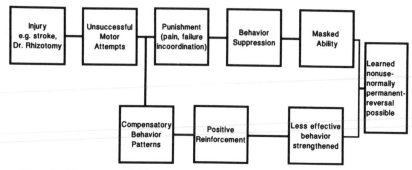

Figure 1. Schematic model for development of learned nonuse. After Tries (1991).

situations in which excess motor disability develops, as will be discussed below.

During the course of this century, several investigators have found that a behavioral technique could be employed in animals to substantially improve a motor deficit resulting from neurological damage (Chambers, Konorski, Liu, Yu, & Anderson, 1972; Lashley, 1924; Ogden & Franz, 1917; Tower, 1940; Yu, 1980). Lashley and Tower, working with monkeys following pyramidotomy, invoked in passing a simple form of the learned nonuse hypothesis as a possible explanation for their specific results. The possibility that this might be a general mechanism was not considered, nor did their hypothesis, based as it was on isolated observations, receive very much attention. However, in terms of the subject of this chapter, it is of interest to note that there are some interesting parallels in terms of the possible participation of a learned nonuse mechanism in the masking of

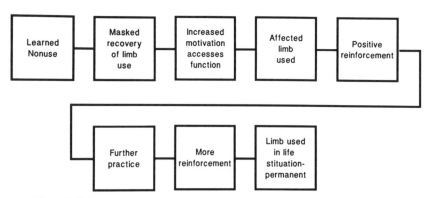

Figure 2. Schematic model of the mechanism for overcoming learned nonuse.

the behavioral capacity actually present both after pyramidotomy and after unilateral forelimb deafferentation.

Direct Test of the Learned Nonuse Hypothesis

All the evidence cited up to this point constitutes indirect evidence for the learned nonuse hypothesis. Consequently, we attempted to test the hypothesis in direct fashion (Taub, 1977, 1980). This involved restraining a deafferented limb in several animals so that they could not attempt to use it for a period of 3 months following surgery. In thus preventing an animal from trying to use the deafferented limb during the period before recovery of function had taken place, one should thereby prevent the animal from learning during that interval that the limb could not be used. Learned nonuse of the deafferented limb should therefore not develop. Thus, the unilaterally deafferented animal should be able to use the deafferented extremity in the free situation, though never again subjected to restraint of the intact limb.

On removing the animals from the restraining situations 3 months after surgery, we found that they were able to use the deafferented limb, and the ability to do so spontaneously reached the level normally exhibited by animals with both forelimbs deafferented. No further interventions were needed to accomplish this result.

Thus, the learned nonuse hypothesis was confirmed by direct test. Suggestive evidence was also obtained during the course of our prenatal deafferentation experiments. In this regard, it is interesting to recognize that life in the physically restrictive uterine environment imposes major constraints on the ability to use the forelimbs (though it does not entirely prevent use of the limbs). Consequently, prenatal deafferentation of a single limb could provide a means of testing the learned nonuse hypothesis. We studied three animals that had received unilateral forelimb deafferentation during the prenatal period and were then placed *in utero* for the remainder of gestation: two when two thirds of the way through gestation and one when two fifths of the way through gestation (Taub *et al.*, 1975b). Early illness and a muscular deformity prevent a clear interpretation of the results from one of the animals deafferented two thirds of the way through gestation. However, the other two animals exhibited purposive use of the deafferented extremity from the first day of extrauterine life, at which time they both employed the limb for postural support during "sprawling" and in pushing to a sitting position. Subsequently, though the intact limb was never restrained, the ability to use the deafferented limb paralleled the development of motor ability in animals given *bilateral* deafferentation on the day of birth. Thus, the results from the prenatally deafferented animals provide additional evidence in favor of the learned nonuse explanation for the lack of purposive movement following unilateral forelimb deafferentation in adolescent monkeys.

Previous Research with Humans

In 1967, I received a visit from Dr. Laurence Ince, an investigator in physical medicine. He observed an experiment employing one of the simple conditioned-response paradigms we were using at the time. A unilaterally deafferented monkey was seated in a restraining chair, and its intact arm was tied to one of the vertical supports of the apparatus, thereby immobilizing it. The monkey's task was to flex its deafferented limb in order to avoid an electric shock to the intact limb. The monkeys learned the avoidance task rapidly and rarely received shock.

Dr. Ince wondered whether a similar procedure might be of value with human patients after stroke; they also had a unilateral motor disability. By this time, the learned nonuse formulation described above had received initial consideration. Since learned nonuse was conceived as a general mechanism that might apply after many types of neural injury, Dr. Ince's cogent suggestion seemed very much worth trying. He transferred the technique used with unilaterally deafferented monkeys to chronic stroke patients with almost no change (Ince, 1969). The unaffected arm was tied to the limb of a chair, and the patient had to make a flexion of brief excursion with the plegic limb in order to avoid electric shock. The study included three patients who had made little use of their affected extremities since experiencing their stroke, which in each case was at least 1 year earlier. The motor status of two of these persons did not change; however, one individual improved substantially, not only in the training situation but also in the life situation. Though the sample size was very small, Ince may well have adventitiously come upon the percentage of stroke patients with chronic motor deficit who can be helped by techniques for overcoming learned nonuse (see below).

An investigator at the same institution, Jacob L. Halberstam, became interested in Ince's results and carried out a larger-scale study with 20 elderly cerebrovascular accident (CVA) patients and 20 age-matched control subjects (Halberstam, Zaretsky, Brucker, & Guttman, 1971). There were some changes. The unimpaired arm was not tied down, and in addition to limb flexion, a second task, lateral movement at the elbow, was added. Otherwise, the procedures were essentially similar. Most of the patients increased the amplitude of their movements with practice in the two conditioned-response tasks, some greatly. There was no report of whether this improvement in movement transferred to the activities of daily life.

One might think that this work would be considered promising. However, it was largely ignored, rarely being referred to in the papers of other investigators. The reason for this lack of attention may be that the techniques employed were at such variance from those employed in physical rehabilitation at the time. Other investigators, not operating within a learned-nonuse context, have used training techniques to obtain some improvements in limb use in chronic stroke patients whose greatly impaired motor function was presumably not amenable to future recovery (Franz, Scheetz, & Wilson, 1915; Balliet, Levy, & Blood, 1986).

Starting in 1981, I was prevented from carrying out my own research for a period of six years (Taub, 1991), and additional time was required to establish a laboratory in the new institution to which I moved. However, it was fortunate that during that time, Dr. Steven L. Wolf of the Emory University School of Medicine, following a pilot case study (Ostendorf & Wolf, 1981), was able to begin an important project that took the restraint portion of the published protocol (Taub, 1980) and applied it to chronic neurological patients (Wolf, LeCraw, Barton, & Jann, 1989). Approximately three quarters of the patients had experienced a stroke, while one quarter had experienced traumatic brain injury. For all patients, at least 1 year had elapsed after brain damage before the beginning of treatment. The experimental intervention involved an attempt to force use of the involved upper extremity by restraining the "good" limb in a sling for a period of 2 weeks. The sling was worn during waking hours, but was removed for sleep and a ½-hr period of exercise. It is important to note that no attempt was made to combine shaping (or any other type of training technique) with the restraint procedure.

Wolf employed 21 tasks to assess motor ability in terms of, depending on the task, speed or force of movement. Different tasks required differential contributions from the distal and proximal musculature. The choice of tasks reflected an eminently appropriate attempt to examine changes as a result of intervention on a joint-by-joint basis. The selection was in part empirical, based on Wolf's prior biofeedback research, and in part based on consultation with vocational rehabilitation counselors in the Greater Atlanta area. Prior to the beginning of the restraint intervention, task performance was tested over a series of six baseline sessions. Patients were again tested during the middle of the 2-week restraint period, at its end, and at four times during the ensuing year.

Most of the patients exhibited improvement on many of the timed tasks, and a substantial number exhibited improvement on all or nearly all of them. On a group basis, improvements were significant for performance on 19 of 21 tasks. However, it was found, surprisingly, that a considerable amount of this improvement occurred during the six baseline sessions, i.e., before the restraint device was applied. For many of the timed tasks, the improvement in performance from the last baseline session to the first postintervention session was not unequivocally greater than might have been expected from a projection of the baseline curve of improvement through an additional (baseline) session. That is, the improvement observed in the session after restraint was removed could conceivably have been the result of the administration of additional training in that testing session itself, rather than being due to the prior restraint. For other timed tasks, there was a more marked improvement between the last baseline session and first postintervention session than would have been expected from a projection of the baseline curve of improvement.

In an effort to deal with the ambiguity produced by the improvement-through-baseline effect, Wolf and co-workers gave five additional subjects ten baseline sessions rather than six. The objective of this procedure was to bring subjects to an asymptote in their motor improvement so that further improvement following restraint of the unaffected arm could be clearly attributable to the restraint procedure. However, for many tasks, this was not clearly the case, and in any event, the postrestraint improvement was sometimes not large as compared with the baseline improvement. When the data for all 21 timed tasks for these five subjects are considered together, there was essentially no change in task performance between the last baseline session and the last treatment or last follow-up session. However, there was a substantial improvement from the *first* baseline session to the end of treatment. This is probably the more significant aspect of the data, as will be discussed below.

The data for the three force or strength tasks show the improvement-through-baseline effect in even more pronounced fashion than the timed tasks. For the 21 primary subjects, there was at least as great, if not greater, improvement during the baseline period than there was during the treatment and follow-up periods.

Systematic data concerning the quality of movement in the activities of daily life were not obtained in the experiment of Wolf and co-workers. Therefore, it is not possible to determine the extent to which there was transfer from the experimental to the life situation.

While not conclusive, the study by Wolf and co-workers and the studies of Ince (1969) and Halberstam and co-workers (Halberstam *et al.*, 1971) raised the possibility that some humans can learn to overcome an inability or reduced ability to use an impaired limb after stroke or traumatic brain injury through the application of one of the techniques designed to overcome learned nonuse. The promising nature of the results stimulated the work of my colleagues and myself at the University of Alabama at Birmingham and guided its planning. The work was carried out in collaboration with Neal E. Miller, Thomas A. Novack, Edwin W. Cook III, William D. Fleming, Cecil S. Nepomuceno, Jane S. Connell, and Jean E. Crago (Taub *et al.*, 1993). It was conducted at the Spain Rehabilitation Center of that institution with the help of its director, Dr. Samuel L. Stover.

An Experiment on Overcoming Learned Nonuse in Humans after Stroke

The design of the experiment represented an attempt to optimize the amount of motor improvement that could be produced in chronic stroke patients and that could be unequivocally attributed to the treatment interventions. We employed both types of techniques that had been used to overcome learned nonuse following unilateral deafferentation in monkeys: not only restraint of the unimpaired limb but also training of the impaired extremity. We also employed a separate-groups design with an attention-comparison group that made it valid to administer only one baseline prerestraint testing session. It was therefore possible to avoid the possibility of an improvement-across-baseline-days effect from affecting the results. In addition, data were obtained on whether the effects of the procedures employed in the clinic had generalized and had an effect on improving the extent and quality of motor function in activities of daily life.

Potential subjects were identified from physician files at the Spain Rehabilitation Center and from the files of Drs. James Halsey and Lindy E. Harrell, of the Department of Neurology of this institution. They were then evaluated in structured examinations first by a physical therapist (J.E.C.), after which the most promising candidates were examined by a physiatrist (W.C.F. or C.S.N.).

The following exclusion criteria were employed: (1) stroke experienced less than 1 year earlier; (2) lack of ability to extend at least 10° at the metacarpophalangeal and interphalangeal joints and 20° at the wrist (the focal criterion); (3) balance problems, including walking at all times with an assistive device; (4) ability to make extensive use of the involved upper extremity so that significant further improvement could not be expected; (5) serious cognitive deficits (as determined from the medical chart, the two examinations noted above, and a battery of cognitive tests); (6) excessive spasticity (not found in any subject meeting criterion 2); (7) serious uncontrolled medical problems; (8) age greater than 75 years; and (9) left arm dominance or left hemiplegia (for ease in test administration with the equipment employed).

Nine persons who met the study's inclusion criteria were randomly assigned to either an experimental group (four) or an attention-comparison group (five). The subjects in the two groups were closely matched in initial motor ability and did not diverge significantly in such demographic characteristics as age (median: restraint group, 65 years; comparison group, 63 years), sex (one male per group), and socioeconomic status. Chronicity ranged from 1.2 to 18 years (median: restraint group, 4.1 years; comparison group, 4.5 years).

For the experimental group, the unaffected limb was secured in a resting hand splint and then placed in a sling; the affected arm was left free. The restraint was to be worn at all times during waking hours except when specific activities were being carried out (e.g., excretory functions, naps, and situations in which balance might be compromised). Each subject agreed to spend well over 90% of waking hours in restraint. The restraint devices were worn for 14 days. On each of the 10 weekdays during this period, patients spent 7 hr at the rehabilitation center and were given a variety of tasks to be carried out by the paretic upper extremity for 6 hr (e.g., eating lunch with a fork and spoon, throwing a ball, playing dominoes or Chinese checkers, card games, writing on paper, writing on a chalkboard, pushing a broom, Purdue Dexterity Board, Minnesota Rate of Manipulation Test).

The procedures given to the comparison group were designed to focus attention on the involved extremity. This was accomplished in three ways:

(1) Patients were told during four periods on separate days that they had much greater motor ability with their affected extremity than they were exhibiting; they were exhorted to focus attention at home on using the affected extremity in as many new activities as possible. Examples were given; record keeping was required and monitored.

(2) Patients received two sessions designated physical therapy, but involving only activities that required neither active movement nor limbering of the involved limb.

(3) Patients were given self-range-of-movement exercises to carry out at home for 15 min a day. In these exercises, the affected extremity was passively moved into a variety of positions by the unaffected extremity. Thus, the involved limb was not given any experience of or training for active movement.

Each of the tests employed to assess motor functions was administered to experimental and comparison subjects just before and immediately after their 2-week intervention period. The Emory Motor Function

Test, developed by Wolf and collaborators at Emory University, was discussed above. Half the items involve simple limb movements without functional endpoints; only four involve complete tasks that are commonly carried out in the life situation. We employed the test because it was clearly an excellent method of assessing basic motor acts. However, the results from this test, while quantitative, have an unknown relationship to a person's ability to perform the activities of daily life (ADL). The Arm Motor Activity Test (AMAT) was developed to provide this information (McCulloch, Cook, Fleming, Novack, Nepomuceno, & Taub, 1988). It consists of 16 compound tasks composed of one to three component tasks performed continuously without the subject's awareness of the component parcellation. Each of the compound tasks is a complete ADL commonly carried out in the life situation (e.g., donning a sweater, picking up a single dried bean on a spoon and bringing it to the mouth, unscrewing a jar cap). Performance on both tests was videotaped and was scored both at time of administration by an experimenter and from the videotape by three clinicians blind to group membership and pre- and postintervention order of test administration. Breaking the tasks of the AMAT down into component segments and timing each component permits the type of quantification possible with simpler actions without interfering with the normal flow of movement characteristic of everyday activity.

A third instrument, the Motor Activity Log, provided information about motor function in the life situation. It consists of 14 common and important activities of daily life from such functional areas as feeding, dressing, and grooming. For each item, the patient must report whether and how well (on a 6-point scale) each activity was performed.

Mean performance times on the two motor-ability tests were significantly faster for the restraint group than for the control group following treatment (Fig. 3). Performance times for the experimental group decreased 30.0% from pre- to postintervention, whereas the mean performance times of the comparison subjects on both tests increased 2.2%. In individual subject statistical tests, all four experimental subjects exhibited significant or near-significant improvement in performance time following restraint (all $ps < 0.06$, median $p = 0.002$), whereas none of the subjects in the comparison group showed significant improvement (all $ps > 0.3$).

Quality of movement and functional ability were significantly improved among experimental subjects relative to control subjects on both the Emory Test and the AMAT at the end of treatment (all $ps < 0.003$). The comparison group did not improve on either scale on either test. On an individual basis, each subject in the experimental group showed a significant improvement on both scales on both tests. None of the comparison subjects exhibited a significant improvement on either scale on either test.

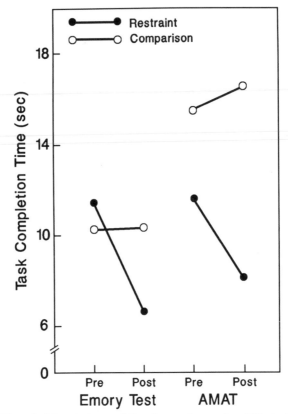

Figure 3. Mean task completion time on two motor ability tests.

The version of the Emory Motor Function Test employed in this experiment has two tasks that assess strength. One task involves lifting progressively increasing weights strapped to the forearm from the surface of a table to the top of a 9-in.-high box. A second task involves measuring grip strength with a dynamometer. The comparison group patients showed a pre- to postintervention increase of 10.0% in the lifting task and a decrease of 8.8% in the grip task. Of the three experimental subjects for whom data are available on the weight-to-box task [the data of one subject (No. 4) were excluded because he exerted test maximum force during pretreatment testing and therefore could not improve further], the first two exhibited a larger pre- to postintervention increase in lifting ability (83.3%) than the comparison subjects, but for grip strength (data from subject No. 4 were available for this task), there was little change (+9.3%). For the last experimental subject, an attempt was made to improve strength by providing brief periods of exercise with pulley weights. This was followed by an 808.9% improvement in the lifting task. No specific training was given in grip; nevertheless, it increased in strength substantially (275%).

During and after restraint intervention, the Motor Activity Log (Fig. 4) indicated that the experimental subjects exhibited a marked increase in their ability to use their affected upper extremity in a wide range of everyday activities, improving from a mean rating of 1.5 ("very little"/ "slight use") to a rating of nearly 4 ("almost normal use"). Most of the improvement was made during the treatment period. However, these gains were retained during the entire 2-year follow-up period, and they even increased somewhat during that time. The subject who improved most between 1 month and 2 years after treatment (No. 1) is the only one who complied with instructions to keep practicing at home the manual dexterity tasks each had been assigned. Improvement from baseline for the restraint group was significant at all times beginning at the second mea-

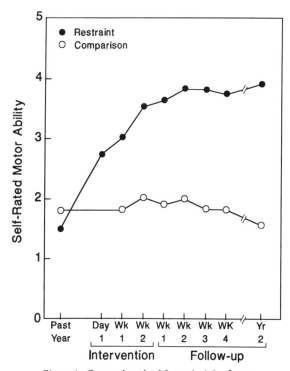

Figure 4. Group data for Motor Activity Logs.

surement point (day 4) of the first week of treatment. The rate of improvement for the group and for each subject individually describes a typical negatively accelerated learning curve. The restraint subjects performed significantly better than the comparison subjects at each point after the beginning of the interventions. In addition, as may be seen from Fig. 5, there was no overlap in the Motor Activity Log scores of the individuals in the two groups after the first week of restraint.

The improvement of the restraint patients in Motor Activity Log scores reflects in part better quality of movement and in part the fact that these patients were able to translate the improvements in the nature of their movements measured in the laboratory into mastery of a large range of activities of daily life that they had not been able to carry out with the affected arm since experiencing their stroke. The new activities engaged in included: brushing teeth, combing hair, picking up a glass of water and drinking, eating with a fork or spoon, and writing, among others. Deter-

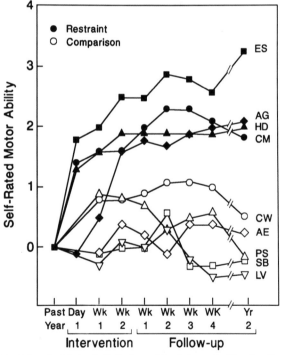

Figure 5. Individual data for Motor Activity Logs. The data are ipsitized so that each subject's pretreatment score is set to zero.

mination on a simple binary basis of whether a subject made no attempt to carry out a given motor activity in contrast with any attempt at all, at whatever level of ability, is a more clear-cut, reliable measure than a multistep rating scale. Table 1 indicates that there was a mean increase of 97.1% in the number of activities on the Motor Activity Log that the patients could carry out 1 month after restraint compared to the period before treatment. The comparable change for the comparison subjects was 14.5%. The difference between groups on this measure was significant after the interventions (U test, $p < 0.01$), but not before. The robustness of the effect is indicated by the fact that differences between groups were statistically reliable even though the sample size was small. At 2 years after treatment, there was no change in the restraint group's ability to perform the new tasks, but the comparison group had lost its small gain. The fact that all four restraint subjects performed at the 14-item maximum for the log at both 4 weeks and 2 years after intervention imposed an artificial ceiling on the improvement that could be recorded for the restraint group

Table 1. Motor Activity Log: Number of Activities of Daily Life That Could Be Performed before and after Interventions[a]

Restraint group					
Subject	Pre	1 Month post	1 Month change (%)	2 Years post	2-Year change (%)
1	5	14	+180.0	14	+180.0
2	14[b]	14	—	14	—
3	9	14	+ 55.6	14	+ 55.6
4	9	14	+ 55.6	14	+ 55.6
		Means:	+ 97.1[c]		+ 97.1[c]
Comparison group					
Subject					
11	3	4	+ 33.3	3	—
12	12	14	+ 16.7	11	− 8.3
13	5	9	+ 80.0	8	+ 60.0
14	14	7	− 50.0	7	− 50.0
15	13	12	− 7.7	11	− 15.4
		Means:	+ 14.5		− 2.7

[a]The maximum possible score is 14.
[b]The ceiling effect in pretreatment performance renders this aspect of HD's data uninterpretable [though her quality of movement improved substantially (see Fig. 5)].
[c]$p < 0.01$ for the comparison between the restraint and comparison groups (Mann-Whitney U test).

on this instrument. Consequently, the data presented in Table 1 probably understate the true improvement of the restraint subjects in activities of daily life.

Neither group showed any pre- to postintervention cognitive change. The lack of change in the restraint group suggests that the improvement on the motor ability measures was not due to some nonspecific effect, such as increased motivation to do well generally or elevated mood, that might have resulted from contact with the project.

In interviews, each of the restraint patients stated that he or she was capable of a greatly expanded range of activities in the life situation. They reported that they had made major gains in what was, in effect, functional independence. This is consistent with the results for the Motor Activity Log. For example, subject No. 2, while her uninvolved arm was in restraint, baked a cake, brought it into the center, cut it into pieces, balanced the pieces on a cake server and placed them on plates, and then served them to project members using only the affected extremity throughout. When two of the experimental patients (Nos. 4 and 1) were asked to sign their names with the involved hand, they said they could not do this and had not been able to since experiencing their stroke. They were asked to try; it was perfectly all right if they could not do the task. Both subjects, to their great surprise, were able to sign their names. The movements were slow, but the signatures were of reasonably good quality (and both speed and quality improved later with practice). Both these patients began signing checks and writing notes in the life situation with the affected hand (which, as noted, had been dominant before they had experienced CVA). This led to part-time clerical employment for one of these subjects. One of her main tasks was answering the phone with the unaffected hand and taking messages with the affected hand. She was thereby able to relieve a self-reported depressed state because she previously "had nothing to do except spend most of my days staring at the four walls of my apartment." Though the comparison subjects also expanded somewhat the extent of the activities carried out by their impaired limb, in no case did this have significance for general functional independence in the life situation.

Recent Clinical Use of the Learned Nonuse Approach

Desai (1991) has used a shortened form of the protocol for overcoming learned nonuse in Houston in conjunction with EMG biofeedback, physical therapy, and occupational therapy in a series of chronic stroke and head injury patients. The data indicate that the motor ability of the patients was greatly improved. While one cannot conclusively isolate which part of the multimodality treatment effect was due to which component, his prior experience with the last three modalities suggests that half the motor improvement was due to the portion of the regimen designed to overcome learned nonuse.

Tries (1989) has described a case in which restraint of the unaffected limb was used with a left hemiplegic patient in the clinic for 12 1.5-hr sessions distributed over 1 month. This treatment followed a course of EMG biofeedback therapy and is reported to have resulted in considerable additional motor improvement.

Relevant Issues for Interpretation of the Data

Were Placebo Factors Involved in the Motor Improvement?   The improvement in the restraint group in the study by Taub and co-workers was superimposed on a median poststroke period of 4.1 years and a median baseline of more than 3 years during which patients had reached a largely unvarying plateau of greatly impaired motor function. These long baselines and the long follow-up period render the results for each subject of increased therapeutic significance. Moreover, the maintenance of gains by restraint subjects over a 2-year posttreatment period and the dissipation of a much more modest effect over the same time interval in comparison subjects argues against a significant contribution from attention/placebo factors to the motor improvement of the restraint group.

The learned nonuse theory states that one of the two main functions of interventions designed to overcome learned nonuse is to increase the motivation to use the affected limb. Since the attention-control procedure in this experiment would undoubtedly result in an increase in this type of motivation, it may be viewed as a type of reduced treatment and is therefore potentially more powerful for comparison purposes than an attention-control procedure alone. This consideration further supports the position that the improvement in movement in the restraint group was not due to the operation of attention/placebo factors.

The Improvement-through-Baseline Effect.   The study of Wolf and associates (Wolf *et al.*, 1989) revealed that simply having chronic stroke patients practice movements in the clinic leads to improvement, often quite marked, in the practiced tasks in patients who, by the traditional wisdom of the field, should be exhibiting no further motor recovery. How can this striking phenomenon be accounted for? One explanation is that the repeated practice constituted a type of training of the target movements. Training, of course, was shown in the deafferentation research with monkeys to be one of the two main methods for overcoming learned nonuse. Thus, the learned nonuse and overcoming learned nonuse models both predict and can fully account for the learning-through-baseline effect.

How Great Was the Motor Improvement?   A related issue is the question of what the appropriate baseline is from which to measure the motor improvement recorded in the experiments performed to date. The learned nonuse formulation states that a major mechanism involved in overcoming the learned nonuse of a limb is increasing the motivation to use it. Thus, just by asking a patient to perform a test task, one is increasing that person's motivation to use a paretic limb in the immediate situation. This factor, by itself, could substantially increase motor ability beyond that which a patient would normally exhibit in the life situation. The Emory Motor Function Test, as noted, consists mainly of isolated movements without independent functional significance. With this type of test, it would not be easy to determine whether initial test performance represented a clear improvement over motor activity in the life situation. However, the AMAT establishes an explicit functional endpoint for each task, thus providing the patient (and the experimenter) with a criterion against which current test performance can be related to life-situation motor activity. It is probably for this reason that we repeatedly encountered the situation on the AMAT that patients were greatly surprised at how well they were able to perform a task. In a number of cases, they performed activities, on being asked to do so, that they had not carried out since the time of their stroke. We did not find this to be the case during the Emory Test.

These considerations, in addition to the improvement-through-baseline effect, suggest that the performance on the first administration of both the Emory Test and the AMAT could represent a substantial improvement over the use to which the paretic limb is normally put in daily life. Using the first test performance as the baseline for assessing the effects of treatment could therefore result in an underestimate of the true improvement that occurred as a result of the therapeutic intervention. Since the Motor Activity Log elicits information about motor function *before* the beginning of participation in the project and its attendant testing, it does not suffer from this disadvantage. The Motor Activity Log involves self-report, and this, of course, has inherent difficulties. However, as already noted, reducing the responses on this test to a dichotomous determination—(1) inability to perform a task at all or (2) ability to perform the task to whatever degree—removes some of the inaccuracies introduced by a rating scale. By this measure (which itself involved a ceiling effect, as described above, and may well have represented an underestimate), motor improvement was more dramatic than on the two laboratory motor tests. This degree of improvement, which is consistent with the day-to-day clinical observations of the staff, could well be the measure least subject to artifact and most reflective of the true treatment effect.

Relative Contributions of Training and Restraint to the Motor Improvement. In the experiment by Wolf and associates (Wolf *et al.*, 1989), the unaffected arm was restrained, but training of the affected arm was not carried out. In the work described above, both techniques were employed. Consequently, a difference in the results in the two studies, where they are directly comparable, could provide an index of the value of training the impaired limb when added to restraint of the unimpaired limb in overcoming learned nonuse. In both experiments, the Emory Motor Function Test was employed, but a different number of testing sessions was given in each phase of the experiments, especially during the baseline period. However, there are some common time points that can serve as the basis for cross-evaluation. In both studies, there was at least one baseline testing session and one testing session at the end of treatment. There were many more baseline testing sessions in the work of Wolf and co-workers than in the present study. However, since the repeated baseline sessions had the effect of improving motor performance, the comparison of the difference between the *first* baseline and last treatment sessions should tend to favor the study of Wolf and co-workers. The results indicate that the median decrease in performance time for all timed tasks was more than three times as great in the study by Taub and co-workers as it was for the 21 primary subjects in the study by Wolf and co-workers by the end of treatment.

The Emory Motor Function Test is comparatively straightforward, and Dr. Wolf kindly invited our research group to his laboratory for training in the administration of this test. Moreover, the restraint procedure, which we also observed in Dr. Wolf's laboratory, is also relatively simple to duplicate. Wolf and co-workers differentiated the tasks on their test by the joints that were primarily involved in performing each. However, since all but one of the timed tasks used by Wolf and co-workers were employed here, it would appear legitimate to use the median decrease in performance time on all tasks to obtain a rough comparison of subject performance in the two studies.

These considerations suggest that adding training to the restraint procedure greatly increases the extent to which learned nonuse can be overcome. This suggestion in no way indicates that training is the more important of the two treatment components, especially with regard to performance in the life situation. Our experiment provides only data relating to the interaction of the two techniques. It seems unlikely that training of the affected limb alone would produce large treatment effects; it is probably the combination of the two techniques that is effective.

Population Potentially Amenable to the Overcoming-Learned-Nonuse Approach. An informal test employed by Wolf for determining the appropriateness of a patient for interventions for overcoming learned nonuse, based on his previous research (Wolf & Binder-Macloud, 1983), involves having a seated person project the affected hand and distal portion of the forearm beyond the edge of a chair's armrest. The patient is asked to first extend the unsupported hand at the wrist and then extend the fingers to the maximum extent possible. Approximately 20–25% of the stroke population with chronic motor deficit can carry out these movements with excursions of at least 20° and 10° at the two locations, respectively (thereby exceeding the second exclusion criterion listed above). All the patients who met this criterion in the work to date exhibited marked motor improvement when given treatment for overcoming learned nonuse. While one would not want to restrain the unaffected limb for 90% of waking hours in patients who had balance problems, this probably would not be a bar to effective therapy by a modified procedure restricted to supervised periods during the day. The percentage of stroke patients with chronic motor deficit who do not meet Wolf's informal criterion, but who would also benefit from this therapeutic approach, is at present unknown. It would clearly not be as high as in the current work, but at least some of these patients might also be helped.

These considerations are of interest, since chronic stroke patients are now a largely untreated population. Moreover, the learned nonuse therapeutic approach makes use of very little equipment, does not involve drugs, involves payment for only a relatively modest amount of therapist time, and has no side effects.

Applicability of the Learned Nonuse Model to Chronic Stroke Patients with Motor Deficit

The results from the experiment described above indicate that in stroke patients identified by the inclusion criteria of this study, motor ability can be significantly increased by interventions that are effective in overcoming learned nonuse. The data are characterized by their consistency; there was virtually no overlap between the experimental and comparison groups in any of the parameters measured. While the sample size was small, the effects were large and were maintained and even increased somewhat over a 2-year follow-up period.

These results can be understood by reference to the models presented in Figs. 1 and 2. The models are set up to indicate that the learned nonuse formulation is as applicable to the case of humans following stroke as it is to monkeys following unilateral forelimb deafferentation. If the neural substrate for a movement is destroyed by CNS injury, no amount of intervention designed to overcome learned nonuse can be successful in helping recover lost function. However, many stroke patients (at a minimum those defined by the inclusion criteria of this project) have considerably more motor ability available than they make use of. As noted earlier in this chapter, the suppression of this additional motor capacity is set up by unsuccessful attempts at movement in the acute postinjury phase. In contrast, attempts to cope with the motor demands of a situation without using the affected extremity would be met, in many cases, with complete or partial success. Neal Miller (1989) correctly includes in this process the reinforcement of awkward and extremely inefficient uses of the affected portion of the body itself during the postinjury period when these are the only movements that can be made. Again, as noted above, rewarded patterns of behavior are strengthened, thus leading to repetition. Hence, the tendency not to use the involved limb and the substitution of "bad habits" (Miller, 1989) would grow with time and would eventually achieve enough strength in some individuals to dominate the situation. Later, when recovery had proceeded to the point where the affected limb could again be used effectively, the hemiplegic patient, like the unilaterally deafferented monkey, would not, because of his history of reinforcement, try to use the affected limb. The inability to make attempted movements in the early postinjury phase is associated with the cortical shock or diaschisis characteristic of that period (Taub, 1977; Taub & Berman, 1963). Recovery from cortical shock occurs over time; increased motor activity should then become increasingly possible, but the suppression of movement would remain unabated and inhibit use of the limb. Even if emotional excitement produced an inadvertent expression of motor ability or if treatment produced motor improvement in the clinic, this newly emerged capacity would have little "strength" and would not compete successfully with the well-learned habit of nonuse. Consequently, the nonuse of the limb would persist and mask indefinitely an underlying capability for extensive motor activity. However, if individuals are correctly motivated to employ this unexpressed ability, they will be able to do so. The procedures employed with the experimental patient group provided the conditions under which various new uses of the limb could be practiced repeatedly, thereby permanently overcoming the motor suppression. Consequently, performance time, quality of movement, and the range of activities engaged in all improved substantially. The results thus suggest that though learned nonuse is an incapacitating condition, it can nevertheless be reversed or overcome by appropriately directing the attention of an impaired subject. This objective can be accomplished to differing extents by a variety of means. Prolonged restraint of the intact limb is effective in facilitating the expression of the latent motor ability, and repeated practice in using the newly emerging motor ability can also be an important factor.

An alternative hypothesis is that the experimental interventions resulted in some type of neural reorganization, perhaps involving sprouting, that permitted improved motor performance. This possibility is rendered unlikely, however, by the speed at which the motor improvement took place. By the end of the first day of restraint, over 50% of the complete improvement observed for the Motor Activity Log had already occurred (see Fig. 4). This result has the appearance of the unmasking of an ability that is already present, rather than the initiation of a neural restitution process.

Excess Motor Disability

Excess motor disability that is substantially greater than appears warranted by the organic condition of the individual is a common clinical observation. Its existence in any individual case often cannot be demonstrated conclusively, since by its nature it involves function that is not being expressed and therefore cannot be observed. In this chapter, we have described experiments indicating that following unilateral deafferentation in monkeys and stroke in humans, there can be substantial excess motor disability that is maintained by a learned nonuse mechanism. However, the disability can be reversed. Similar results involving the use of techniques for overcoming learned nonuse following stroke have been obtained by Wolf and co-workers (Wolf et al., 1989) and by a number of other investigators (Desai, 1991; Halberstam et al., 1971; Ince, 1969; Tries, 1989). The extensive new motor function, which typically develops too rapidly for the learning of new motor skills to be involved, indicates that the motor ability being expressed had been latent, awaiting only the application of an appropriate therapeutic intervention. We have also reviewed evidence that excess motor disability can also occur following pyramidotomy and other motor lesions in monkeys (Chambers et al., 1972; Lashley, 1924; Ogden & Franz, 1917; Tower, 1940; Yu, 1980). Of particular additional interest is the fact that Wolf and co-workers (Wolf et al., 1989) have used a technique for overcoming learned nonuse in traumatic brain injury patients with predominantly unilateral motor involvement to improve motor performance substantially, thereby suggesting that the pretreatment deficit involved excess motor disability. Desai (1991) has obtained similar results in clinical work.

The models for the development and overcoming of learned nonuse in Figs. 1 and 2, respectively, are stated in general terms. The reason is that the formulation presumably identifies a general mechanism that operates in a variety of conditions, not just after the neurological injuries just specified. The formulation indicates that any type of organic damage that results in an initial inability to carry out a function establishes the conditions of reward and punishment (contingencies of reinforcement) conducive to the development of learned nonuse; the operation of this mechanism becomes superimposed on and strengthens the organically determined inability to carry out the function. If the anatomical or biochemical substrate the impairment of which led to the initial deficit recovers or heals, learned nonuse could still hold recovery of function in check unless it is overcome. Until now, the application of the learned nonuse mechanism has been studied only with respect to neurological impairment of an upper extremity. However, according to the formulation, the mechanism could also apply to other types of function such as speech (as in aphasia); other portions of the body, such as a lower extremity; or nonneural injury, such as skeletal system damage.

There follows a discussion of a partial list of conditions that could in some cases produce excess motor disability that is at least partly due to the operation of the learned nonuse mechanism. For these cases, that portion of the deficit due to learned nonuse would be reversible by the application of an appropriate technique.

1. Peripheral Nerve Damage.   After a peripheral nerve is severed, regeneration usually takes place. Reflex testing may indicate that motor pathways have been repaired, but in the case of some patients, purposive use of the limb is permanently impaired. Much can go awry in the regeneration process, but the possibility remains that in some cases, the full range of motor function possible is being suppressed by learned nonuse, especially if the nerve damage is primarily unilateral. I am indebted to Dr. Wolf for noting that overcoming learned nonuse techniques should not be employed in cases of peripheral nerve damage unless one has made certain that there is electromyographic demonstration of reinnervation of target muscles; even then, it might be wise to limit movement efforts for the first postinjury year, since excess contractions could possibly lead to fatigue that might result in regression in the nerve-regeneration process.

2. Spinal Cord Injury.   Following trauma to the spinal cord, there is frequently a period of shock or diaschisis during which motor function is impaired in regions below the level of injury. Subsequently, unless transection has occurred, some or all of the lost motor capacity returns. In my deafferentation experiments, for example, a remarkable amount of motor function was observed in the hindlimbs of monkeys with spinal cords that had suffered severe damage in the upper thoracic region as a result of progressive compression from scar tissue formation and the action of overlying muscle following the extensive laminectomy required by intradural brachial dorsal rhizotomy. In some animals, postmortem examination revealed that only a flattened ribbon of spinal cord remained in the focal region of damage, usually T1 or T2 through T4. Nevertheless, on casual examination, hindlimb function was sometimes indistinguishable in these monkeys from that of intact animals. In this situation, the damage is undoubtedly progressive and can probably be adjusted to slowly. In contrast, some humans who receive a sudden traumatic insult to the spinal cord exhibit a permanent motor loss that seems far in excess of what is warranted by the amount of injury that has apparently been sustained, as determined by neurological examination and direct visualization at surgery. Moreover, there can be major differences between individuals in amount of function recovered, though tests of reflex function suggest that similar amounts of neural substrate remain intact.

3. *Urinary and Fecal Incontinence.* Tries (1991) has suggested that many cases of incontinence are the result of learned nonuse, and their remediation by biofeedback involves an overcoming of this suppressive mechanism. These views are discussed in the next section, on the use of biofeedback in rehabilitation medicine.

4. *Other Conditions.* What appears to be excess motor disability is often observed after fractured hip, other broken bones, and arthritis, among other conditions. For example, a fractured bone in a limb heals, but the elderly patient continues to exhibit reduced use of that extremity. A fractured hip heals, but the patient does not resume normal activity. An arthritic condition goes into partial or complete remission, but the patient remains loath to use the affected portions of the body. In the case of fractured bones, the reason for the deficit clearly might be the muscular deconditioning that occurred during the skeletal healing. However, the enforced period of nonuse following the fracture of a bone (and the flare-up/remission pattern in some patients with arthritis) fits the requirements for the development of learned nonuse; it would start in the period of enforced nonuse or exacerbation and then inappropriately continue in some patients into the posthealing or remission period.

The large individual differences in amount of recovery exhibited in each of the types of neurological and nonneurological injury discussed above, when a similar amount of organic damage appears to be present, have frequently caught the attention of clinicians. The formulation underlying this chapter suggests that learned nonuse can be an important contributory factor in explaining some of these puzzling differences in amount of recovery of function. This consideration is advanced here simply as a hypothesis. One reason it may be of interest is that at present, there is no effective treatment for excess motor disability. When it is recognized, there is little that can be done about it—and in most cases it is not looked for or recognized. In contrast, the overcoming learned nonuse model suggests a new type of treatment and gives the clinician something concrete that can be tried as an alternative to the benign neglect of current practice. In short, the hypothesis is testable and clinically relevant.

Overcoming Learned Nonuse and the Use of Biofeedback in Rehabilitation Medicine

It is generally recognized that the results from the use of EMG biofeedback for the rehabilitation of movement are quite variable. Sometimes it is effective; indeed, sometimes it works so rapidly that its effects appear to be "almost miraculous" (Olton & Noonberg, 1980, p. 286)—but very often it does not work at all, or produces effects in neuromuscular measures without resulting in the ability to make better use of a limb (Wolf, 1983). What is the reason for this variability and for the fact that improvement is often remarkably rapid? One reason for lack of improvement undoubtedly relates to amount of pretreatment deficit (Wolf & Binder-Macloud, 1983) and, presumably, the extent of the CNS injury. When the damage is sufficiently great, no behavioral technique can produce significant functional improvement. However, when there is success, especially in those cases in which the rapidity of improvement is apparently miraculous, learned nonuse may be a factor. That is to say, very large, rapid changes in motor function do not suggest a learning or relearning process; learning processes are typically gradual. What rapid improvement does suggest is that the motor capacity was already there, but was latent. A candidate mechanism that could accomplish the masking of latent motor capacity would be learned nonuse.

Biofeedback has all the necessary characteristics to be an excellent technique for increasing motivation so that learned nonuse can be overcome, thereby unmasking suppressed movements. It focuses the attention on the effort to be made and provides an encouraging context within which improvement can be elaborated. In this regard, it is similar to restraint of the uninvolved limb. Dr. Susan Middaugh has provided an excellent account of this effect (Middaugh, 1989, p. 18):

The first thing I found out in the course of treating patients was that simply wearing a white coat, attaching electrodes to muscles, and using terminology like "augmented sensory feedback" (the term in use at the time) could produce an immediate, and at times dramatic, increase in a patient's ability to voluntarily contract a partially paralyzed muscle, even before I turned the feedback display on! It was clear that biofeedback was a novel situation which gets the patient's attention. In addition, the patients liked to work with EMG feedback. Simply being able to demonstrate to the patient, in a very concrete and direct way, that a partially paralyzed muscle was not "dead" and that it did respond to the patient's efforts to voluntarily contract or relax it, had positive motivational effects—even though the physical therapist had usually been telling the patient the very same thing. In short, EMG biofeedback often made the patient a better patient, and this enhanced the therapeutic exercise process whether or not the patient used the information provided by the biofeedback display to guide trial-by-trial attempts to relearn voluntary muscle control.

This is not the whole story. Dr. Middaugh then presents data indicating that biofeedback can contribute to the reeducation of motor function. However, one must now also consider the possibility that part of the effect that biofeedback produces in a rehabilitation setting is the result of its being a good means of overcoming learned nonuse.

Tries (1991) has made a similar point with respect to urinary incontinence and the use of a biofeedback technique that is remarkably effective in the treatment of a large number of cases of incontinence. The initial work was with fecal incontinence (Engel, Nikoomanesh, & Schuster, 1974; Whitehead, Burgio, & Engel, 1985; Whitehead & Shuster, 1987), but presumably because of the congruence of neural innervation, a similar technique was also found to be effective in many cases of urinary incontinence (Burgio & Burgio, 1986; Burgio, Whitehead, & Engel, 1985; Middaugh, Whitehead, Burgio, & Engel, 1989). The procedure involves step-wise filling of the bladder or rectum with fluid and manometric feedback display of external anal sphincter pressure, abdominal (rectal) pressure, and, in the case of urinary incontinence, bladder pressure. In the typical experiment, only two to five feedback training sessions are given, each consisting of only three trials, but striking progress (sometimes apparently complete remission) is sometimes achieved after the first session. The mechanism usually introduced to explain these results is the reeducation of neuromuscular control of the anal or urinary sphincters and the related muscular apparatus. The thrust of Tries's argument, however, is that the process is usually too rapid, especially when it takes only one or two sessions, for it to be only neuromuscular education.

One point requires clarification here to avoid confusion: On the one hand, it is argued that if appropriate motor function is established within a very few sessions following a long period of nonfunction or serious dysfunction, learning or relearning cannot be the sole process involved because the time frame is insufficient. On the other hand, it is also the case that learned nonuse is explicitly formulated in terms of reinforcement or learning mechanisms. Why, then, does the speed of the process exclude neuromuscular reeducation from being the sole mechanism involved, while it does not exclude overcoming learned nonuse? The reason is that different types of learning processes are involved in each case. Motor-skill learning typically requires considerable time, even when the skill to be learned is relatively simple, and learning a new coordination for the precisely timed and complex muscular interactions of the excretory processes clearly cannot be considered a simple motor act. Even if reestablishing continence required only resetting the timing parameters of a central motor program regulating that process, training or retraining of this process could hardly be expected to take just one or two three-trial session(s). In contrast, a learned suppression of movement can be overcome very rapidly if the motivation to regain the lost function is increased sufficiently and if this is done in an appropriate manner. Accomplishing substantial transfer from the training to the life situation may require considerable practice or overtraining of the newly regained ability, but the all-important initial demonstration of motor competence can take place very rapidly.

Tries employs the learned nonuse mechanism as an explanation that is more consistent with the very brief training that is often sufficient to produce the dramatic improvement in continence frequently observed with the use of biofeedback. She suggests that during a period when adequate neuromuscular control of elimination is not possible, because of either injury, pregnancy, change in neuromuscular status as a result of aging, or some other cause, inappropriate muscular habits are developed in an effort to reduce the extremely aversive consequences of incontinence. The improper habit, which is better than nothing, is rewarded and develops strength in the same fashion as does the use of just three limbs to carry out the activities of daily life after stroke or somatosensory deafferentation. When the proper neuromuscular coordination later becomes possible because of recovery of function or healing, the improper habit, which has acquired great strength through repeated reinforcement, prevents its performance. (In the case of aging, the proper coordination was presumably always possible, but it would have required a change in pattern of neural activation of the muscles. The old neuromuscular control process that was appropriate to the musculature before the deconditioning and other changes produced by aging, and that is now dysfunctional, sets up the conditions under which learned nonuse can develop.) Thus, there is a component of treatment with biofeedback for incontinence (and in the rehabilitation field in general) that does not consist of retraining the old, correct habit; that habit may already be there. It consists instead in overcoming the new, inappropriate habit that is suppressing or masking the older, correct one. As noted above, the process of lifting a conditioned suppression of behavior can be rapid.

It should be reemphasized that the overcoming-learned-nonuse mechanism is not being offered here as an explanation that supplants neuromuscular reeducation as the process responsible for increased continence resulting from biofeedback training. The two are viewed as complementary mechanisms that can function synergistically. The point being made, though, is that learned nonuse could well be involved in the process, and this is a point now worth considering in terms of its experimental and clinical implications.

Summary

1. Following deafferentation of a single forelimb, monkeys do not use the affected limb.

2. Two types of behavioral techniques can be employed to induce a monkey to employ the deafferented extremity: restraint of the unaffected limb and training of the affected limb.

3. The same two techniques can be used to greatly improve motor function of the affected upper extremity of many chronic stroke and traumatic brain injury patients.

4. These results are explained in terms of the operation of a learned nonuse mechanism that develops in the early postinjury period and that usually acts to permanently suppress attempts to use the affected extremity. The existence of the learned nonuse mechanism received direct demonstration in experiments with deafferented monkeys. The techniques that restore motor function are effective because they overcome learned nonuse.

5. It is proposed that learned nonuse is responsible for a portion of the motor disability in excess of that which seems warranted by the organic damage often noted by clinicians in such conditions as peripheral nerve damage, spinal cord injury, aphasia, urinary and fecal incontinence, nonuse of a prosthetic limb after unilateral amputation, fractured hip, fracture of other bones, and arthritis.

6. It is further proposed that biofeedback is an excellent method for overcoming learned nonuse of motor function and that this mechanism is involved, along with neuromuscular reeducation, in many instances in which biofeedback is successful in the area of rehabilitation medicine. This

is the case especially when the recovery is very rapid, as often happens in the treatment of fecal and urinary incontinence.

ACKNOWLEDGMENTS.   The research with human stroke patients was supported in part by grants from the Biomedical Research Support Grant Program, National Institutes of Health (S07 RR07178), Bethesda, Maryland, and the Center for Aging, University of Alabama in Birmingham.

I thank Dr. Samuel L. Stover for help in implementation of the study at the Spain Rehabilitation Center, University of Alabama at Birmingham; Drs. James Halsey and Lindy B. Harrell, Department of Neurology, University of Alabama at Birmingham, for access to their patient files; Dr. Louis B. Penrod for advice; and Bayer Cheng and Monica Stanberry for help during conduct of the experiment. I also thank Dr. Steven L. Wolf for his invaluable suggestions at the inception of the study and Drs. Wolf and Neal E. Miller for a critical reading of the manuscript.

The theoretical portion of the chapter was presented at the 63rd Annual Congress of Rehabilitation Medicine, Baltimore, Maryland, October 22, 1986; the human stroke data were included in presentations at the annual meeting of the American Physiological Society, Montreal, Canada, October 11, 1988, and at the 97th Annual Convention of the American Psychological Association, September 13, 1989.

References

Balliet, R., Levy, B., & Blood, K. M. T. (1986). Upper extremity sensory feedback therapy in chronic cerebrovascular accident patients with impaired expressive aphasia and auditory comprehension. *Archives of Physical Medicine and Rehabilitation*, *67*, 304–310.

Bossom, J. (1972). Time of recovery of voluntary movement following dorsal rhizotomy. *Brain Research*, *45*, 247–250.

Bossom, J., & Ommaya, A. K. (1968). Visuo-motor adaptation (to prismatic transformation of the retinal image) in monkeys with bilateral dorsal rhizotomy. *Brain*, *91*, 161–172.

Burgio, K., & Burgio, L. (1986). Behavior therapies for urinary incontinence in the elderly. In J. Ouslander (Ed.), *Clinics in geriatric medicine: Urinary incontinence*, Vol. 2 (pp. 809–827). Philadelphia: W. B. Saunders.

Burgio, K., Whitehead, W., & Engel, B. (1985). Urinary incontinence in the elderly. *Annals of Internal Medicine*, *103*, 507–515.

Chambers, W. W., Konorski, J., Liu, C. N., Yu, J., & Anderson, R. (1972). The effects of cerebellar lesions upon skilled movements and instrumental conditioned reflexes. *Acta Neurobiologiae Experimentalis*, *32*, 721–732.

Denny-Brown, D. (1966). *The cerebral control of movements* (Chapter 4). Liverpool: Liverpool University Press.

Desai, V. (1991). Report on functional utility score change in nine chronic stroke or closed head injury patients receiving a training program for overcoming learned nonuse as part of a multimodality treatment program. In N. E. Miller (Chair), *Overcoming learned nonuse and the release of covert behavior as a new approach to physical medicine.* Symposium conducted at the meeting of the Association for Applied Psychophysiology and Biofeedback, Dallas, March, 1991.

Eidelberg, E., & Davis, F. (1976). Role of proprioceptive data in performance of a complex visuomotor tracking task. *Brain Research, 105,* 588–590.

Engel, B. T., Nikoomanesh, P., & Schuster, M. M. (1974). Operant conditioning of retro-sphincteric responses in the treatment of fecal incontinence. *New England Journal of Medicine, 290,* 646–649.

Franz, S. T., Scheetz, M. E., & Wilson, A. A. (1915). The possibility of recovery of motor functioning in longstanding hemiplegia. *Journal of the American Medical Association, 65,* 2150–2154.

Gilman, S., Carr, D., & Hollenberg, J. (1976). Limb trajectories after cerebellar ablation and deafferentation in the monkey. *Archives of Neurology, 33,* 390–394.

Goldberger, M. E. (1974). Recovery of movement after CNS lesions in monkeys. In D. Stein (Ed.), *Recovery of function after neural lesions.* New York: Academic Press.

Goldberger, M. E., & Murray, M. (1974). Restitution of function and collateral sprouting in the cat spinal cord: The deafferented animal. *Journal of Comparative Neurology, 158,* 37–54.

Halberstam, J. L., Zaretsky, H. H., Brucker, B. S., & Guttman, A. (1971). Avoidance condition-ing of motor responses in elderly brain-damaged patients. *Archives of Physical Medicine and Rehabilitation, 52,* 318–328.

Ince, L. P. (1969). Escape and avoidance conditioning of response in the plegic arm of stroke patients: A preliminary study. *Psychonomic Science, 16,* 49–50.

Kimble, G. S. (1961). *Hilgard and Marquis' conditioning and learning* (2nd ed.). New York: Appleton-Century-Crofts.

Knapp, H. D., Taub, E., & Berman, A. J. (1958). Effect of deafferentation on a conditioned avoidance response. *Science, 128,* 842–843.

Knapp, H. D., Taub, E., & Berman, A. J. (1963). Movements in monkeys with deafferented forelimbs. *Experimental Neurology, 7,* 305–315.

Lashley, K. S. (1924). Studies of cerebral function in learning: V. The retention of motor areas in primates. *Archives of Neurology and Psychology, 12,* 249–276.

Lassek, A. M. (1953). Inactivation of voluntary motor function following rhizotomy. *Journal of Neuropathology and Experimental Neurology, 3,* 83–87.

Liu, C., & Chambers, W. W. (1958). Intraspinal sprouting of dorsal root axons. *American Medical Association Archives of Neurological Psychiatry, 79,* 46–61.

Liu, C. N., & Chambers. W. W. (1971). A study of cerebellar dyskinesia in the bilaterally deafferented forelimbs of the monkey (*Macaca mulatta* and *Macaca speciosa*). *Acta Neuro-biologiae Experimentalis, 31,* 263–289.

McCulloch, K., Cook, E. W., III, Fleming, W. C., Novack, T. A., Nepomuceno, C. S., & Taub, E. (1988). A reliable test of upper extremity ADL function. *Archives of Physical Medicine and Rehabilitation, 69,* 755.

Middaugh, S. J. (1988). Biofeedback and applied psychophysiology from a rehabilitation perspective. *Biofeedback and Self-Regulation, 16,* 18–20.

Middaugh, S. J., Whitehead, W. E., Burgio, K. L., & Engel, B. T. (1989). Biofeedback in urinary incontinence in stroke patients. *Biofeedback and Self-Regulation, 14,* 3–19.

Miller, N. E. (1989). Biomedical foundations for biofeedback as a part of behavioral medicine. In J. V. Basmajian (Ed.), *Biofeedback: Principles and practice for clinicians* (pp. 5–15). Baltimore: Williams & Wilkins.

Mott, P. W., & Sherrington, C. S. (1895). Experiments upon the influence of sensory nerves upon movement and nutrition of the limbs. *Proceedings of the Royal Society of London, 57,* 481–488.

Munk, H. (1909). *Über die functionen von hirn und ruckenmark* (pp. 247–285). Berlin: Hirschwald.

Ogden, R., & Franz, S. I. (1917). On cerebral motor control: The recovery from experimentally produced hemiplegia. *Psychobiology, 1,* 33–50.

Olton, D. S., & Noonberg, A. R. (1980). *Biofeedback: Clinical applications in behavioral medicine.* Englewood Cliffs, NJ: Prentice-Hall.

Ostendorf, C. G., & Wolf, S. L. (1981). Effect of forced use of the upper extremity of a hemiplegic patient on changes in function. *Journal of the American Physical Therapy Association, 61,* 1022–1028.

Sherrington, C. S. (1931). Quantitative management of contraction in lowest level of contraction. *Brain, 54,* 1–28.

Skinner, B. F. (1938). *The behavior of organisms.* New York: Appleton-Century-Crofts.

Stein, B. M., & Carpenter, M. W. (1965). Effects of dorsal rhizotomy upon subthalamic dyskinesia in the monkey. *Archives of Neurology, 13,* 567–583.

Taub, E. (1976). Motor behavior following deafferentation in the developing and motorically mature monkey. In R. Herman, S. Grillner, H. J. Ralston, P. S. G. Stein, & D. Stuart (Eds.), *Neural control of locomotion* (pp. 675–705). New York: Plenum Press.

Taub, E. (1977). Movement in nonhuman primates deprived of somatosensory feedback. *Exercise and Sports Sciences Reviews,* Vol. 4 (pp. 335–374). Santa Barbara: Journal Publishing Affiliates.

Taub, E. (1980). Somatosensory deafferentation research with monkeys: Implications for rehabilitation medicine. In L. P. Ince (Ed.), *Behavioral psychology in rehabilitation medicine: Clinical applications* (pp. 371–401). New York: Williams & Wilkins.

Taub, E. (1991). The Silver Spring Monkey incident: The untold story. *CFAAR Newsletter, 4(1),* 1–8.

Taub, E., & Berman, A. J. (1963). Avoidance conditioning in the absence of relevant proprioceptive and exteroceptive feedback. *Journal of Comparative and Physiological Psychology, 56,* 1012–1016.

Taub, E., & Berman, A. J. (1968). Movement and learning in the absence of sensory feedback. In S. J. Freedman (Ed.), *The neuropsychology of spatially oriented behavior* (pp. 173–192). Homewood, IL: Dorsey.

Taub, E., Bacon, R., & Berman, A. J. (1965). The acquisition of a trace-conditioned avoidance response after deafferentation of the responding limb. *Journal of Comparative and Physiological Psychology, 58,* 275–279.

Taub, E., Ellman, S. J., & Berman, A. J. (1966). Deafferentation in monkeys: Effect on conditioned grasp response. *Science, 151,* 593–594.

Taub, E., Perrella, P. N., & Barro, G. (1973). Behavioral development following forelimb deafferentation on day of birth in monkeys with and without blinding. *Science, 181,* 959–960.

Taub, E., Goldberg, I. A., & Taub, P. B. (1975a). Deafferentation in monkeys: Pointing at a target without visual feedback. *Experimental Neurology, 46,* 178–186.

Taub, E., Perrella, P. N., Miller, E. A., & Barro, G. (1975b). Diminution of early environmental control through perinatal and prenatal somatosensory deafferentation. *Biological Psychiatry, 10,* 609–626.

Taub, E., Williams, M., Barro, G., & Steiner, S. S. (1978). Comparison of the performance of deafferented and intact monkeys on continuous and fixed ratio schedules of reinforcement. *Experimental Neurology, 58,* 1–13.

Taub, E., Miller, N. E., Novack, T. A., Cook, E. W., III, Fleming, W. C., Nepomuceno, C. S., Connell, J. S., & Crago, J. E. (1993). Technique to improve chronic motor deficit after stroke. *Archives of Physical Medicine and Rehabilitation, 74,* 347–354.

Tower, S. S. (1940). Pyramidal lesion in the monkey. *Brain*, *63*, 36–90.

Tries, J. (1989). EMG biofeedback for the treatment of upper extremity dysfunction: Can it be effective? *Biofeedback and Self-Regulation*, *14*, 21–53.

Tries, J. M., (1991). Learned nonuse: A factor in incontinence. In N. E. Miller (Chair), *Overcoming learned nonuse and the release of covert behavior as a new approach to physical medicine*. Symposium conducted at the meeting of the Association for Applied Psychophysiology and Biofeedback, Dallas, March, 1991.

Twitchell, T. E. (1954). Sensory factors in purposive movement. *Journal of Neurophysiology*, *17*, 239–254.

Whitehead, W. E., & Schuster, M. (1987). Biofeedback in the treatment of gastrointestinal disorders. In J. Hatch, J. Fisher, & J. Rugh (Eds.), *Biofeedback: Studies in clinical efficacy* (pp. 179–188). New York: Plenum Press.

Whitehead, W. E., Burgio, K. L., & Engel, B. (1985). Biofeedback treatment of fecal incontinence in geriatric patients. *Journal of the American Geriatrics Society*, *33*, 320–324.

Wolf, S. L. (1983). Electromyographic biofeedback applications to stroke patients: A critical review. *Physical Therapy*, *63*, 1448–1455.

Wolf, S. L., & Binder-Macloud, S. A. (1983). Electromyographic biofeedback applications to the hemiplegic patient: Changes in upper extremity neuromuscular and functional status. *Journal of the American Physical Therapy Association*, *63*, 1393–1403.

Wolf, S. L., Lecraw, D. E., Barton, L. A., & Jann, B. B. (1989). Forced use of hemiplegic upper extremities to reverse the effect of learned nonuse among chronic stroke and head-injured patients. *Experimental Neurology*, *104*, 125–132.

Wylie, R. M., & Tyner, C. F. (1981). Weight-lifting by normal and deafferented monkeys: Evidence for compensatory changes in ongoing movements. *Brain Research*, *219*, 172–177.

Wylie, R. M., & Tyner, C. F. (1989). Performance of a weight-lifting task by normal and deafferented monkeys. *Behavioral Neuroscience*, *108*, 273–282.

Yu, J. (1980). Neuromuscular recovery with training after central nervous system lesions: An experimental approach. In L. P. Ince (Ed.), *Behavioral psychology in rehabilitation medicine: Clinical applications* (pp. 402–417). Baltimore: Williams and Wilkins.

PART VI

Long-Term Stress

The two chapters in this final section review some psychophysiological and psychological variables in the effects of long-term stress in two very different settings. Chapter 14, by A. J. W. Taylor and M. M. Brown, provides a look at individual responses in small, isolated groups during a year in Antarctica. Chapter 15, by Tores Theorell, reviews several of his studies on long-term stress in ordinary work settings in Sweden.

The chapter by Taylor and Brown first describes the authors' elaborate methods for assessing subjects in isolation in Antarctica and for transmitting data back to their laboratory in New Zealand, some of it by satellite. The research was hindered by a relatively small number of subjects, but the researchers take advantage of their small sample sizes to report on many interesting individual effects. In general, it appeared that the single most powerful source of behavioral influence was the isolated group itself, that is, relationships among the subjects, rather than the weather or the long nights. The authors also point up the inevitable importance of certain personality factors, such as dominance and achievement-orientation, in determining social and emotional reactions. The research has implications for future research on isolated groups in terms of selection and training of subjects, data-processing procedures, and the development of advisory systems.

In the final chapter, Theorell looks at a number of selected parameters of responding in subjects exposed to long-term stress, especially job strain. The author points out that some physiological variables, such as immunoglobin and plasma testosterone, show complex and even anamolous associations with job strain. Other variables, especially blood pressure and heart rate, more consistently correlate positively with job strain, although the age of the worker apparently determines whether the effects will be observed during working hours or also at home at night. Theorell also observes that some psychological variables may interact with physiological parameters—including emotional support, depression, and feelings of powerlessness—influencing the degree and direction of effect of job strain. Attempts, like Theorell's, to examine the effects of long-term stress are especially significant in light of its greater impact on health relative to the more customary short-term stressors imposed in laboratory analyses.

CHAPTER **14**

Quartets in Antarctic Isolation

A. J. W. Taylor and M. M. Brown

The best of psychological research is empirical, replicable, related to previous findings in the discipline, and incorporated as appropriate with findings from related disciplines; it offers solutions for maximizing human performance and raises questions for further study. The rest falls short in some major respect while still making some contribution to the corpus of knowledge and providing opportunities for researchers to gain experience in their search for facts.

The project to be reported in this chapter was supported by an international ecological organization in return for honorary consultancy work on the preparation and debriefing of a series of four-person parties that wintered over in the Antarctic each year from 1986 until the present time. Any conflict between the consultant and researcher roles was minimal, because advice proffered frequently was not taken!

Methods

Subjects and Preparation

The study involved 14 subjects from 25 to 43 years old, 5 of whom where women (including one who wintered two successive years because of special circumstances). They were from seven different countries; for six, English was their second language. They were brought together in New Zealand for various periods of training before leaving by ship to

A. J. W. TAYLOR and M. M. BROWN • Psychology Department, Victoria University of Wellington, Wellington, New Zealand.

Clinical Applied Psychophysiology, edited by John G. Carlson, A. Ronald Seifert, and Niels Birbaumer. Plenum Press, New York, 1994.

spend 12 or 13 months at a well-designed and provisioned base in Antarctica that had been especially constructed for them. Their object was to monitor the primary and secondary impact of humans on the Antarctic ecology, and they were selected as a group for their ability to run scientific programs, to maintain the field and base equipment, and to operate a complete communications network.

The subjects were also selected for the personal stability they might have displayed previously under somewhat comparable circumstances—as well as for the compatibility they had engendered during a 2-month training period they spent in New Zealand before going South to Antarctica. At that latter stage, and when possible, the consultant's role was to spend one day with them to deal with any obvious problems and to help them prepare for the year ahead.

The preparation for the ensuing year was essentially of the self-help kind that was designed to make the subjects sufficiently resilient and responsible for detecting and managing any difficulties that might arise among them. It involved the consideration of any given personal emotional, occupational, and social deficits, and the acquisition of techniques for conflict resolution that they could use to advantage when necessary (Cornelius, Faire, & Hall, undated). In return, the subjects were invited to cooperate in a behavioral research project by providing data at regular intervals with which their progress might be monitored and any patterns be detected.

For the first three groups, the monitoring was done retrospectively at the debriefing when each party returned from Antarctica with a batch of such questionnaires as they had been sufficiently motivated to complete each month while they were away. The researcher's only other contact with them had been through telephone calls from the subjects when they experienced difficulty with their relationships, and from him when he wished to keep in touch. Then, in 1989, through a chance realization that modern technology could be used to advantage, a computerized form of the questionnaires and tests was developed and put into operation, and the results were transmitted back to the researcher by Inmarset satellite each month (Taylor, 1989a).

There were, of course, the necessary preliminaries to be overcome by way of programming the material, of establishing the equivalence of the paper and computer questionnaires, of ensuring the confidentiality of responses, of testing the systems, and of financing the operation. But with the help of the subjects, their organization, technicians, and postgraduate students (Alty, 1990), the new scheme for data acquisition, transmission, and reception was put into operation, and to some extent it proved to be effective. Moreover, the method of data collection obviated the problems that would certainly have arisen had it been necessary for a psychologist to be present *in situ* to try to observe the group without being part of it.

Instruments

Turning now to the actual data and the parameters of behavior to which it related, the purpose was to detect changes in the health, personality, and social interaction of subjects that previous studies with larger isolated groups had led researchers to expect (Palinkas, 1986; Taylor, 1987). The procedure was to select such shorter forms of relevant questionnaires as would be psychometrically robust, economical for time required in responding and processing, and acceptable to the subjects. The questionnaires and rating scales used in the study were:

1. Adaptability Questionnaire (ADQ)—9 items (Cazes, Rivolier, Taylor, & McCormick, 1989)
2. General Health Questionnaire (GHQ)—20 items (Goldberg, 1979; as presented by Siegert, McCormick, Taylor, & Walkey, 1987)
3. Hopkins Symptom Checklist (HSCL)—21 items (Green, Walkey, McCormick & Taylor, 1988)
4. MacKay Stress-Arousal Checklist (MSACL)—45 items (MacKay, Cox, Burrows, & Lazzerini, 1978)
5. SYMLOG Adjective Rating Form (SARF)—26 items (Bales & Cohen, 1979)
6. Ways of Coping List (WOCL)—48 items (adapted from Folkman & Lazarus, 1980)

To these were added certain cognitive tests to measure reaction time, visual discrimination, and short-term memory that were adapted from those used by the International Bio-medical Expedition to the Antarctic (Rivolier, Goldsmith, Lugg, & Taylor, 1988). An opportunity was also taken with one party to include an appraisal of cortisol and melatonin measures, and this assessment confirmed the peak readings of cortisol with stressful experience and of melatonin with daylight.

Obviously, the selection of research parameters, of related instruments, and of procedures is largely a matter of the researchers' theoretical orientation, personal experience, preference, and familiarity of usage with subjects under comparable conditions—providing they meet the standard criteria for relevance, reliability, validity, ease of administration and scoring, and consumer acceptance. But in the present case, these obligations were even more critical, because of the lack of comparable matched control groups, as well as the inability to control the enterprise either for the group as a whole or for individual subjects once they were down in the Antarctic with the sea routes frozen for a year and no access by aircraft. The small number of subjects in the study also obliged the researcher to inspect the data for indicators and trends and to report them with due caution (rather than to dismiss them because they were drawn from too small a research population to be appropriate for conventional and powerful multivariate statistical analysis). Such are the realities of ongoing applied research and the challenges for behavioral scientists who choose to respond to them.

Results

The computer presentation of the correct discrimination task, the incorrect discrimination task, and the number of digits recalled for the four subjects in one particular Antarctic party showed marked mean variations as the season progressed (Fig. 1). These variations raised once again the question of cognitive fluctuations among isolated people (Taylor, 1989b), but because of the small size of the group, such variations can only point to the need for a more extensive study. Unfortunately, the computer presentation of the reaction-time test faltered because of temporary technical and logistic problems.

The initial computer presentation of the questionnaires that was attempted with one party produced individual results that were comparable to those of the pencil-and-paper format on three of the forms: HSCL (Fig. 2), GHQ (Fig. 3), and MSACL (Fig. 4).

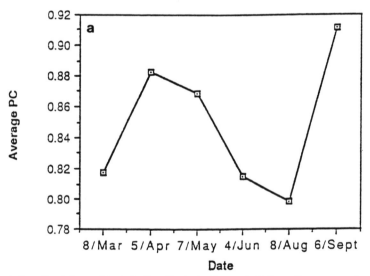

Figure 1. Results of four subjects in the discrimination and digit-recall tests over the year. (a) Average percentage of correct discriminations; (b) average percentage of incorrect discriminations; (c) average number of digits recalled.

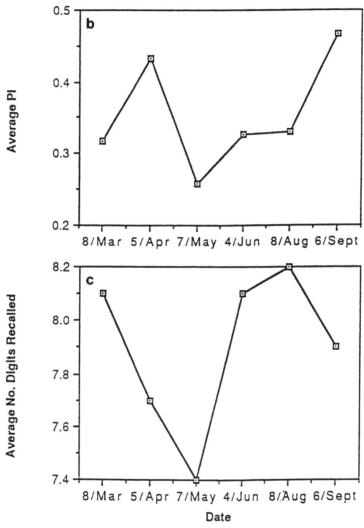

Figure 1. (*Continued*)

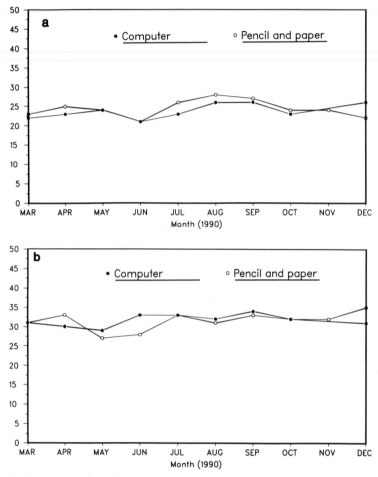

Figure 2. Comparison of pencil-and-paper mode and computer-mode scores on the HSCL. (a) Subject 13; (b) subject 14; (c) subject 15; (d) subject 16.

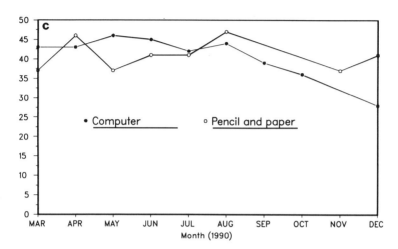

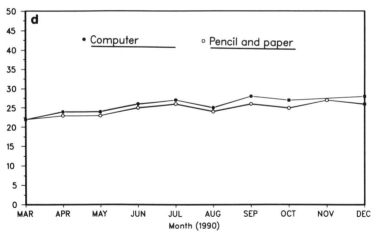

Figure 2. (Continued)

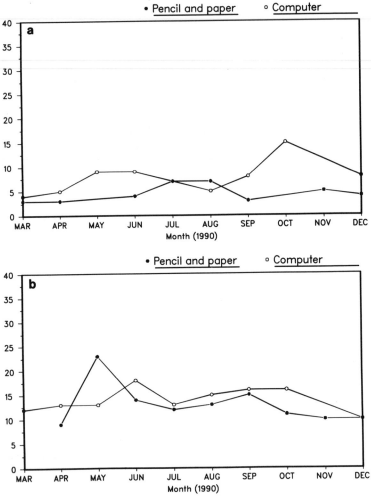

Figure 3. Comparison of pencil-and-paper mode and computer-mode scores on the GHQ. (a) Subject 13; (b) subject 14; (c) subject 15; (d) subject 16.

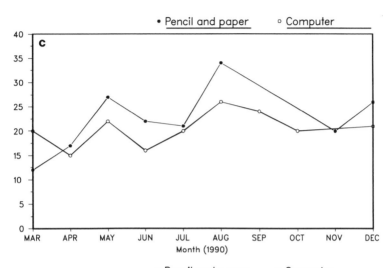

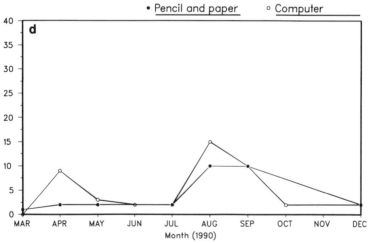

Figure 3. (Continued)

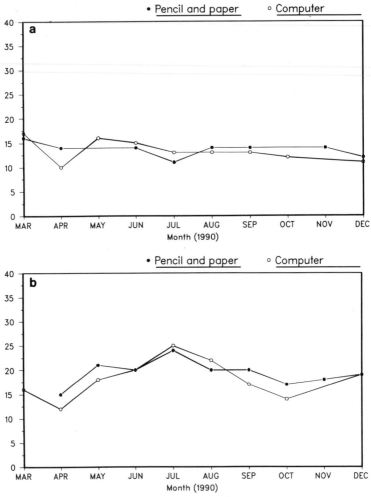

Figure 4. Comparison of pencil-and-paper mode and computer-mode scores on the MSACL. (a) Subject 13; (b) subject 14; (c) subject 15; (d) subject 16.

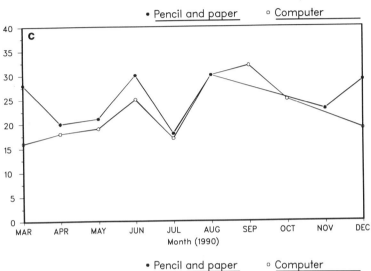

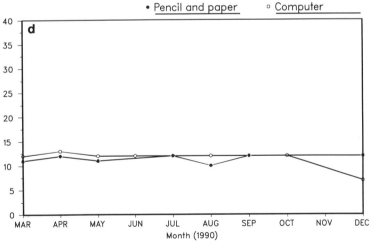

Figure 4. (Continued)

However, each individual produced different scores on the computer and questionnaire formats of the ADQ (Fig. 5) and the WOCL (Fig. 6). In each instance, and allowing for smoothing of the graphs where appropriate, the computer format produced more revelations of discomfort than did the pencil-and-paper format [cf. Sawyer, Sarris, Quigley, Baghurst, & Kalucy (1990), who observed informants in a clinical series]. The increase in candor might have arisen because, unlike the three tests previously reported as producing comparable results, the ADQ and the WOCL required semistructured rather than structured responses to given items. Therefore, the results showed that the computer form of presentation was a viable option to incorporate in the present research.

However, to make the best use of available data, the pencil-and-paper records provided by the subjects for eight data-gathering points or more were regarded as sufficiently complete to be included. Using this criterion, such records were found to have been given by eight subjects, incomplete records were given by five, and no records at all were given by three. The records of the composite eight subjects from different parties who completed the pencil-and-paper records showed (1) consistently higher levels of HSCL symptoms for three subjects [in descending order, subjects 15, 6, and 13 (Fig. 7A)]; (2) higher feelings of GHQ illness for three subjects [in descending order, subjects 15, 14, and 12 (Fig. 7B)]; (3) higher MSACL stress and arousal scores for three subjects [in descending order, subjects 15, 14, and 12 (Fig. 7C)]; (4) greater difficulty in ways of coping for two subjects [in descending order, subjects 15 and 14 (Fig. 7D)]; and (5) greater difficulty in ADQ adaptation for three subjects [in descending order, subjects 15, 14, and 10 (Fig. 7E)].

These results showed that subject 15 stood out among all others in the completed series of five measures for the problems he was experiencing, and subject 14 was somewhat similar (Table 1). Closer inspection of monthly returns showed that three others were consistently above the remainder only on one measure each, and there were a few subjects whose scores peaked only occasionally during the year, for example, subject 7 on GHQ in July, subject 6 on MSACL, and subject 7 again on WOCL in March and October.

A closer examination of the frequency of stressful periods reported on the WOCL by all four subjects in the group that included subjects 15 and 14 showed that subject 15 reported stress nine times, subject 14 reported stress five times, and, perhaps not surprisingly, their compatriots each reported stress four times. Also, the typical pattern of response for subject 15 was to indulge in avoidance and wishful thinking and to seek social support rather than to give more attention to the problem (Table 2).

However, the latter was still his major method of problem-solving, as indeed it had been for all subjects without exception; the point, though, is that his antagonist, subject 14, was the only other person with a tendency to use emotional reactions and, in his case, only avoidance (Fig. 8).

The stressors reported by the subjects in this same group were more interpersonal and personal, rather than occupational or related to the particular deprivations and hazards of their environment. The interpersonal stressors arose primarily from a continuous power struggle between the appointed leader and another member of the group and from their differences in task orientation. Personal antipathy quickly developed between the two main contestants, with the other two being relatively powerless in their company—apart from one who established a mutually supportive emotional relationship with the leader for a time that resulted in the inevitable complications when she brought it to a stop.

Both the unchanging and changing pattern of interpersonal affiliations was brought out clearly by the group average form of the SYMLOG Field Diagram Form, an example of which is shown in Fig. 9. This particular SYMLOG showed that the group was cohesive when the summer support staff had left them, although even at that early stage the struggle for dominance referred to in the previous paragraph had begun.

By midwinter, the leadership usurper (subject 14) had become the most dominant and negative force and the least task-oriented, and the others set him apart—and the two subjects outside this contest for leadership were the most positive in their expression of feelings. By the end of the year, one of the latter had become less positive about the others, but was quite alone in her drive to complete various assignments before returning home. Finally, the group resumed its familiar pattern of the one persistently dominant and negative person being set apart from the other three.

The results confirm that the long period of Antarctic isolation was extremely stressful for some and a disappointment and a trial for others. For all, it fell far short of their expectations. Although the experience produced no clinical and physical symptoms of stress, it did produce psychological indicators that are often a precursor. To take but two subjects as an example—i.e., the two locked in the leadership struggle in the group just reported—on the HSCL they both had elevated feelings of distress, and the designated leader (subject 15) had additional somatic distress and performance difficulty (Table 3).

Apart from midwinter, when the rival had a high MSACL stress score, the leader's scores were again consistently well above those of the others in

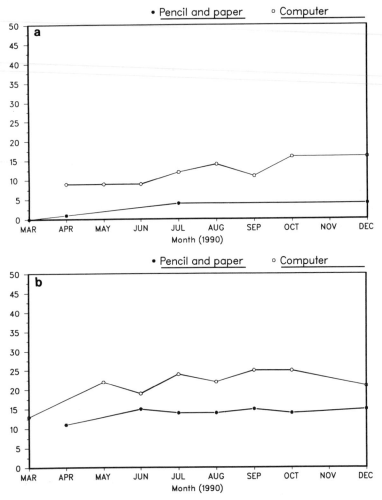

Figure 5. Comparison of pencil-and-paper mode and computer-mode scores on the ADQ. (a) Subject 13; (b) subject 14; (c) subject 15; (d) subject 16.

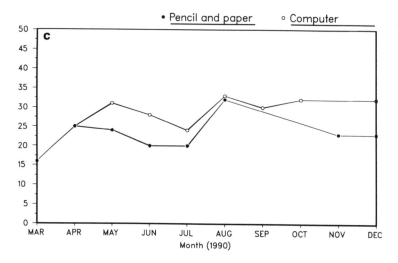

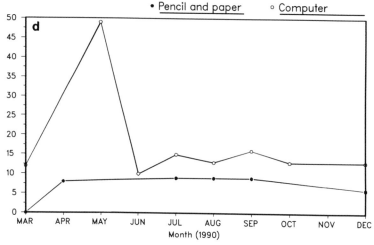

Figure 5. (Continued)

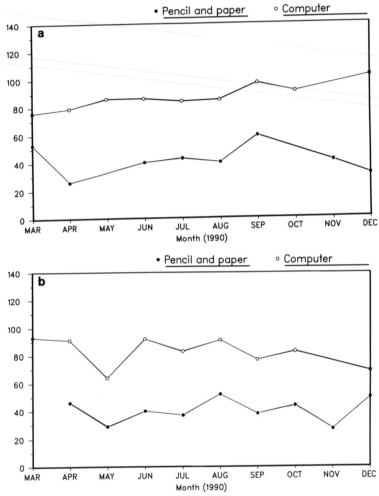

Figure 6. Comparison of pencil-and-paper mode and computer-mode scores on the WOCL. (a) Subject 13; (b) subject 14; (c) subject 15; (d) subject 16.

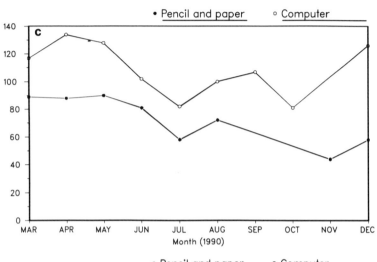

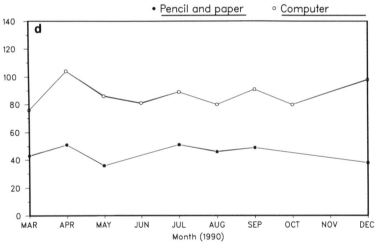

Figure 6. (Continued)

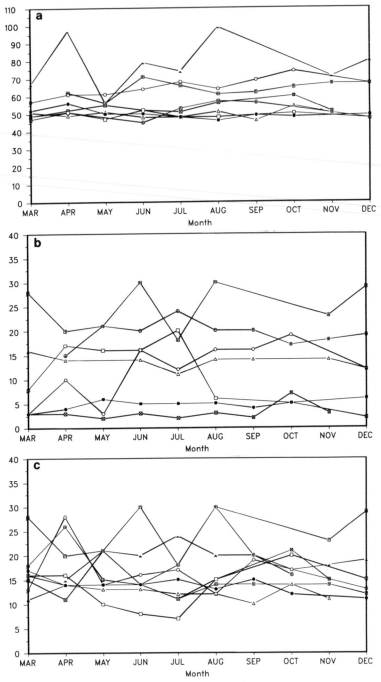

Figure 7. Comparison of scores for all expeditions 1986/1987–1990/1991. (a) HSCL; (b) GHQ; (c) MSACL; (d) WOCL; (e) ADQ.

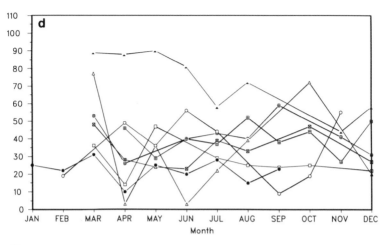

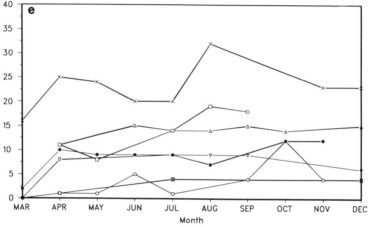

Figure 7. (Continued)

Table 1. Rankings of Subjects
on the Most Negative Levels of Tests Used

	Test				
Subject	HSCL	GHQ	MSACL	WOCL	ADQ
15	1	1	1	1	1
14	—	2	2	2	2
12	—	3	3	—	—
6	2	—	—	—	—
13	3	—	—	—	—

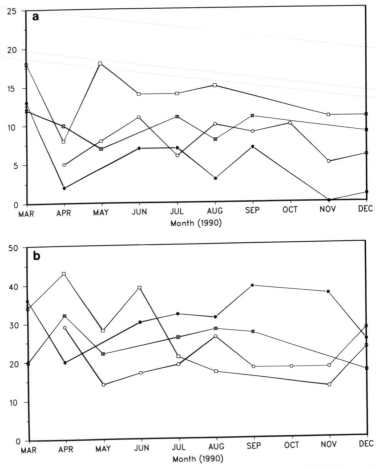

Figure 8. Comparison of WOCL scores for all team members of the 1990/1991 expedition. Subscales: (A) 1—Seeking Social Support; (B) 2—Problem Focused Coping; (C) 3—Self Blame; (D) 4—Wishful Thinking; (E) 5—Avoidance. Subjects: (●) 13; (○) 14; (□) 15; (⊠) 16.

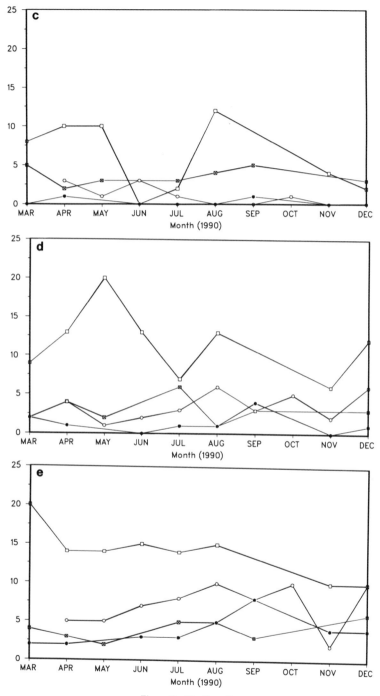

Figure 8. (Continued)

Table 2. Mean WOCL Scores for the 1990/1991 Group

Subject	Category[a]				
	SSS	PF	BS	WT	AV
13	5.0	31.25	0.25	1.25	3.88
14	7.78	23.37	1.00	3.56	7.22 (3)
15	13.63	27.25	6.00	11.63	14.00
16	9.71	21.5	3.57	3.00	4.00
Group	8.97	25.84	2.63	4.88	7.38

[a](SSS) Seeks social support; (PF) performance focus; (BS) blames self; (WT) wishful thinking; (AV) avoidance.

his party—although his arousal scores did show some fluctuations in comparison with those of the others that remained high and constant (Table 4).

Similarly, the GHQ scores of this same pair of antagonists were consistently above the mean on feelings of general illness, sleep disturbance, and anxiety and dysphoria, but only for the leader were they high on depression (Table 5).

Neither of the two contestants was without intellectual insight, but despite their previous training in conflict resolution, they were unable to act on it. A degree of self-awareness could be inferred from their SYMLOG replies, and in particular from those they gave just before midwinter—conceivably the most stressful seasonal period of their whole Antarctic year. At that time, the leader (subject 15) thought himself as apart from the group, and far less friendly, more dominant, and achievement-oriented than he would wish to be. But the group average put him otherwise—i.e., within the group, but less dominant, more friendly, and slightly more achievement-oriented than he thought himself to be. Not so his rival for dominance (subject 14), who thought himself within the group but some-

Table 3. Mean HSCL Scores
for the 1990/1991 Group

Subject	Distress		Performance difficulty
	General	Somatic	
13	27.63	14.3	8.63
14	34.67	15.00	14.44
15	37.00	19.25	21.63
16	27.29	15.14	9.57

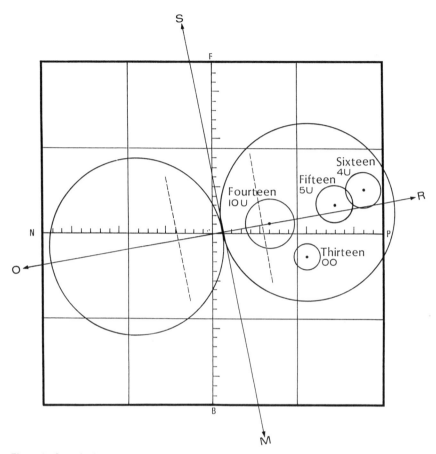

Figure 9. Sample SYMLOG Field Diagram Form. S = Scapegoat direction; M = Mediator direction; O = Opposite circle; R = Reference circle; N = Negative direction; P = Positive direction; F = Forward, task oriented; B = Backward, emotionally expressive. Figure indicates a unified group with all subjects clustered within the reference circle, with subject 14 the most dominant and subject 13 the least, and the same subject 14 the least positive and subject 16 the most positive. Subject 16 is the most task oriented, and subject 13 the only emotionally expressive member of the group.

one who wished to be more dominant yet more friendly and a little more achievement-oriented. In his case, the group average put him right outside the group in the unfriendly and not achieving sector, and it gave him the same and the most dominating position that he gave himself.

Of the other two persons in the same intensively studied group, subject 13 saw himself in midwinter as a submissive, friendly, mild

Table 4. Mean MSACL Scores
for the 1990/1991 Group

Subjects	Stress	Arousal
13	1.5	12.13
14	7.00	12.33
15	13.75	11.13
16	0.00	11.43

achiever, and his ideal was to be just a little more so on all three dimensions. He came closer to seeing himself as the group saw him than did any other member, and his doing so kept him in the reference group. Finally, subject 16 saw herself as within the group, friendly, and achievement-oriented, but neither dominant nor submissive. She wished she were more friendly, but less achievement-oriented and more submissive. But the group average perception put her well outside the group in her dimensions of friendship and achievement orientation, and it regarded her as slightly more submissive than she thought herself.

Further reflections on the dimension of self-awareness came in response to unstructured questions. For example, the leader admitted that he could be a real grouch; that he was anxious when in the field away from base; that he was not always honest; that he complained too much, blamed things on his teammates unfairly, was pushy, and did not compromise. He felt controlled, trapped, confused, and angry. It hurt him to be near his antagonist, and he appealed to the researcher for professional help in that matter. With regard to the behavior-monitoring research, he said that he had discovered some upsetting and some positive things about himself. As he stated it: "The accounting has made me think objectively [and] honestly [but it] can be disturbing . . . no one likes seeing their weaknesses."

Table 5. Mean GHQ Scores for the 1990/1991 Group

Subject	General illness	Sleep disturbance	Anxiety and dysphoria	Depression
13	1.25	2.75	0.50	0.00
14	3.26	5.33	3.56	0.56
15	5.38	6.00	5.75	5.25
16	1.71	2.29	0.14	0.00

The challenger for leadership refused to work as hard as two of the others right from the beginning, and by midwinter he chose not to sit with them at the same table. He said that *had* it been possible, he would have left the base entirely, because he was afraid of being "incarcerated" there with the others for another six months. He felt that he needed more time to devote to his work than the others were giving him, and he thought that they did not appreciate the work he was doing. He also expressed some skepticism about the value of the behavioral research, as people with personality problems often do.

A third member of the party, and a relatively innocuous one, felt that the leader had abandoned his role and that the challenger was selfish and moody. Personally, he felt that nobody in the group valued *his* work, and nobody was interested in him as a person, especially when he had news that his father had died and he wanted to share his sorrow. Instead, he went for long walks to be as isolated physically as he felt emotionally. After midwinter he said: "We don't live as a group of friends or of people trained to be friends. . . . I felt like begging for company." Like the leader, he welcomed the monthly discharge of feelings that compliance with the research provided by saying: "I've been waiting for this test. I feel free to express with it. If you have some advice let me know. It will be hard for me to trust again . . . these questions help to some extent."

The fourth member tried early to mediate, but when she realized she could not please everyone, she challenged her own motives for trying. She became close to the leader for a time, but withdrew again because of the effect of the relationship on the others in the small group and because of his strong negative and assertive behavior. Thereafter, she carried on her work with devotion and sought to bring rationality to bear on the quarreling dissidents. The outcome brought her positive rewards that, unfortunately, she complained, could not be registered on the psychological tests. But she did write: "I have enjoyed doing these tests, and they were good in the way that they made me sit down and think of why this and that had happened and why I reacted the way I did. I think I have learned a lot from it, not only about myself but also about other people."

However, on debriefing, both separately as individuals and collectively as a group when they returned to New Zealand, none of this particular party gave the impression that he or she was in a state of emotional instability that would require professional intervention. Rather, they were all angry, bored, and so disappointed with each other that they were ready to go their separate ways. They had been together too long in close confinement in an isolated, insulated, and emotionally negative group, and they had insufficient resilience and resources from which to generate a flexible pattern of positive relationships to meet their current needs.

Discussion and Conclusions

It might not be too far-fetched to claim that the data reported herein meet the plea from Ursin and colleagues (Ursin, Bergan, Collet, Endresen, Lugg, Maki, Matre, Molvaer, Muller, Olff, Pettersen, Sandal, Vaernes, & Warncke, 1991), because they were derived from reliable and valid instruments, and were obtained from small groups with an international membership that included both sexes and operated under field conditions. If they do not fill that need, they certainly give credence from the field to the data reported long ago from the experimental laboratory by Haythorn (1973). They indicated the same power of the personality variables of dominance in causing conflict, and of shared affiliation and achievement in creating cohesion among long-duration small groups, as were found originally with 10-day small groups of submariners. Also, the data emphasized the importance of selecting people with the appropriate mix of such variables for practical real-life assignments.

Overall, and despite the inevitable gaps in the data, the study showed that a year of Antarctic isolation is relatively stressful for small groups of even the most dedicated of individuals with somewhat related previous experience of the prevailing conditions. It shows that the stressors were more interpersonal and personal than otherwise, and leaves open to conjecture whether they might have been greater had the focus group not received some training in techniques of stress reduction and conflict resolution beforehand. But the question remains whether the training program might have been intensified in all interpersonal areas and whether the criteria and methods of personnel selection needed an overhaul.

Concerning the study itself, the usual questions can be raised concerning the value to be placed on data from small groups, especially when on occasion individuals chose for whatever reason not to respond (Leon, McNally, & Ben-Porath, 1987; Ursin, Etienne & Collet, 1990a). But the convergence and consistency of data from clinical, psychometric, sociometric, structured, unstructured, and observational sources gave it credibility. The outcome confirmed the shrewd comment of an early clinician that the critical mental stresses of exploration are not so much those imposed on the human being by climate, geography, or disease as the complexity of relationships (Pozner, 1965). If the occasional expression of resistance to participation in the research can be taken as a measure of personal discomfort and anxiety, rather than of other perhaps more legitimate dissatisfactions, regular participation can itself provide a welcome relief for the discharge of feelings and an opportunity for making outside contact at a personal level.

The problem for managers and researchers is to encourage research subjects to continue their commitment to responding, whatever the complexity of their relationships. At least they can now mention the cathartic benefit to be derived by subjects who complete their monthly returns. But their task could also be made easier were researchers to eliminate redundancies and irrelevancies, e.g., by omitting the longer HSCL but retaining the shorter GHQ, and by removing questions 1, 2, 5, and 6 from the ADQ. The latter might also be made more acceptable were it to include more items that touch on psychological well-being rather than on psychological distress. Not that the ADQ necessarily induces a mental set to report the pathological in groups that are under stress, but the inclusion of positive items would extend the range of options to which the subjects could respond.

The implications of this study would reinforce the work of behavioral scientists who are involved as consultants and researchers with the various space agencies. It shows that unremitting attention must be paid to the selection and training of even the most competent and dedicated volunteers who have committed themselves to work in small groups in isolation. It also shows that procedures need to be worked out that will ensure the flow of data from subjects once an enterprise has begun. Then, an advisory system needs to be put into place that could be brought into operation to reduce personal and interpersonal tensions, should they arise. The outcome should facilitate both the direct and the indirect attainment of mission objectives.

References

Alty, R. T. B. (1990). *The equivalence of written and computer formats of three questionnaires.* Master's thesis. Wellington, NZ: Victoria University.

Bales, R. I., & Cohen, S. P. (1979). *SYMLOG: A system for the multi-level observation of groups.* New York: Free Press.

Cazes, G., Rivolier, J., Taylor, A. J. W., & McCormick, I. A. (1989). *Arctic Medical Research, 48,* 185–194.

Cornelius, H., Faire, S., & Hall, S. (undated). *Conflict resolution network: A trainers manual* (5th ed.). Chatswood, New South Wales, Australia: Conflict Resolution Network.

Folkman, S., & Lazarus, R. S. (1980). An analysis of coping in a middle-aged community sample. *Journal of Health and Social Behaviour, 21,* 219–239.

Goldberg, D. (1979). *Manual of the general health questionnaire.* Windsor, U.K.: NFER Publishing.

Green, D. E., Walkey, F. H., McCormick, I. A., & Taylor, A. J. W. (1988). Development and evaluation of a 21 item version of the Hopkins Symptom Checklist in New Zealand and United States respondents. *Australian Journal of Psychology, 40,* 61–70.

Haythorn, W. H. (1973). The mini-world of isolation: Laboratory studies. In J. E. Rasmussen (Ed.), *Man in isolation and confinement* (Chapter 8). Chicago: Aldine.

Leon, G. R., McNally, C., & Ben-Porath, Y. S. (1987). *Personality characteristics, mood, and coping patterns in a successful North Pole Expedition team.* University of Minnesota. Private circulation, p. 24.

MacKay, C., Cox, T., Burrows, G., & Lazzerini, T. (1978). An inventory for the measurement of self-reported stress and arousal. *British Journal of Social and Clinical Psychology, 17,* 283–284.

Palinkas, L. A. (1986). Health and performance of Antarctic winter-over personnel: A follow-up study. *Aviation, Space, and Environmental Medicine, 57,* 954–959.

Pozner, H. (1965). Mental fitness. In E. G. Edholm & A. L. Bacharach (Eds.), *A practical guide for those going on expeditions* (pp. 77–97). Bristol: Wright.

Rivolier, J., Goldsmith, R., Lugg, D. J., & Taylor, A. J. W. (Eds.). (1988). *Man in the Antarctic: The scientific research of the International Biomedical Expedition to Antarctic.* London: Taylor & Francis.

Sawyer, M., Sarris, A., Quigley, R., Baghurst, P., & Kalucy, R. (1990). The attitude of parents to the use of computer-assisted interviewing in a child psychiatry service. *British Journal of Psychiatry, 157,* 675–678.

Siegert, R. J., McCormick, I. A., Taylor, A. J. W., & Walkey, F. H. (1987). An examination of reported factor structures of the General Health Questionnaire and the identification of a stable replicable structure. *Australian Journal of Psychology, 39,* 87–98.

Taylor, A. J. W. (1987). *Antarctic psychology.* Wellington, NZ: Department of Scientific and Industrial Research.

Taylor, A. J. W. (1989a). The collection and transmission of behavioral data by computer and satellite. In Guo Kun (Ed. in Chief), *Proceedings of the International Symposium on Antarctic Research* (pp. 355–359). Tianjin: China Ocean Press.

Taylor, A. J. W. (1989b). Polar winters: Chronic deprivation or transient hibernation? *Polar Record, 25,* 239–246.

Ursin, H., Etienne, J. L., & Collet, J. (1990). An Antarctic crossing as analogue for long-term manned spaceflight. *European Space Agency Bulletin, 64,* 45–49.

Ursin, H., Bergan, T., Collet, J., Endresen, I. M., Lugg, D. J., Maki, P., Matre, R., Molvaer, O., Muller, H. K., Olff, M., Pettersen, R., Sandal, G. M., Vaernes, R., & Warncke, M. (1991). Psychological studies of individuals in small, isolated groups—in the Antarctic and in space analogues. *Environment and Behavior,* Special Polar Psychology Issue, *23,* 766–781.

CHAPTER 15

Notes on the Use of Biological Markers in the Study of Long-Term Stress

Tores Theorell

The development of applied physiology relevant to the stress researcher has been rapid during recent decades. This development means that it is now possible to record minute changes in the blood concentration of hormones, immunoglobulins, and lipoproteins, as well as the urinary and salivary excretion of several hormones. Furthermore, it is possible to follow physiological functions, such as electrical activity in the brain and the heart, as well as blood pressure measured at regular intervals in a fully automated way throughout day and night. One of the problems is that there are too many parameters that could be studied. Accordingly, it is important to give thought to the choice of parameters. In this chapter, I do not intend to present a comprehensive review of this field, but rather to give examples of the use of relevant markers and issues that have to be raised in the interpretation of results.

In most studies of the relationship between psychological stress reactions and biological changes, the stressors have been of short duration. To the clinician, however, long-term stress reactions are more relevant than short-term reactions, since they are of greater significance to health. But long-term reactions that last for months may be difficult to study because there is biological adaptation, which means that receptors change in number and sensitivity, and that changes not only in hormone release but also in synthesis and breakdown may be part of the long-term stress reaction

TORES THEORELL • National Institute of Psychosocial Factors and Health, 17177 Stockholm, Sweden.

Clinical Applied Psychophysiology, edited by John G. Carlson, A. Ronald Seifert, and Niels Birbaumer. Plenum Press, New York, 1994.

itself. Accordingly, we should look for relationships that persist despite all these difficulties and also take interest in the time dimension itself.

Change in Cross-Sectional Correlation Patterns with Change in Job Strain

The most frequent way of analyzing the relationship between psycho-socially straining situations and biological markers is to make correlations between the marker level and the reported psychosocial stress level at the same time. In a study that was performed in our institute, workingmen and women aged 25–60 were asked to participate four times during a year with intervals of 3–4 months. On each occasion, they were asked to describe in a questionnaire various aspects of psychological demands and decision latitude. An index for demands and another index for decision latitude were calculated, and the ratio between them, job strain, was calculated. The effect of seasonal variations on biological markers was minimized due to the way in which participants were recruited at the start of the study. Each individual's level of job strain was subsequently rated. In the figure presented herein, the highest level of job strain is displayed to the left and the lowest level to the right. The same individuals have been studied on all four occasions.

Table 1 shows changes in immunoglobulin G (IgG) in relation to job-strain level in these individuals (Theorell, Orth-Gomér, & Eneroth, 1990a). It can be seen that there is a small but significant rise in IgG with rising job-strain level in the total studied group. It can be observed, however, that most of this rise took place in the group of subjects who reported that they had poor emotional support in their general life situation. In this group, a substantial increase in IgG level took place. There was no relationship between IgG level and social support as long as the job-strain level was low—rather, as long as the subjects had a level of job strain that was low for them as individuals. When the job-strain level increased, emotional support in the life situation became progressively more and more important to the IgG level. Furthermore, the correlation between job strain and IgG was almost significantly negative (-0.23, $p < 0.10$) when the job-strain level was at its peak, but very far from significant when the job-strain level was low.

How can we explain these seemingly contradictory findings, and what conclusions can we draw from them? We have assumed that the job-strain measures reflect the perceived situation at work during the past weeks and months. Accordingly, a rising job-strain level may reflect a stressor that lasts for several weeks. The measure of emotional support in

Table 1. Mean Immunoglobulin Levels in Different Adequacy
of Social Support Groups on Different Levels of Job Strain[a]

Group	Mean log	SD log	Antilog
	(g/liter)		
Least strain			
Low support	1.00	0.18	10.0
Intermediate support	0.96	0.11	9.1
High support	0.93	0.10	8.5
Next-to-least strain			
Low support	1.03	0.14	10.7
Intermediate support	0.97	0.08	9.3
High support	0.93	0.10	8.5
Next-to-worst strain			
Low support	1.04	0.10	11.0
Intermediate support	0.97	0.12	9.3
High support	0.96	0.09	9.1
Worst strain			
Low support	1.08	0.12	12.0
Intermediate support	0.96	0.09	9.1
High support	0.95	0.08	8.9

[a]From Theorell et al. (1990a). Number in each group: Low support, 11 or 12; intermediate support, 11; high support, 25–27.

the general life situation, on the other hand, reflects a longer-lasting state that may have relevance for the individual's ability to cope with stressors. When job strain was low (to the right in the figure), the individuals reported the level that they may have been used to for a very long time; when job strain was high (to the left), however, they had been forced to exhaust some of their extra resources and to mobilize energy that was reflected in a rising systolic blood pressure during work hours in the present study (see Fig. 1) and perhaps also to mobilize immune defenses because of the symbolic threat to the organism that the long-lasting stressor imposes—reflected in rising IgG levels. The mobilization may be more intense when rising job strain is combined with low emotional support in the general life situation. When this condition has lasted for a long time, there may be a risk that IgG mobilization results in depletion of resources, which may explain why a negative correlation may arise between job strain and IgG. Such negative correlations have also been observed in other cross-sectional analyses (Endresen, 1991). We concentrated these analyses on IgG levels, since IgG is a very slow-reacting immunoglobulin—clearly an advantage when long-lasting stressors are being studied.

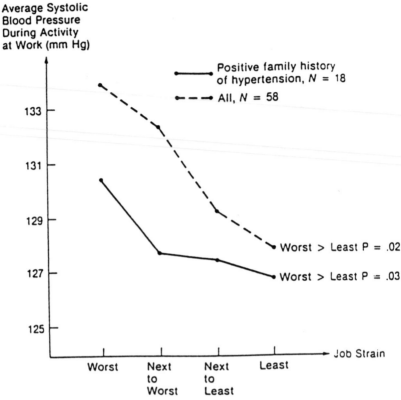

Figure 1. Systolic blood pressure during working hours in relation to changes in job strain (longitudinal data). From Theorell *et al.* (1988). Reprinted with permission of the Helen Dwight Reid Educational Foundation. Copyright 1989.

Another observation that may be of interest partly reflects the same phenomenon. Plasma testosterone levels tended to decrease with increasing job strain in the male participants (see Table 2), at least among those with sedentary jobs. Plasma testosterone is less stable than IgG. Accordingly, observations from minimum and next-to-minimum job-strain observations and from maximum and next-to-maximum job strain, respectively, were combined in this table. A cross-sectional analysis of the correlation between job strain and plasma testosterone showed a significantly *positive* association on the occasions with the maximum and next-to-maximum job-strain levels. This association gradually disappeared with increasing job strain (correlation coefficients from highest to lowest job strain being 0.10, n.s.; 0.24, n.s.; 0.33, $p < 0.05$; 0.31, $p < 0.05$).

Table 2. Mean Plasma Testosterone Concentration (millimoles/liter)
in Sedentary and Physically Strenuous Work Groups during "Worst"
to "Next-to-Worst" and Least to Next-to-Least Job-Strain Periods[a]

Group	Worst and next-to-worst job strain	Least and next-to-least job strain
Sedentary ($N = 23$)	23.7	27.7
Physically strenuous ($N = 21$)	25.2	25.1

[a]From Theorell et al. (1990). The men were 25–60 years old (mean: 43). F (sedentary/strenuous) = 0.06, not significant; F (strain period) = 3.96, $p = 0.05$; F (interaction strain × sedentary/strenuous) = 4.25, $p = 0.05$.

A parallel observation of the relationship between self-reported total alcohol intake per week (based on a questionnaire asking specifically about ingested amounts of beer, wine, and hard liquor) and plasma testosterone showed that there was a significantly negative correlation between alcohol intake and plasma testosterone at peak job strain, but not on other occasions (correlations from lowest to highest job strain: -0.36, $p < 0.05$; -0.24, n.s.; -0.25, n.s.; -0.06, n.s.). The self-reported level of alcohol intake did not change with increasing job strain.

In summary, in the case of plasma testosterone in the male participants, we observed a significantly positive association between job strain and plasma testosterone that disappeared when the individuals reached job-strain levels that were unusually high for them. Alcohol intake has a negative association with plasma testosterone levels during such periods. It was as though alcohol did not matter for testosterone levels as long as the individuals did not have unusually high job-strain levels.

An additional theme that was illustrated by this study was the fact that two personal characteristics, namely, depressive tendency (reported in diaries with notes approximately once an hour during four different workdays) and family history of hypertension, were both related to the long-term physiological reaction pattern. In male subjects with depressive tendency, there was a relatively high level of reported sleep disturbance throughout the whole study period, whereas in other subjects, sleep disturbance reports clearly increased with job strain. Similarly, plasma prolactin levels increased markedly with job strain in these subjects. In subjects with a family history of hypertension, a different pattern was observed—there were decreasing plasma prolactin levels with increasing job strain, and reported sleep disturbance levels were relatively low and increased markedly with increasing job strain. These findings illustrate that personal characteristics may either attenuate or strengthen associations between long-term stressors and biological stress markers. In the case of depression tendency, we may be dealing with an activation of the dopaminergic system. In the case of family history of hypertension, the explanation may be psychological—subjects in this group have been reported to have more alexithymic traits than other subjects (Jorgensen & Houston, 1986). They may accordingly tend to react with more direct psychophysiological activation and disregard psychological appraisal of difficulties. The explanation could be also be physiological—the fact that subjects with family history of hypertension react with more pronounced sympathoadrenal activation may influence other physiological systems (Theorell, 1990).

What Is the Relationship between Acute Physiological Reactions during a Crisis Situation and Resulting Long-Term Difficulties?

A recent study by our group may illustrate some of the complex relationships between a dramatic life event and its long-term consequences. A longitudinal study has been performed on a group of subway drivers who happened to have been driving a train when a person fell or jumped in front of the train and was hurt or killed. This person under train (PUT) experience is impossible to anticipate; it may lead to long-term absenteeism because of illness, particularly if the person was seriously injured (not so much if the person died or was only mildly injured); and it is frequently associated with a slowly deteriorating perception of the psychosocial climate in the work site during the first year that follows—as though the person receives good emotional support immediately after the accident, but then during the following months feels forgotten and left with depressing thoughts about it (Theorell, Leymann, Jodko, Konarski, Norbeck, & Eneroth, 1992).

What psychophysiological markers were studied and what were the relationships? All parameters—blood pressure in the supine position after 10 min rest, concentrations of cortisol, prolactin, and testosterone in plasma, and indices of depression, phobic anxiety, and sleep disturbance—were recorded 3 weeks, 3 months, and 1 year after the PUT experience. A matched control group of subway drivers who had not had the PUT experience during the study period was recruited.

Systolic and diastolic blood pressure, degree of depression and phobia, and plasma concentrations of cortisol and testosterone did not change significantly during the study period in any of the groups. Sleep disturbance as well as plasma prolactin concentration were increased in the PUT group during the acute phase, that is, 3 weeks after the event, but subsequently decreased to control-group levels (for prolactin, see Fig. 2).

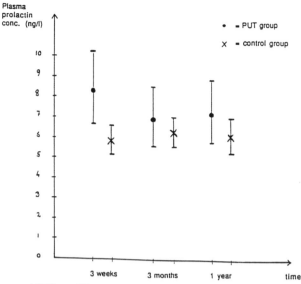

Figure 2. Means and 95% confidence intervals of plasma prolactin (computations based on logarithms) on each occasion following the PUT event in the PUT group (N = 13) and the control group (N = 15). Only men who had measurements for all occasions were included. From Theorell *et al.* (1992).

Accordingly, the expected acute reaction did occur. Prolactin secretion is mostly parallel to feelings of depression in combination with powerlessness (Theorell, 1992), and sleep disturbance is a normal reaction to this kind of situation. These acute reactions, however, were not associated with long-term sickness absenteeism. On the other hand, a high depression score and a high plasma cortisol concentration 3 weeks after the PUT event (both of which did not increase significantly during this period) did predict an increased risk of having long-term sickness absenteeism during the interval 3 months to 1 year after the event.

The pattern of associations indicated that the PUT event increased the risk of long-term sickness absenteeism, but that this risk had nothing to do with the degree of acute psychophysiological reaction during the first weeks after the event. On the other hand, a depressive state with high plasma cortisol level during this period indicated a high risk of long-term sickness absenteeism. One interpretation of this finding may be that a depressive state (for reasons other than the PUT) at the time of the PUT event in combination with the PUT experience contributed to long-term sickness absenteeism.

Blood Pressure Recordings at Night and at Work

Recently, we have had the opportunity of exploring the association between job-strain and blood pressure levels using special measurement techniques both for the exposure (job strain) and the dependent blood pressure variable.

Long-term stressors may be underestimated by subjects who are prone to develop early primary hypertension. Studies have shown that subjects with a family history of hypertension tend to report very few stressors at work (Theorell, 1990), and it could be suspected that this may be due to alexithymia. If this is true, one way of avoiding individual negative bias is to use group data only and, accordingly, disregard what subjects report regarding their own perception of the work environment. An occupational classification has been constructed from which inferences can be made regarding the psychological demands, decision latitude, social support, physical demands, and occupational hazards in occupations on the Swedish labor market (Johnson, Stewart, Fredlund, Hall, & Theorell, 1990). The classification is based on Swedish surveys of randomly selected working men and women. The tables give separate scores for men and women, for those below and above 45 years of age, and for those who have been working for up to 5, between 5 and 20, and finally for more than 20 years. According to the theory, those who are working in an occupation with a high psychological-demand score and a low decision-latitude score are exposed to a long-lasting stressor and accordingly should have high blood pressure. In this study, psychological demand was divided by decision latitude.

Blood pressure was recorded by means of fully automated equipment every 10 min during 24 hr (Theorell, de Faire, Johnson, Hall, Perski, & Stewart, 1991). The study sample was recruited from a population screening of men. Those who had borderline blood pressure (85–95 diastolic) on three different occasions were asked to participate in the study; accordingly, the study included only subjects with more pronounced blood pressure reactivity than those in the normal population. Those with jobs classified as physically demanding according to the tables were analyzed separately from those with jobs that were not physically demanding.

The results indicated that subjects in jobs with high job-strain levels had higher diastolic blood pressure levels than others. This was particularly significant at night and remained significant after adjustment for age and body mass index (see Fig. 3). The findings are of interest in view of a somewhat similar study in a much younger sample of men performed some years ago by our group. In this case, there was a difference between the groups in the expected direction only during working hours (only

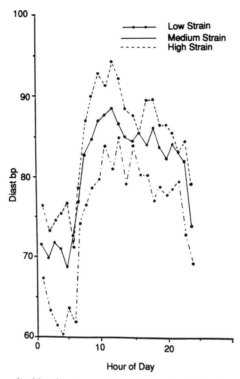

Figure 3. Mean diastolic blood pressure for each of the 24 hr in men with borderline hypertension working in occupations without heavy physical demands. From Theorell *et al.* (1991).

between those in the study group that had a propensity to blood pressure elevation) and only for diastolic blood pressure. These results may be explained by the fact that the present sample was much older—chronic changes in the vessels could now have resulted from the high systolic blood pressure levels during the working hours for several years. The new study does indicate the importance of measuring blood pressure during night when the conditions are more basal.

It was also of interest that the exclusion of subjects with physically demanding occupations made the findings much clearer. Studies in our institute have pointed at the importance of recording heart rate continuously during day and night in the study of the effects of social support on heart rate (Undén, Orth-Gomér, & Elofsson, 1991) and on the rate of progression of coronary atherosclerosis, according to coronary arteriography (Perski, Olsson, Landou, de Faire, Theorell, & Hamsten, 1992). The findings of these studies have shown that subjects who report a low level of social support at work have higher heart rates than others even at night; furthermore, those who have a relatively high heart rate at night have a faster progression of coronary atherosclerosis than others. The latter findings could not be explained by heart muscle damage or accepted risk factors for coronary heart disease.

In conclusion, continuous monitoring of blood pressure and heart rate may be valuable tools in the study of long-term stress.

References

Endresen, I. M. (1991). *Psychoimmunological stress markers in working life*. Doctoral thesis. University of Bergen, Norway.

Johnson, J. V., Stewart, W., Fredlund, P., Hall, E. M., & Theorell, T. (1990). Psychosocial job exposure matrix: An occupationally aggregated attribution system for work environment exposure characteristics. *Stress Research Reports No. 221*. Stockholm: National Institute for Psychosocial Factors and Health.

Jorgensen, R. S., & Houston, B. K. (1986). Family history of hypertension, personality patterns and cardiovascular reactivity to stress. *Psychosomatic Medicine, 48,* 102–117.

Perski, A., Olsson, G., Landou, C., de Faire, U., Theorell, T., & Hamsten, A. (1992). Minimum heart rate and coronary atherosclerosis: Independent relations to global severity and rate of progression of angiographic lesions in men with myocardial infarction at young age. *American Heart Journal, 123,* 609–613.

Theorell, T. (1990). Family history of hypertension—an individual trait interacting with spontaneously occurring job stressors. *Scandinavian Journal of Work and Environmental Health, 16* (Suppl. 1), 74–79.

Theorell, T. (1992). Prolactin—a hormone that mirrors passiveness in crisis situations. *Integrative Physiological and Behavioral Science, 27,* 32–38.

Theorell, T., Perski, A., Ahmstadt, T., Sigala, F., Ahlberg-Hulten, G., Svensson, J., & Eneroth, P. (1988). Changes in job strain in relation to changes in physiological state. *Scand. J. Work Env. Health., 14,* 189–196.

Theorell, T., Orth-Gomér, K., & Eneroth, P. (1990a). Slow-reacting immunoglobulin in relation to social support and changes in job strain: A preliminary note. *Psychosomatic Medicine, 52,* 511–516.

Theorell, T., Karasek, R. A., & Eneroth, P. (1990b). Job strain variations in relation to plasma testosterone, fluctuations in working men—a longitudinal study. *J. Internal Med., 227,* 31–36.

Theorell, T., de Faire, U., Johnson, J., Hall, E., Perski, A., & Stewart, W. (1991). Job strain and ambulatory blood pressure profiles. *Scandinavian Journal of Work and Environmental Health, 17,* 380–385.

Theorell, T., Leymann, H., Jodko, M., Konarski, K., Norbeck, H. E., & Eneroth, P. (1992). "Person under train" incidents: Medical consequences for subway drivers. *Psychosomatic Medicine, 54,* 480–488.

Undén, A.-L., Orth-Gomér, K., & Elofsson, S. (1991). Cardiovascular effects of social support in the work place: Twenty-four-hour ECG monitoring of men and women. *Psychosomatic Medicine, 53,* 50–60.

Index